From the
Ground Up

From the
Ground Up

James Villas

Hundreds of Amazing Recipes

from Around the World for

Ground Meats, including Beef, Chicken,

Pork, Seafood, and More

WILEY

John Wiley & Sons, Inc.

Copyright © 2011 by James Villas. All rights reserved
Published by John Wiley & Sons, Inc., Hoboken, New Jersey
Published simultaneously in Canada

For general information on our other products and services or for technical support, please contact our Customer Care Department within the United States at (800) 762-2974, outside the United States at (317) 572-3993 or fax (317) 572-4002.

Wiley also publishes its books in a variety of electronic formats. Some content that appears in print may not be available in electronic books. For more information about Wiley products, visit our web site at www.wiley.com.

Library of Congress Cataloging-in-Publication Data

Villas, James.
  From the ground up / James Villas.
    p. cm.
  Includes index.
  ISBN 978-0-470-57165-1 (pbk.)
  1. Cooking. 2. Cookbooks. I. Title.
  TX714.V5436   2011
  641.5—dc22   2010036221

Printed in the United States of America

10 9 8 7 6 5 4 3 2 1

For

JEAN ANDERSON

Peerless Food Expert,

Fellow Tar Heel, and

Beloved Friend

Contents

Preface

Just a couple of years ago, my personal passion alone for dishes featuring ground meats, poultry, and seafood would have been reason enough to write a comprehensive, international cookbook on the subject. Today, however, in a lean age of rampant inflation, when a single sirloin strip steak in the supermarket easily costs $15.00, a pound of bacon can set you back six bucks, whole organic chickens and deli chicken salad are more than $6.00 a pound, and both fresh shrimp and lobsters are priced as luxury foods, the topic of economical ground meats has almost a timely urgency about it. And even if the wolf were not hovering at the door these days, I would still insist that a fascinating style of cooking has been at best trivialized and at worst sadly neglected for far too long.

For most American cooks, ground or chopped meats, poultry, and seafood mean only burgers, meat loaf, meatballs, chili, possibly chicken or turkey salad and clam dip, and few are even aware that some of the most glorious and unusual dishes in the international culinary repertory are based exclusively on a vast array of ground, chopped, minced, diced, and shredded items. From the lowliest American hashes and fish cakes, British pasties and rissoles, German molds and sausages, and South American fritters and puddings, to more sophisticated French terrines and soufflés, Italian pasta stuffings and *ragù*, Greek dolmades, and certain Indian lamb curries, the variety of delectable specialties is utterly staggering. In fact, I'll go so far as to argue that ground meat, poultry, and seafood dishes constitute a veritable global cuisine in themselves, and that, faced with an ever-expanding inventory of reasonably priced ground beef, veal, pork, lamb, chicken, and turkey now available in all supermarkets, adventurous cooks today are ready to be introduced to authentic Cajun boudin and Charleston hobotee, English and Canadian ground meat and seafood pies, Spanish potted minced meats, French seafood quenelles, Italian poultry cannelloni, Hungarian meat and seafood croquettes, and various Russian and Asian rolls and balls.

While the main objective in this book is to provide lots of easy, straightforward, and blessedly economical recipes for delectable dishes from around the world based on all the packaged staples found in our markets, it is also my purpose to encourage you to develop the habit of grinding, mincing, and chopping some of your own ingredients, much the same way that more and more serious cooks are now putting up pickles and preserves, making genuine yeast breads, smoking their own meats, and foraging for wild fruits and nuts. First, the major advantage of using a manual or electric food grinder or food processor is that it allows you not only to choose exact cuts and portions of meat, poultry, or seafood to be ground but also the freedom to control ingredient proportions— fats, seasonings, and other additives—and textures. Second, the truth is that even the most helpful butchers will rarely custom-grind any raw poultry, fresh seafood, or special cuts of pork as a precaution against cross-contamination of other meats ground in the same machine, so that when it comes to making most of the wonderful sausages in this book, your only option is a reliable grinder or food processor. And third, there can be no question as to the thriftiness of processing your own ingredients, especially when they're found on sale in the market. As anyone knows who's ever turned out a silky shrimp or tangy ham spread, spicy pork tacos or crusty salmon croquettes, or, perhaps most important of all, a freshly ground all-American hamburger with just the right texture and flavor, nothing is more delicious, satisfying, and, yes, fun than dishes prepared from scratch.

Since there are so many variables in the ingredients, equipment, cooking techniques, and even terminology pertaining to the production of ground dishes, I can't emphasize enough the importance of carefully reading the Introduction of this book before making your first canapés; creating your first sumptuous loaf, casserole, or soufflé; stuffing your first pasta or vegetable; and grinding meats or seafood for your first turnovers and sausages. Not, by any means, that many of the recipes are particularly challenging or time-consuming, but the information and tips provided

Nothing is more delicious, satisfying, and, yes, fun than dishes prepared from scratch.

will quickly familiarize you with most of the basics involved in this exciting style of cooking.

Over the years, I've encountered other champions of ground dishes, but perhaps none was so zealous as the legendary cookbook author and food editor of *The New York Times*, Craig Claiborne. Here was an intrepid gourmand who had sampled, cooked, and relished every exotic edible from French *coulibiac* of salmon to Greek lamb's head soup to Chinese sea slugs, yet when we were sipping Champagne one evening and I asked Craig to name his absolute favorite dish in the entire world, he didn't blink an eye before answering, "Anything made with ground meat." Once you, too, delve into some of the toothsome dishes in this book, I think you'll understand what he meant.

Introduction

An Inventory of Ground Meats, Poultry, and Seafood

Beef

Prepackaged supermarket ground beef (or hamburger) is produced from various cuts of meat with different ratios of lean to fat and priced accordingly. Ground beef, which is generally made from the trimmings of shank, plate, brisket, and chuck, contains the most amount of fat (25 to 33 percent), is the cheapest, and shrinks dramatically when cooked. Ground chuck contains 15 to 20 percent fat, has well-balanced, juicy flavor and texture, and is moderately priced. Ground round is the leanest common variety (10 to 12 percent fat), and while it is ideal for certain dishes, it makes a dry burger if cooked more than medium-rare or not fortified with additional ground fat. The most expensive style is ground sirloin, which has succulent flavor and texture so long as it, like ground round, contains sufficient fat. For burgers, I use mostly ground chuck (or a mixture of chuck and round), and for other dishes, my general preference is either lean chuck or round. (Note: Virtually all freshly ground beef is pinkish red on the surface and reddish brown on the interior. This is totally natural and safe and is due simply to the fact that all beef oxidizes to a bright red color when exposed to air.)

For home-ground beef, the best cuts are boned chuck (preferably first-blade), shank, flank, and meaty short ribs, as well as brisket and what is marketed as "stew meat," all of which have the right lean-fat ratio. Top or bottom round, rump, sirloin, and "London broil" are also delicious when ground with a little chilled suet or fatback, and when rump or bottom-round roasts are on sale, I often buy large ones so that I can grind part of the meat and fat for burgers, meat loaf, hash, pasties, meatballs, and the like. Any cut of beef should be trimmed of heavy sinew and gristle before grinding.

Veal

Just 20 years ago, it was virtually impossible to find (exorbitantly priced) packaged ground veal in all but the most upscale markets, but today, with much of the country's obsession with lean, "light" meats, ground veal is now almost as widely available as ground pork. Furthermore, because of the greater demand, not only is the quality of ground veal (like the whole cuts of meat themselves) better, but the price is also considerably cheaper than before. Ground veal has a subtle, elegant, sweet savor, but its true glory is its affinity for an amazing range of ingredients (tomatoes, onions, anchovies, bacon, tarragon, nutmeg) and its suitability for meat loaves, meatballs, roulades, croquettes, and pasta fillings. The downside is that, since ground veal can be up to 95 percent lean meat, it does not make juicy patties or loaves by itself and must be mixed with fattier meats or other moist ingredients before being cooked. Packaged ground veal should be creamy pink in color, cold to the touch, and showing no signs of leakage. Veal is very perishable and keeps no more than 1 or 2 days in the refrigerator. (Note: If, for some reason, ground veal is unavailable, ground turkey breast, or even ground lean pork, can often be substituted in many recipes.)

For home-ground veal, shoulder has the best flavor and ratio of lean meat to fat and connective tissue, but also acceptable (and cheaper) are boned shank, flank, neck, and breast. Young, tender veal is one meat that does not have to be trimmed of sinew and gristle before being ground.

Pork and Ham

Most of today's pork is considerably leaner than it was 20 years ago due to different breeding methods of hogs, feeds, and packers who trim more fat from carcasses. While there can be no doubt that some of the succulence of primal cuts has disappeared along with the fat and calories, it's also true that most of the packaged ground pork found in supermarkets—produced generally from shoulder butt or picnic and trimmings from the pig's belly and sides—can still have a ratio of up to 25 percent of the flavorful fat necessary to make good sausage, meatballs, pâtés, burgers, and certain pies, chilies, and forcemeats. If the color of packaged ground pork is too pinkish red, I don't hesitate to ask a butcher to grind some shoulder with a little fatback (a request that may or may not be satisfied since, with lingering fears of harmful bacteria and cross-contamination, many butchers refuse to grind pork—or poultry—in a machine that is also used to grind other meats and that must be thoroughly washed after each and every batch). And when it comes to making bulk sausage, I'm so particular about lean-to-fat ratio that I always grind my own pork and fat instead of risking the packaged products in supermarkets. Do beware of any ground pork that is too pale or has a greenish-brown tinge, and never store ground pork for more than 2 or 3 days in the refrigerator.

For home-ground pork, shoulder butt or picnic is by far the best cut of meat (especially when it's on sale for as little as 99 cents a pound), but boned hocks (shanks) or rib chops from the loin, country-style ribs, fresh ham (leg), and lean belly also make delicious ground pork.

As for cooked or smoked ham, I've never seen packaged ground ham in any supermarket. Nor can you depend on butchers to grind ham you've bought, for the same safety reasons they're hesitant to grind any cooked or smoked meats in a machine also used to grind raw pork. On the other hand, no meat is easier to home-grind in a meat grinder or food processor than lean smoked or country ham (which rarely has more than 5 percent fat), and, actually, for most of the recipes in this book that call for ground ham, you can just

If the color of packaged ground pork is too pinkish red, I don't hesitate to ask a butcher to grind some shoulder with a little fatback.

as easily use ham that has been finely chopped or minced with a knife.

Lamb

Scattered throughout this book are recipes for lamb patties, balls, dumplings, pies, and even chili, all made with ground or minced lamb that is now available packaged in most supermarkets. Do note, however, that much ground lamb is produced from trimmings that may include too much strong-tasting fat, and that if you do opt to ask a butcher to grind lamb for you (and he or she is willing), be sure to specify shoulder, which has just the right proportion of lean to fat to make it juicy and delectable. Boned arm and blade chops, cutlets, and fatty leg sold as "stew meat" also make delicious ground lamb if you decide to grind your own meat and want to economize. In any case, just remember that since all lamb is finely grained and relatively tender, it should never be ground more than once.

Liver and Kidneys

There are generally three types of red-meat liver found in grocery stores, none of which is available ground. The most delicate, moist, mild, and expensive is soft, rosy red calf's liver, which is sold either fresh or packaged in frozen slices. Beef liver is purplish red, firmer, and considerably stronger in flavor, but when home-ground to make meatballs, dumplings, meat loaves, and sausages, it can be savory and succulent. The strongest, least tender, and cheapest variety is pork liver, which can be ground for pâtés, liverwurst, puddings, and sausage. To prepare liver for grinding or chopping, peel off any outer membrane and cut away heavy connective tissue and globs of fat. Because of the soft texture, any liver is difficult to grind unless it is first cleaned, cut into strips, and firmed up by sautéing briefly in a little butter or oil. All fresh liver is extremely perishable and should be used within 24 hours of purchase.

Although kidneys have never been a popular variety meat in the United States, in other countries they are highly prized and often chopped or ground to make all sorts of spreads, pies, dumplings, and casseroles. Tender, delectable lamb or veal kidneys can usually be found in upscale markets or ordered from butchers. To prepare them for cooking, halve the kidneys lengthwise, remove the outer fat and membrane, and then cut out any knobs of fat and tubes. Beef and pork kidneys are considerably stronger in flavor, but since they're also more muscular, they can be delicious when split and trimmed of all fat and tubes, ground or minced, and seasoned well. When buying kidneys, make sure they smell fresh and sweet. Quite often in this book, ground or minced kidneys can make an interesting substitute in recipes that call for ground smoked ham, ham hock, or pork butt. As with all variety meats, liver and kidneys are very perishable and should be kept in the refrigerator for no longer than a couple of days before using.

Tongue and Sweetbreads

While still not as popular in the United States as throughout Europe, flavorful beef and veal tongue and delicate beef, veal, and pork sweetbreads (the thymus gland of young animals) are now available in better markets and are superb when ground, chopped, or shredded for various terrines, salads, loaves, and sausages. Very muscular in texture and ideal for grinding, whole (never ground) beef tongue is marketed fresh, corned, pickled, and smoked and must be slowly simmered for 3 to 4 hours before using. Veal tongue, which is more tender, is almost always sold fresh and requires 2 to 2½ hours of poaching. (Lamb and pork tongues are much smaller, usually precooked and ready to eat, and are appropriate only for salads when shredded.) To prepare any cooked tongue for grinding, chopping, or shredding, peel off the skin and cut away the root, any small bones, and gristle.

The richest, most luxurious, and fragile sweetbreads are milky white, fine-grained veal sweetbreads, available whole both fresh and frozen and utterly delectable when broken up and sautéed in butter or mixed with other chopped meats in casseroles or gratins. Young beef and pork sweetbreads are darker, coarser, more strongly flavored, and perfect for grinding with other meats and/or vegetables to make elegant sausages, pâtés, croquettes, and the like. All sweetbreads must be soaked in water overnight and the outer membranes carefully removed before cooking, and they are so perishable that they should be used the same day they're purchased. If you need to obtain fresh sweetbreads directly from a butcher, do be warned that in larger cities, most sweetbreads are often sent immediately to upscale restaurants, and that elsewhere there could be a wait of 2 or 3 days if the butcher has to special-order the sweetbreads from a supplier.

Chicken and Turkey

Just a decade ago, when I needed ground raw chicken or turkey for pâtés and terrines, soup dumplings, patties, croquettes, hash, and various savory pies, I had no alternative but to grind my own, since few butchers would risk cross-contamination by grinding fresh poultry in machines used also to grind meats. Today, both types of fresh, packaged ground poultry are widely available in grocery stores under major brand names, both are economical, and both are safe so long as they're used by the expiration date on the package. Also available now are rolls of frozen ground organic chicken and turkey—white and dark meat. For me, commercial ground chicken or turkey meat (which is mostly breast) is far too lean to use by itself and is much juicier when combined with ground pork or sausage or moistened with cream or half-and-half. If, however, fat consumption is an issue, these ground poultry meats provide a good alternative to most ground red meats. As for giblets (the gizzard, heart, and liver) and necks, they are never marketed ground, chopped, or minced. All fresh ground chicken and turkey should be used by the expiration date on the package. Frozen ground chicken or turkey should be used within 2 days of being thawed.

All fresh ground chicken and turkey should be used by the expiration date on the package.

For home-ground chicken, skinless, boneless breasts are easiest to deal with and, of course, are lean, but for more juicy flavor, the best parts are boned and skinned thighs and drumsticks, as well as highly economical gizzards. Large, firm, skinless, boneless turkey breasts and meaty wings are easy to grind and have more flavor than their chicken counterparts, but again, for ultimate rich and succulent flavor, nothing beats the darker meat from relatively inexpensive turkey thighs, drumsticks, and gizzards. As for soft chicken and turkey livers, to facilitate grinding or mincing, they should first be firmed up by sautéing briefly in a little butter.

Fish and Shellfish

It may come as a surprise to most Americans that there is a whole international repertoire of ground, minced, chopped, and shredded fish and shellfish dishes, but, as this book clearly illustrates, the number of delectable seafood spreads, bisques and chowders, salads, quiches and soufflés, and quenelles is virtually endless. Since few butchers will grind any form of seafood, never does a food processor come in handier than when grinding, mincing, chopping, or pureeing fresh fish and shellfish. Whether raw or cooked, the best fish generally for most dishes in this book are such lean, firm-fleshed varieties as pike, cod, haddock, salmon, halibut, red snapper, perch, and sturgeon, while the fresh shellfish I use most are shrimp, lobster, clams, claw or lump crabmeat, and large sea scallops. Also ideal for grinding, pureeing, or mashing are salt cod, sardines, canned tuna packed in oil, pickled herring, and smoked salmon, haddock, and trout. All fresh fish should be rinsed well, patted dry, covered snugly with plastic wrap, and stored for no longer than 2 days in the coldest area of the refrigerator before using. Even more perishable is fresh shellfish. I always rinse raw shrimp and never store it in the refrigerator for more than 2 days (maybe 3 days for cooked shrimp). Cooked lobster meat and crabmeat, as well as fresh shucked clams, should be stored in their original containers for no longer than 2 days, but frozen lobster tails in their original wrappers will keep for up to 2 months in the freezer. I never rinse shucked scallops, storing them, if necessary, in a tightly covered glass or ceramic (never metal) container in the refrigerator for 1 to 2 days. I do not buy canned shrimp, lobster, crabmeat, or scallops, but canned salmon and minced clams are acceptable for certain dishes.

Fundamental Equipment for Home Grinding

Meat Grinders

Available in stores and on the Internet in various models, sizes, and weights, manual or electric home meat grinders are indispensable to cooks seriously interested in producing many of the dishes in this book. (Note: KitchenAid brand stand mixers are equipped to handle a separate, inexpensive meat-grinding attachment.) For durability, trustworthiness, and grinding the toughest meats and poultry, nothing beats an old-fashioned, manual, cast-iron or stainless steel grinder (with coarse and fine cutting plates) that clamps or suctions to a counter or table. The one I still use is the one I inherited from my mother, who inherited it from her mother. I also own a 300-watt electric machine with a stainless steel housing, 3 cutting plates, a sausage attachment, and forward-reverse action that can grind about 3 pounds of meat or poultry per minute. For both grinders, foods need to be cut into relatively small chunks, and to avoid bad clogs, any bone fragments, gristle, and tough tendons should be removed before grinding. With most electric models, you must remove the knife and plate to clean clogs; with others, you can simply turn the worm in reverse. If fats build up inside the cutter housing of a grinder after steady use, it's best to disassemble the machine, wash all parts in hot, sudsy water, and reassemble. (Another option is to grind one or two slices of bread to clean the feed screw.) To keep the metal parts of a grinder rust-free after washing, always dry them thoroughly and rub with a little cooking oil. Manual home grinders generally cost between $30 and $75 and electric ones between $100 and $200. It is always essential to read a manufacturer's instructions carefully.

Food Processors

Throughout this book, I often specify a food processor or offer the option of a meat grinder or food processor for grinding foods for certain dishes. Food processors are indeed miraculous machines that are ideal when it comes to grinding, mincing, or pureeing meats, poultry, and seafood for dips, spreads, pâtés, mousses, and other styles of dishes. Generally, a standard medium processor with a powerful motor and pulse button that can be engaged while churning is all you need, the only trick being developing an expert "trigger finger" that allows you to pulse ingredients to exactly the right texture without reducing them to mush. The one disadvantage of food processors (as with some electric meat grinders) is that red meats, poultry, and game with tough gristle and sinew can entangle the blades and stall the motor of even the most rugged machines, meaning you must scrupulously trim various cuts and portions before processing them. For the best grinding results with the metal chopping blade, never process more than about a cup of cut-up or portioned ingredients at a time, scraping the processed contents of the work bowl into a container between batches. For a coarse grind, zap the pulse button on and off three or four times; for a medium grind, five or six times; and for a fine grind or puree, hold down the button continuously till the desired consistency is attained. Since the various food processor manufacturers usually have specific instructions and tips for getting the most benefits from their machines, be sure to read your manual carefully and follow the advice.

Knives and Cleavers

While many primary ingredients in this book can often be chopped, diced, minced, shredded, and even slivered in a food processor, I still depend invariably on a standard, heavy, sharp chef's knife or a lighter, razor-sharp Japanese chef's knife (the Global brand is unique and inimitable) to produce the results I want with no risk of overprocessing. To bone lesser cuts of meat (blade beef chuck, pork necks and arm steaks, veal shank and breast), most poultry intended for grinding, and fish, I also use a good boning knife, and to trim tough connective tissue, gristle, and tendons from meats, turkey legs, and the like, I couldn't work without a razor-sharp paring knife. For hacking any ingredients with thick bones

For the best grinding results with the metal chopping blade, never process more than about a cup of cut-up or portioned ingredients at a time.

(and often for rapid mincing), it's always good to have a heavy, old-fashioned Chinese cleaver on hand.

Bowls and Spoons

I draw attention to bowls only because, obvious as they may seem to any facet of cooking, they are particularly important when dealing with bulky ground meats, poultry, and seafood, which often must be mixed by hand or stirred with a spoon. In my kitchen, the bigger and heavier the bowl, the better, and a good rule of thumb is to use a glass or ceramic bowl that measures about double the volume of the ingredients being mixed. As for mixing spoons, nothing beats sturdy wooden ones with long handles for durability and a good grip.

Pans, Dishes, and Molds

Unless a recipe in this book calls for a nonreactive enameled or stainless steel skillet or saucepan (which does not react unpleasantly to acidic ingredients like tomatoes, citrus, and vinegar), feel free to use any cast-iron, aluminum, copper, or other piece of equipment in your collection. If a specific size of skillet or pan is not indicated, use a medium one (usually an 8- to 9-inch skillet or 1-quart saucepan). A 9- to 10-inch pie plate, tart pan, or quiche dish, a 9 by 5 by 3-inch glass or metal loaf pan, a 5-cup soufflé dish, attractive 1½- and 2-quart ovenproof casseroles, and various small ramekins and molds are also needed for many of the recipes.

Sausage Funnels and Casings

If you grind sausage in a meat grinder without a sausage attachment or in a food processor, you will need a funnel with which to stuff the sausage into a casing for links. Different styles and sizes of sausage funnels can be found in most kitchen supply stores and online (separately or in sets), and funnel kits that fit meat grinders with various plate diameters are also available. Most funnels are plastic and inexpensive. Natural hog, sheep, and collagen sausage casings can be acquired from some butchers and occasionally in large grocery stores, but since very few large store butchers now grind any sausage, you may have to either find a small-time professional who still does or resort to ordering packaged casings online in 50-foot lengths. (Produced from a meat gelatin and marketed in sticks or cups, collagen casings are used today for most commercial sausage.) Natural hog and sheep casings are preserved in salt and should be rinsed before using. Natural casings can be stored in the refrigerator for up to 1 year; collagen casings require no refrigeration but should be kept in a cool area. All sausage casings are inexpensive, and, generally, 1 pound of sausage needs about 2 feet of standard casing. For added flavor and a slightly crackly texture, I prefer natural casings to the collagen ones. (Note: Sausage-making is a fairly intricate art, and since there are many details about equipment and procedures that extend beyond the scope of the recipes in this book, I recommend that anyone seriously interested in the subject buy a good specialized book.)

Practical Information and Tips

Testy Terminology

If the meats, poultry, and seafood that are coarsely chopped, shredded, slivered, mashed, or pureed throughout this book seem pretty self-explanatory, those that are ground, minced, and finely chopped (especially in a food processor) may create a bit more confusion. Although there is no exact science to defining such culinary terms, at least to my mind *ground* indicates the finest texture of the three, followed by the coarser *minced*, followed by the even coarser *finely chopped*. At times, the difference in these textures can be negligible, so it might be best just to let individual taste and common sense be your guide.

The Chill Factor

Although it is not indicated in many recipes in this book, chilling most raw meats, poultry, and seafood briefly in the freezer before grinding or mincing them not only facilitates the procedure but also helps preserve flavorful juices. This is particularly true when using a food processor, the point being to firm up the texture of the food so that it offers some resistance to the metal blade and quickly flakes instead of being reduced to a paste. Super-chilled meats also pass much more easily through a meat grinder. The fattier the item, the longer it should be chilled, but generally, about 30 minutes in the freezer should suffice to produce a firm grinding texture.

Butcher as Best Friend

Nobody seriously interested in producing many of the international dishes featured in this book can afford to be without a knowledgeable, skillful, and friendly butcher—at a grocery store, in an upscale deli, or at an almost extinct neighborhood butcher shop. More often than not today, the majority of whole and ground provisions that you need are readily available in the well-stocked cases of markets, but where do you turn when you want a greater or lesser ratio of fat in ground beef chuck or dark-meat turkey for burgers, when you need pristine fatback to add to home-ground veal or to line a terrine for pâté, when you decide to grind last-minute sausage and don't have enough casings, or when fresh lamb kidneys, veal sweetbreads, full-flavored old hens, or salt cod are simply not available in a market's display case? Butchers are not magicians, most follow strict safety standards when it comes to what they will and will not grind, and sometimes their suppliers simply cannot provide the particular organic pork, fowl, or game that a customer demands. But in general, a reliable butcher can often make the difference between mediocre and memorable Pennsylvania Dutch scrapple, French brandade, Latin American picadillo, and true German bratwurst. As my wise mother used to say over and over, "When you find a good butcher, treat him like family."

As my wise mother used to say over and over, "When you find a good butcher, treat him like family."

Packaged Mixes and Combos

Today you see them in almost all markets: packages of anonymous, reasonably priced mixed ground meats, as well as combos comprised of distinctly separate grinds of beef, pork, and veal, marketed mainly for meat loaves. More often than not, these products (like "stew meat") contain mainly meat trimmings, and while there's really no way to determine the quality of the meats or the ratio of lean to fat, generally I find the mixtures respectable enough and certainly ideal if you're on a tight budget and don't have the time to grind your own. In all likelihood, the meats will be no better or worse than individually packaged ground ones, and a distinct advantage to the combos is that you can either mix the ground meats together for loaves, patties, chilies, meatballs, croquettes, and pies or use them separately for sausages, forcemeats, and sauces.

A Few Choice Words on Fat

There's not a single recipe in this book that bows to some people's overinflated and misconceived obsession with fats, and the reasons are simple. First, fat is what gives ground and chopped meats, poultry, and seafood much of their succulence and appealing texture, as anyone knows who's sunk teeth into a juicy hamburger made with ground beef chuck, chicken salad or croquettes made with the ground meat of a fatty old stewing hen, and fish cakes made with silky ground or minced salmon with its nice ratio of fat. Second, the amount of added fat needed to enhance ground lean meats, fowl, and seafood is virtually negligible in my recipes, thus precluding any drastic health threats to the calorie- and cholesterol-conscious. And third, the truth is that, contrary to popular perception, nothing is less appetizing than a patty made with ultra-lean, bone-dry chopped beef fillet or turkey breast, a pork pie prepared with fatless loin instead of tender shoulder, sausages that are tough due to lack of fat, or a shrimp quiche that's not moistened with just a tablespoon of bacon grease. Nobody dislikes excess fat more than I do, which is why I drain off most grease from fatty ground meats that have been browned for chilies, certain pies and casseroles, and all sauces. But to reject lesser (and usually inexpensive) cuts of meat, dark poultry parts, and such fish as salmon, herring, and trout just because they have a higher fat content than other varieties is both senseless and foolish.

Better Safe than Sad

Anybody who reads the newspaper today is aware of the risks of bacterial contamination with meats, poultry, and seafood that are not handled and cooked properly, and never should more precaution be taken than when dealing with ground and chopped raw items that, by their very nature, are doubly exposed to factors that can cause safety problems. Common sense dictates that any unused packaged or home-ground meats should be kept tightly covered in the refrigerator for no longer than about 2 days, and while I never hesitate to prepare beef, veal, or lamb patties, balls, loaves, dumplings, and croquettes till just cooked through, I am careful to cook all ground pork dishes and sausages till well done (not meaning, of course, till dry and tasteless). Also, when I grind my own raw meats (especially pork), I make sure that all parts of the meat grinder or the blades and bowl of the food processor have been washed in sudsy water, and, like professional butchers, never would I grind raw beef, veal, or lamb after grinding raw pork, poultry, or seafood (which, despite all precautions today, could harbor dangerous parasites or bacteria) without first thoroughly washing all the equipment.

Due to careful handling and/or preservatives, the packaged ground chicken and turkey found in markets can be deemed safe, and so long as you respect the expiration date on the label and keep the product well-chilled, there should be no spoilage problems. Suffice it to say that when I grind or chop my own raw poultry, there's not a finger, working surface, knife, or machine part that comes in contact with the meat that isn't washed with soap and water afterward. As for fresh seafood, my only real precaution is to keep the fish or shellfish tightly covered and icy cold in the refrigerator for no more than 1 or 2 days.

Dos and Don'ts of Storage and Freezing

All ground raw meats and poultry are highly perishable, especially those that are prepackaged in the supermarket, and I go out of my way to use packaged goods the same day I buy them and not grind or chop any whole cuts or pieces till I'm ready to start cooking. If I do need to store ground meats and poultry (which happens especially when they're on sale and I buy in quantity), I wrap them freshly in plastic wrap, place them in zip-top plastic bags (in separate batches, if necessary), and store them in the refrigerator for no longer than 2 days or the freezer for up to about 3 months (any longer and they risk freezer burn and lose significant moisture). Carefully wrapped in plastic wrap and sealed in resealable zip-top plastic bags, fresh meat and poultry sausage keeps well in the refrigerator for up to a week and for about 2 months in the freezer. I allow all frozen chopped meats and poultry to thaw in the refrigerator overnight—never on the open counter.

Any fresh fish I plan to grind I buy the same day and never keep in the refrigerator for more than a few hours. I do not freeze ground fish, and I discard any that is not used in cooking. Fresh uncooked shellfish that I intend to grind, chop, dice, or flake I usually buy the same day, and any that must be stored is wrapped tightly in plastic and kept in the refrigerator for no more than a day. The only shellfish I freeze is shrimp I find on sale, and when frozen in cartons filled with water, the shrimp maintain their firm texture for up to about 2 months. I never freeze fresh crabmeat, scallops, clams, oysters, mussels, or cooked lobster meat, but when carefully wrapped in plastic wrap and sealed in zip-top bags, fresh seafood sausages can be frozen for up to a month.

Jazzing Up

No foods are more versatile than ground or chopped meats, poultry, and seafood, and while this book is full of unusual domestic and foreign recipes, there are literally dozens of novel ways to jazz up the more familiar dishes we prepare on a regular basis. Chopped steaks, for example, can be given altogether new taste

I allow all frozen chopped meats and poultry to thaw in the refrigerator overnight— never on the open counter.

and texture by mixing different ground meats together, stuffing them with blue, goat, or another unexpected cheese, or adding minced onions, carrots, garlic, olives, or herbs to the mixture; or by enhancing the meat with a little barbecue sauce, tomato puree, sour cream, or rolled oats and spices softened in milk. Lamb, veal, or pork meatballs can be seasoned with curry powder or spiked with finely chopped dill pickles, chutney, capers, and even anchovies, and they (like meat loaves) can be lightened with club soda or broth, both of which have a leavening effect in any ground meat dish. For meat loaves made with ground beef, ham, or turkey, a layer of hard-boiled eggs hidden in the middle makes a delightful surprise when the loaf is sliced, and, by the same token, any ordinary seafood croquettes or cakes with a few tiny boiled shrimp buried in the centers suddenly become a special treat. The possibilities for jazzing up ground dishes are endless, and I urge you to use your imagination and common sense throughout this book.

Appetizers, Canapés, and Dips

French Country Pâté

No ground meat specialty is more subtle and glorious than a genuine French country pâté served with toasted French bread and the tiny, tart pickles known as cornichons, and this has been my standard recipe for as long as I can remember. Pork fat is essential for a perfect texture, so unless you want a dry pâté, don't skimp on this important ingredient. Equally important to the texture is the weighting down of the pâté after it has cooked, and I find nothing is handier than a board I cut specially to fit inside the mold and on which I place a brick or a few canned goods. The pâté should be served just chilled, not cold.

Makes 8 to 10 servings

1 pound fresh pork fat
1 pound lean pork shoulder
½ pound cooked ham
¼ pound chicken livers, trimmed
4 garlic cloves, peeled
2 tablespoons heavy cream
2 large eggs
¼ cup brandy
1 teaspoon salt
1 teaspoon freshly ground black pepper
¼ teaspoon ground allspice
¼ teaspoon dried thyme
¼ cup all-purpose flour

1. Thinly slice about one-quarter of the pork fat and line a 1½-quart pâté mold or terrine with the slices, allowing the long ends to hang outside the mold. Set aside.

2. In a food processor, finely grind the remaining pork fat, pork shoulder, and ham and scrape the mixture into a bowl. Place the chicken livers, garlic, cream, eggs, and brandy in the food processor and grind coarsely. Add about one-third of the pork and ham mixture to the livers and grind just till well blended.

3. Preheat the oven to 400°F.

4. Scrape the contents of the food processor into the mixture in the bowl, add all the remaining ingredients, and stir till well blended and smooth. Fill the prepared mold with the pâté mixture and fold the overhanging strips of pork fat over the top. Cover tightly with heavy foil, place the mold in a shallow baking pan with about 2 inches of water, and bake for 3 hours. Remove the foil and continue baking till the top of the pâté is slightly crusted, about 20 minutes.

5. Remove the pan from the oven, place a board or another pan or dish that is slightly smaller than the mold on top of the baked pâté, stack heavy objects on top, and weight the pâté till it is completely cooled and the texture is firm (about 3 hours). (There will be an overflow of fat after weights are placed on top.)

6. Chill the pâté overnight. Bring almost to room temperature before serving in thin or medium slices.

Kentucky Country Ham Mousse

Makes about
5 cups

Kentucky produces some of the South's greatest cured country ham, but as any Rebel cook knows, it's always a problem wondering what to do with the hardened ends and odd pieces of any baked ham. This molded mousse is one delicious solution, and thanks to the miracle of the food processor, it is not only relatively easy but also fairly quick to prepare—not counting the chilling time required. Garnished with sprigs of watercress, parsley, or rosemary, the mousse is ideal for a cocktail buffet. Ordinary smoked ham can be substituted, but the mousse will not have half the flavor.

4 tablespoons (½ stick) butter
¼ cup all-purpose flour
1 cup milk, heated
1 tablespoon Dijon mustard
¼ teaspoon powdered sage
Cayenne pepper to taste
¼ cup Madeira
2 large egg yolks
½ cup heavy cream
2 tablespoons unflavored powdered gelatin
½ cup chicken broth
1 pound cured country ham, trimmed of fat and cut into chunks
Watercress, parsley, or rosemary sprigs for garnish

1. In a heavy saucepan, melt the butter over moderate heat, add the flour, and whisk the roux for 1 minute. Gradually add the milk, reduce the heat to low, and whisk the mixture till very thick. Add the mustard, sage, cayenne, and Madeira and stir till very well blended.

2. In a small bowl, combine the egg yolks and heavy cream, whisk till well blended, and stir in a little of the hot sauce. Add the mixture to the hot sauce and continue cooking over low heat, whisking till thickened.

3. In another small bowl, soften the gelatin in the chicken broth for 5 minutes, then stir it into the hot sauce. Place the ham into a meat grinder or food processor, grind finely, and stir into the sauce.

4. Scrape the mixture into a 1-quart mold, cover with plastic wrap, and chill for at least 6 hours. Unmold the mousse on a large serving dish, garnish the edges with watercress, and serve with rectangles of toast or crackers.

Garnished with sprigs of watercress, parsley, or rosemary, the mousse is ideal for a cocktail buffet.

Spanish Chorizo–Stuffed Mushrooms

Makes 4 to 6 servings

Approach a bar in Madrid or Barcelona for a glass of crisp fino sherry and this is one of the many tempting tapas you might find on a colorful plate. I like to serve the stuffed mushrooms as an appetizer preceding any seafood and rice casserole, but they're also perfect for a formal buffet. Spanish-style chorizo sausage is now available at most delis and markets, but if you're unable to find it, substitute ⅓ cup of finely chopped pepperoni. My favorite mushrooms for this dish are cremini or medium shiitakes, which have much more flavor than the ordinary button variety.

2 tablespoons olive oil, plus more for brushing mushrooms

1 Spanish chorizo sausage, skinned and finely chopped

1 small onion, finely chopped

1 garlic clove, minced

1 dozen large mushrooms (about 1 pound), stems finely chopped and caps reserved

2 tablespoons sherry

½ cup dry bread crumbs

1 large egg yolk, beaten

2 tablespoons minced fresh parsley leaves

Salt and freshly ground black pepper to taste

1. Preheat the oven to 375°F.

2. In a large skillet, heat the oil over moderate heat, add the chorizo, and stir for 1 minute. Add the onion, garlic, and mushroom stems and stir till the mushrooms release most of their liquid, about 5 minutes. Add the sherry and let cook till it is evaporated. Add the bread crumbs, stir till well blended, and remove from the heat. Stir in the egg yolk, parsley, and salt and pepper till well blended, and set the filling aside.

3. Brush the mushroom caps with a little olive oil and arrange them in a large baking dish. Fill the caps with equal amounts of the filling, mounding it, and bake till golden, about 10 minutes. Serve hot or warm.

Scottish Deviled Kidney Spread

In Scotland, a spicy spread such as this (as well as the Scottish organ meat sausage called haggis) would most often be made with beef or pork kidneys, but since these robust organs are an acquired taste, I recommend that you use much milder, utterly delectable lamb or veal kidneys. When shopping for any kidneys, look for those that are firm, with even color and no dry spots, and remember that kidneys are very perishable and should never be held in the refrigerator for more than a day. Since they are relatively delicate, lamb and veal kidneys should be broiled in butter just till the interiors are pinkish and never overcooked to prevent toughness.

2 tablespoons fruit chutney, finely chopped

2 tablespoons Dijon mustard

2 teaspoons prepared English mustard

2 tablespoons fresh lemon juice

1 teaspoon salt

Freshly ground black pepper to taste

16 whole lamb kidneys (about 2 pounds), trimmed of fat and membranes and split lengthwise

4 tablespoons (½ stick) butter, melted

¼ cup chopped fresh parsley leaves

**Makes about
1½ cups**

1. In a large, shallow glass baking dish, combine the chutney, mustards, lemon juice, salt, and pepper and stir till well blended. Add the kidneys, turn to coat evenly on all sides, cover with plastic wrap, and let stand for 2 hours, turning periodically.

2. Preheat the oven broiler.

3. Pour the butter into a shallow baking pan, add the kidneys (reserve the chutney mixture), turn to coat, and broil till just pink inside, about 3 minutes on each side. Transfer the kidneys and butter to a food processor, add the chutney mixture and parsley, and grind the mixture to a smooth paste.

4. Scrape the paste into a crock, chill for about 30 minutes, and serve with crackers.

When shopping for any kidneys, look for those that are firm, with even color and no dry spots.

Appetizers,
Canapés,
and Dips

Greek Lamb, Raisin, and Pine Nut Spanakopitas

In Greece, the small, crispy triangles called spanakopitas are made with everything from feta cheese to spinach to a variety of meats, and since they can be assembled far in advance, frozen, and popped in the oven for last-minute canapés or a first course, I'm never without a tray full. Those made with minced lamb shoulder, raisins, and pine nuts are particularly delectable, but if the lamb presents a problem, ground beef shoulder or round is almost as good. Frozen phyllo dough is now available in all markets; just be sure to keep the sheets covered with a damp towel as you work so they don't dry out.

Makes 3 to 6 servings

¼ cup olive oil
1 medium onion, minced
1 garlic clove, minced
¾ pound lean lamb shoulder, minced
½ cup toasted pine nuts
½ cup seedless dark raisins, chopped
2 tablespoons minced fresh parsley leaves
Salt and freshly ground black pepper to taste
6 sheets phyllo pastry (fresh or frozen, thawed if frozen)

1. In a large skillet, heat 2 tablespoons of the oil over moderate heat, add the onion and garlic, and stir till golden, about 5 minutes. Add the lamb and stir till lightly browned, about 3 minutes. Transfer to a bowl, add the nuts, raisins, parsley, and salt and pepper, stir till well blended, and set aside.

2. Preheat the oven to 400°F. Brush a large baking sheet with part of the remaining oil and set aside.

3. Cut a phyllo sheet in half crosswise, place a half sheet on a work surface, and cover the remaining sheets with a damp towel to prevent drying out. Spoon a full tablespoon of the lamb mixture on the middle of the sheet, leaving the bottom edge and sides uncovered. Fold the bottom edge up over the mixture, fold in the sides, and roll the pastry into a triangle. Repeat with the remaining sheets and mixture.

4. Arrange the spanakopitas on the prepared baking sheet, brush with the remaining oil, and bake till golden and crisp, about 20 minutes. Serve hot.

French Rillettes of Pork

French pork rillettes are one of the most glorious appetizers ever conceived, and I've never served a crock or ramekin that wasn't wiped clean by guests. Traditionally, rillettes are made by shredding the cooked, tender, unctuous meats with two forks, but so long as you don't over-grind, they can be prepared quickly in a food processor. Packed into small ramekins, the rillettes could be served as individual appetizers, but I prefer simply to place a large crock with a big basket of toasted French bread rounds in the middle of the table and let guests help themselves. Do try to make the rillettes a day in advance and place in the refrigerator to allow the flavors to meld.

Makes 8 to 10 servings

2 pounds boneless pork shoulder

¾ pound fresh pork fat

1 medium onion, minced

1 garlic clove, minced

Herb bouquet (½ teaspoon dried thyme, 2 bay leaves, 3 whole cloves, and 2 parsley sprigs tied in cheesecloth)

Salt and freshly ground black pepper to taste

2 cups chicken broth

1 cup dry white wine

1. Trim off any skin on the pork shoulder and cut the meat and fat into 2-inch chunks. Place the meat, fat, onion, garlic, herb bouquet, and salt and pepper in a casserole or large saucepan. Add the broth, wine, and enough water to cover by 1 inch, bring to a boil, reduce the heat to low, cover, and simmer till the meat is very tender, about 3 hours, skimming from time to time. Uncover the casserole and continue simmering till the liquid has evaporated and the meat is cooking in the fat, about 1 hour.

2. Transfer the meat to a heavy bowl and let the fat cool to room temperature in the casserole. Shred the meat with two heavy forks (or grind coarsely in a food processor), add the cooled fat, and continue working with the fork till the mixture is smooth and silky—almost a heavy paste. Taste for salt and pepper, pack the rillettes in small ramekins or a large crock, cover with plastic wrap, and refrigerate for at least 24 hours. Serve with small rounds of toasted French bread.

Charleston Hobotee

Makes
6 servings

Today, chefs in the Carolina Lowcountry are rediscovering many of the area's glorious specialties that can be traced back to the plantation era, the one salient exception being this luscious curried meat custard that no doubt derives from the Malaysian import bobotie and that I recall eating as a child at the old Fort Sumter Hotel in Charleston. Legend has it that, a century and a half ago, hobotee was mainly a breakfast dish prepared with whatever ground or minced meats happened to be on hand, but like my Southern mother and grandmother, I've always served it (with glasses of sherry) as a first course at any seafood meal. I think the dish is most subtle when made with minced or finely chopped cooked veal (the original probably involved lamb), but by all means use either roasted beef round or pork loin if that's what's most readily available.

3 tablespoons butter
1 medium onion, finely chopped
2 tablespoons curry powder
1½ cups finely chopped cooked veal, beef, or pork
1 slice white bread, soaked in milk and squeezed dry
2 tablespoons chopped almonds
2 tablespoons fresh lemon juice
2 large eggs
½ teaspoon sugar
Salt to taste
1 cup half-and-half
Dash of ground white pepper
6 small bay leaves

1. Preheat the oven to 300°F.

2. In a skillet, melt the butter over moderate heat, add the onion, and cook, stirring, till softened, 2 to 3 minutes. Add the curry powder and cook, stirring, 2 minutes longer. Transfer the onion to a bowl, add the meat, bread, almonds, lemon juice, one of the eggs, the sugar, and salt and blend thoroughly.

3. Butter six ½-cup ramekins and divide the meat mixture equally among them. In another bowl, combine the remaining egg, the half-and-half, and white pepper and whisk till well blended. Pour equal amounts of the cream mixture into the ramekins, garnish the tops with a bay leaf, and bake till golden, about 25 minutes. Serve hot.

Like my Southern mother and grandmother, I've always served it (with glasses of sherry) as a first course at any seafood meal.

Spiced Chicken and Ham Spread

Makes about
2½ cups

This is one of the best ways I know to use up leftover chicken and/or ham, and I've also been known to turn the remains of a roast pork loin or turkey breast into a similar spread intended for canapés. Feel free to substitute a few chopped capers for the sweet pickle, and by all means play around with different spices or herbs.

1 cup chopped cooked chicken
1 cup chopped cooked ham
1 tablespoon chopped sweet pickle
1 tablespoon grated lemon rind
4 tablespoons (½ stick) butter, softened
⅛ teaspoon grated nutmeg
Salt and freshly ground black pepper to taste
Tabasco sauce to taste

In a food processor, combine the chicken, ham, pickle, and lemon rind and grind almost to a puree. Scrape the mixture into a bowl, add the butter, nutmeg, salt and pepper, and Tabasco, and mix till well blended and smooth. Cover with plastic wrap and chill for about 30 minutes. Serve on thin rounds of rye bread or crackers.

Yorkshire Potted Ham Canapés

Yorkshire, in northern England, is known for its superlative hams, and locals learned centuries ago that one of the best ways to deal with leftover ham was to grind it, pot it with sweet farm butter and various seasonings, and use the spread to make all sorts of canapés. Technically, this potted ham should be covered with about ⅛ inch of clarified melted butter and chilled for a couple of hours to be authentic, but I don't find that at all necessary. Ideally, genuine English "brown bread" would be used for these canapés, but given that impracticality, thin whole-wheat toast is almost as good. At an informal supper, I might also simply place a crock of this spread and a basket of toast on the table and let guests help themselves.

1½ cups finely ground lean ham
3 large hard-boiled eggs
1 tablespoon minced sweet pickle
8 tablespoons (1 stick) butter, softened
¼ teaspoon dry mustard
Salt and freshly ground black pepper to taste
Rectangles of thin whole-wheat toast, crusts removed

Place the ham in a bowl. Press the egg yolks through a sieve into the bowl and discard the egg whites. Add the pickle, butter, mustard, and salt and pepper to the bowl, beat with a wooden spoon till the mixture is smooth, pack into a crock, and chill for 30 minutes. Serve with the toast rectangles.

Makes about
2 cups

Appetizers,
Canapés,
and Dips

17

Russian Chopped Chicken Liver

Makes about 2½ cups

At most Jewish delis and restaurants in the United States, chopped chicken liver has evolved mainly as a fairly coarse, mild spread often served with chopped raw onions, but in Russia, *pashet* is not only ground to an almost silky texture but is also flavored with everything from bacon to spices to strong spirits to sweet pickle juice. You can sauté the onions and livers in chicken fat, but for the best flavor there's really nothing like bacon grease rendered from bacon that is then ground with the other ingredients. This spread can be frozen very successfully, but do time things so it can be served slightly chilled.

2 slices bacon, chopped
2 medium onions, chopped
1½ pounds chicken livers, trimmed and halved
2 hard-boiled eggs, finely chopped
¼ teaspoon grated nutmeg
Salt and freshly ground black pepper to taste
2 tablespoons brandy
Paprika for sprinkling

1. In a large, heavy skillet, fry the bacon over moderate heat till it renders most of its grease, about 5 minutes. Add the onions and livers and stir for 5 minutes. Cover the pan, reduce the heat to low, and simmer 5 minutes longer. Remove from the heat, let cool, and reserve the pan juices.

2. In a food processor, combine the bacon, onions, and livers, grind to a coarse puree, and scrape into a bowl. Add the reserved pan juices, eggs, nutmeg, salt and pepper, and brandy and beat with a wooden spoon till fluffy, about 5 minutes. Transfer the mixture to a serving bowl, smooth the top with a rubber spatula, sprinkle paprika over the top, and serve slightly chilled or at room temperature with toast or pumpernickel rounds.

Italian Chicken Liver and Mushroom Crostini

It's been said that Italian cooks know how to make a feast with ordinary toast, and these luscious crostini made with ground chicken livers, mushrooms, capers, and Marsala are a perfect example. Traditionally, the toasts are served as an appetizer before grilled fish or pasta, but you can just as easily use smaller pieces of bread and pass the crostini as a canapé. I think day-old Italian bread works even better than fresh for these rich toasts. Do be careful not to overcook the livers; they should remain pink inside.

¼ cup olive oil
3 tablespoons butter
1 large onion, finely chopped
1 cup sliced mushrooms
3 tablespoons capers, chopped
3 tablespoons Marsala wine
Salt and freshly ground black pepper to taste
½ pound chicken livers, trimmed and coarsely chopped
Ten to twelve ½-inch-thick slices Italian bread
Minced fresh parsley leaves for garnish

1. Preheat the oven to 375°F.

2. In a large skillet, heat 2 tablespoons each of the oil and butter over moderate heat, add the onion and mushrooms, and stir till softened and all the mushroom liquid is evaporated. Add the capers, Marsala, and salt and pepper, stir till most of the wine is evaporated, and scrape the mixture into a food processor.

3. Add 1 tablespoon of the remaining oil plus the remaining 1 tablespoon butter to the skillet, add the chicken livers, stir till they are slightly browned but still pink inside, and transfer to
(continued)

Makes 10 to 12 crostini

Appetizers, Canapés, and Dips

19

the food processor. Grind the mixture to a coarse puree, scrape into a bowl, and set aside.

4. Place the bread slices on a large baking sheet, brush with the remaining 2 tablespoons oil, and toast them in the upper third of the oven till crisp, about 7 minutes. Spread the liver mixture equally on the toasts and sprinkle the parsley over the tops.

Do be careful not to overcook the livers; they should remain pink inside.

Austrian Poultry, Meat, and Hazelnut Terrine

What I love about this relatively simple terrine is not only the wonderful combination of disparate flavors but also the way it freezes well so long as it's wrapped tightly in foil. Do feel free to experiment with different ground meats and poultry (veal, turkey, game, chicken giblets), nuts, and liqueurs, and by all means add a few chopped herbs to the mixture if you want to heighten the flavor even more. Remember that the texture of this terrine should be fairly coarse, meaning that care must be taken not to grind the meats and poultry to a puree. Also, the terrine is best if served only slightly chilled.

Makes 8 to 10 servings

1 pound skinless, boneless chicken breasts
½ pound boneless pork shoulder, coarsely chopped
¼ pound fresh pork fat, coarsely chopped
¼ pound chicken livers, trimmed and coarsely chopped
4 juniper berries, crushed
2 tablespoons kirsch liqueur
Salt and freshly ground black pepper to taste
¼ cup chopped hazelnuts
2 bay leaves

1. Cut one of the chicken breasts into 6 or 7 thin slices, wrap in plastic wrap, and set aside in the refrigerator. Coarsely chop the remaining breasts and place in a large bowl. Add the pork shoulder, pork fat, chicken livers, juniper berries, kirsch, and salt and pepper, toss, cover with plastic wrap, and let marinate overnight in the refrigerator.

2. Preheat the oven to 300°F. Grease a 10-inch-long rectangular terrine or loaf pan and set aside.

(continued)

Appetizers, Canapés, and Dips

3. Transfer the ingredients in the bowl to a food processor, grind coarsely, and scrape the mixture back into the bowl. Add the hazelnuts and stir till well blended. Pack half the mixture into the prepared terrine, arrange the reserved chicken strips over the top, and add the remaining mixture, smoothing the top with a rubber spatula. Place the bay leaves on top and cover the terrine tightly with foil. Place the terrine in a large roasting pan with enough hot water to come halfway up the sides and bake till firm and a knife inserted in the center comes out dry, 1 to 1¼ hours. Let cool, then chill for at least 3 hours before serving in slices.

French Duck Liver Terrine with Pistachios

Now that fresh duck liver is more readily available in our markets, there's really no excuse for not preparing one of the most luscious terrines of the entire French culinary repertoire. Do not listen to those who say that cured, commercial bacon (with its smoky flavor) can be substituted for fresh pork fat in this dish, and if you can't find packages of sliced fatback in the market, get into the habit, as I have, of collecting and freezing any excess surface fat trimmed from pork loins and shoulders just for use in terrines such as this one. Although the terrine can be served the day after it's prepared, I prefer to let it mellow in the refrigerator for at least 2 days. As for the duck liver itself (which weighs between 1 and $1\frac{1}{2}$ pounds), it should be held in the refrigerator no longer than one day before being used.

Makes
8 servings

2 pounds thinly sliced chilled pork fatback
1 pound fresh duck liver, cut into chunks
1 pound lean pork shoulder, cut into chunks
2 slices white bread, soaked in ¼ cup milk and squeezed dry
1½ tablespoons all-purpose flour
1½ teaspoons salt
½ teaspoon ground cinnamon
½ teaspoon ground allspice
½ teaspoon freshly ground black pepper
¼ teaspoon grated nutmeg
⅛ teaspoon ground cloves
⅛ teaspoon ground cardamom
¼ cup brandy
¼ cup shelled and coarsely chopped pistachio nuts
2 teaspoons dried thyme
6 bay leaves
French cornichons

(continued)

Appetizers,
Canapés,
and Dips

23

1. Line a 2-quart terrine or loaf pan with about half of the sliced pork fatback, allowing enough to hang over the edges to cover the top when filled with forcemeat.

2. Run the duck liver, pork shoulder, and all but 3 or 4 slices of the remaining fatback through the fine blade of a meat grinder. In a food processor, combine the bread with the ground meats, add the flour, salt, cinnamon, allspice, pepper, nutmeg, cloves, cardamom, and brandy and reduce to a thick paste. Add the nuts and spurt the machine just long enough to blend well.

3. Preheat the oven to 325°F.

4. Scrape the forcemeat into the prepared terrine, pat and push with your fingers to remove any air from the mixture, dampen your hands, and fold the overhanging fat over the top. Pat and smooth to make a neat loaf, sprinkle the thyme over the top, place the bay leaves in a row across the top, and carefully arrange the remaining slices of fatback over the terrine.

5. Place the terrine in a large roasting pan with enough hot water to come halfway up the sides and bake till a knife inserted in the center comes out dry, about 2 hours. Remove and discard the top slices of fatback, cover the terrine with foil, fit a board or smaller pan or plate on the top, weight down with a brick or canned goods, and let cool till the terrine is firm.

6. Serve the terrine in medium slices with the cornichons.

Montauk Clam Fritters

You could use fresh minced clams (preferably East Coast quahogs or cherrystones or West Coast butter or razor clams), plus their juices, for these fritters, but since the canned varieties are already cooked (and fully acceptable in flavor and texture), I prefer them, since the risk of overcooking (and toughening) the clams is reduced. Be sure to watch the fritters carefully and remove them from the oil just as they turn brown. Although the fritters make an ideal appetizer, they can also be dropped into the oil by the teaspoon and served as a cocktail canapé.

Makes
4 servings

One 10½-ounce can minced clams, drained and juice reserved
1 large egg, beaten
1 teaspoon fresh lemon juice
1 tablespoon finely chopped fresh parsley leaves
1 cup all-purpose flour
1 teaspoon baking soda
¼ cup milk
2 tablespoons butter, melted
Salt and freshly ground black pepper to taste
Cayenne pepper to taste
Vegetable oil for shallow frying

1. In a bowl, combine the clams, egg, lemon juice, parsley, flour, and baking soda and stir till well blended. Blend the reserved clam juice with the milk and add just enough to the clam mixture to make a firm batter, stirring well. Add the butter, salt and pepper, and cayenne and stir till well blended.

2. In a large, heavy skillet, heat about ¼ inch of oil over moderate heat and, in batches, drop the batter by full tablespoons into the oil. Fry till cooked through and browned, 2 to 3 minutes, turning once. Drain on paper towels and serve hot.

Appetizers,
Canapés,
and Dips

25

Key West Conch Fritters

Makes
4 servings

Long associated with Key West, Florida, conch fritters are made with the small local mollusk in the large pink shell and sold at joints all along the busy streets. Since the meat is naturally tough, it must be tenderized by being either pounded repeatedly or finely ground, and never is a food processor handier than when dealing with this delicacy. Do not over-fry these chewy fritters, and while they can be served with tartar and other sauces as a first course, I prefer just a few squeezes of lime juice on mine. Since fresh conch (when it's available) is so perishable, you're best off using the canned or frozen product, both of which are already cleaned and fully acceptable.

½ pound canned or frozen conch meat (if fresh, foot and orange fin removed)

2 tablespoons fresh lime juice

1 small onion, minced

½ small green bell pepper, seeded and minced

1 garlic clove, minced

Salt and freshly ground black pepper to taste

Cayenne pepper to taste

1 large egg, beaten

1 cup whole milk

1 cup all-purpose flour

1 teaspoon baking powder

Vegetable oil for frying

Lime wedges for garnish

1. Dice the conch finely, place in a food processor, and grind till finely minced. Transfer to a glass bowl, add the lime juice, and toss well. Cover with plastic wrap and refrigerate for 30 minutes.

2. Add the onion, bell pepper, garlic, salt and pepper, cayenne, egg, and milk to the minced conch and stir till well blended.

3. In a large bowl, combine the flour and baking powder and stir till well blended. Gradually add to the conch mixture, stir till a thick batter forms, cover, and refrigerate for 1 hour.

4. To fry the fritters, heat about 2 inches of the oil in a large, heavy saucepan over moderately high heat and, in batches, drop tablespoons of the conch batter into the oil. Turning frequently, fry till golden brown, 4 to 5 minutes. Drain on paper towels. Serve immediately with the lime wedges to be squeezed over the fritters.

Brazilian Salt Cod Fritters

Makes 6 to 8 servings

Although generally imported from Spain or Portugal, dried salt cod (*bacalhau*) is a staple in Brazilian cooking, and nothing is more popular than these mild, crispy fritters served most often as an appetizer at informal seafood dinners. Do remember that all salt cod must be soaked in several changes of fresh water to leach out the salt and tame the strong flavor, and note that while the fish might be marketed as boneless, there are usually a few tiny bones that must be removed before chopping or grinding. I also like to serve these fritters at casual lunches with a big tossed salad, bread sticks, and a flinty white wine. At one time, salt cod in this country was readily available only in Latin, Asian, and Italian markets, but today it can be found in wooden flats at most large grocery stores.

1 pound boneless dried salt cod
2 tablespoons olive oil
1 medium onion, minced
2 tablespoons finely chopped fresh cilantro
½ teaspoon paprika
¼ teaspoon grated nutmeg
2 cups mashed potatoes
3 large eggs, beaten
Freshly ground black pepper to taste
½ cup milk, or more as needed
Vegetable oil for deep frying

1. Place the cod in a baking pan with enough water to cover and let soak for 8 to 10 hours, changing the water twice.

2. Change the water a third time, bring to a low boil, and simmer the cod for about 15 minutes. Drain the cod, cut into chunks, and discard any skin and bones.

3. In a large skillet, heat the olive oil over moderate heat, add the cod and onion, and stir till the fish flakes easily with a fork, about 5 minutes. Transfer to a food processor, add the cilantro, paprika, and nutmeg, grind to a coarse puree, and scrape into a bowl. Add the mashed potatoes, eggs, and pepper and stir till well blended. Gradually add enough of the milk to give the mixture a tight consistency.

4. Heat about 2 inches of vegetable oil in a deep fryer or heavy pot to 375°F on a thermometer. Roll the cod mixture into balls about the size of a walnut, drop them in batches into the hot oil, fry till golden and crisp, 2 to 3 minutes, and drain on paper towels.

5. Serve hot.

Do remember that all salt cod must be soaked in several changes of fresh water to leach out the salt and tame the strong flavor.

Smoked Salmon-Stuffed Eggs

Makes 6 to 8
servings

Smoked haddock, halibut, cod, or sturgeon can also be used to make the filling for these eggs, but whichever you choose, I find the texture is much more delectable if only half the fish is pureed and the other half is finely chopped. Although fresh chives and dill seem like natural seasonings for any smoked fish mixture, do feel free to experiment with chopped or minced olives, capers, anchovies, lemon rind, bacon, and the like. These eggs are great for buffets and picnics.

8 large hard-boiled eggs
¼ pound smoked salmon
4 ounces cream cheese, softened
2 tablespoons minced fresh chives
2 tablespoons minced fresh dill
Salt and freshly ground black pepper to taste
Small dill sprigs for garnish

1. Cut the eggs in half lengthwise, press the yolks through a sieve into a bowl, and reserve the whites. In a food processor, grind half the salmon to a puree and scrape into the bowl with the egg yolks. Finely chop the remaining salmon and add to the bowl. Add the cream cheese, chives, minced dill, and salt and pepper and stir till well blended and smooth.

2. Connect a star tube to a pastry bag, fill the bag with the salmon mixture, and pipe it evenly into the egg white cavities. Garnish the tops of each egg half with a sprig of dill.

Portuguese Sardine- and Caper-Stuffed Eggs

In Portugal, I've had these eggs stuffed with fresh sardines that are grilled and mashed with any number of other ingredients, but frankly, I find the canned fish packed in oil (preferably Portuguese, French, or Italian) to have a more distinctive flavor. Obviously, the eggs can be served at receptions, but since the filling is rich, they also make a beautiful first course served with Parmesan toast or fat sesame sticks and a dry white wine. Because of the fragile texture of sardines, do not use a food processor to make this filling, since it might end up being a liquidy mush.

Makes
8 servings

8 large hard-boiled eggs
Two 3¾-ounce cans skinless, boneless sardines packed in oil, drained
2 tablespoons capers, minced
1 tablespoon red wine vinegar
⅓ cup sour cream
2 tablespoons minced fresh parsley leaves
Salt and freshly ground black pepper to taste
Finely chopped pimentos for garnish

1. Cut the eggs in half lengthwise, press the yolks through a sieve into a bowl, and reserve the whites. In another bowl, mash the sardines with a fork till smooth; add the sieved yolks, capers, vinegar, sour cream, parsley, and salt and pepper, and stir till well blended and smooth.

2. Connect a star tube to a pastry bag, fill the bag with the sardine mixture, and pipe it into the egg white cavities. Garnish the top of each egg half with a few chopped pimentos.

Appetizers,
Canapés,
and Dips

31

Maryland Deviled Crab

Makes
4 servings

All over the Chesapeake Bay area of Maryland (and down through coastal Virginia and the Carolinas), deviled crab has long been a favorite appetizer in homes and seafood houses, and I don't hesitate for a second to classify the dish as one of America's greatest contributions to world gastronomy. One key to superlative deviled crab (in addition to careful seasoning) is to add just enough bread crumbs to bind the mixture; in fact, if you really want to highlight the moist, sweet crabmeat, you may choose (as I sometimes do) not to sprinkle additional bread crumbs on top and settle for just a little drizzled butter. Although the crab is "deviled" with dry mustard, paprika, and a few shakes of Tabasco, I must confess I always like a small bottle of Tabasco within arm's length at my table.

½ cup half-and-half

½ cup mayonnaise

2 large hard-boiled eggs, finely chopped

1½ teaspoons dry mustard

1 teaspoon paprika

1 tablespoon Worcestershire sauce

1 tablespoon fresh lemon juice

Tabasco sauce to taste

2 scallions (part of green tops included), minced

1 small red bell pepper, seeded and minced

½ teaspoon salt

1 pound fresh lump crabmeat, picked over for shells and cartilage and well flaked

1 cup fine dry bread crumbs

2 tablespoons butter, melted

1. Preheat the oven to 375°F. Butter four 4-ounce ramekins or crocks and set aside.

2. In a bowl, whisk together the half-and-half and mayonnaise till well blended; add the eggs, mustard, paprika, Worcestershire, lemon juice, and Tabasco, and stir till well blended. Add the scallions, bell pepper, and salt and stir till well blended. Gently fold in the crabmeat and ½ cup of the bread crumbs till well blended and divide the mixture equally among the prepared ramekins. Sprinkle the remaining bread crumbs equally over the tops, drizzle each with butter, and bake till golden and bubbly, about 30 minutes.

3. Serve hot.

Greek Taramasalata

Makes 6 to 8
servings

Available in jars at virtually all grocery stores, *tarama* is salted cod or carp roe that for centuries in Greece has been ground with bread crumbs, yogurt or cream, olive oil, and seasonings and eaten on pita bread as an appetizer or snack. I also like to stuff the mixture in quartered celery ribs or use it as a dip for various raw vegetables at cocktail parties, and my Greek grandfather loved nothing more than to add a couple of spoonfuls of the spread to his cucumber salads.

12 ounces *tarama*
¼ cup dry bread crumbs
¾ cup plain yogurt
3 tablespoons Greek or Italian olive oil
2 tablespoons fresh lemon juice
¼ teaspoon paprika
Cayenne pepper to taste
Lightly toasted morsels of pita bread or Melba toast rounds
Fresh rosemary leaves for garnish

1. In a food processor, combine the *tarama* and bread crumbs and grind to a paste. Add the yogurt, oil, lemon juice, paprika, and cayenne and grind to a puree. Scrape the mixture into a bowl, cover with plastic wrap, and chill for 1 hour.

2. To serve, spread the mixture evenly on pita morsels or Melba toast, arrange on a serving plate, and garnish the tops with one or two rosemary leaves.

Singapore Crabmeat and Peanut Toasts

These toasts make an unusual canapé reminiscent of decadent hotel lounges in Singapore, and nothing is simpler or quicker to prepare. If you prefer a more dramatic presentation, you could grind the peanuts separately and sprinkle them over the crabmeat before baking, but personally, I love the nuts mingled with all the other flavors. For the right texture, be sure to flake the crabmeat fairly well.

Makes
24 toasts

¼ cup roasted peanuts

1 garlic clove, chopped

3 tablespoons fresh lemon juice

1 tablespoon sesame oil

¼ teaspoon cayenne pepper

½ pound fresh lump crabmeat, picked over for shells and cartilage and flaked

2 scallions (white parts only), minced

Salt and freshly ground black pepper to taste

½ cup mayonnaise

6 slices white loaf bread (crusts removed), toasted and quartered

Minced fresh parsley leaves for garnish

1. Preheat the oven to 450°F.

2. In a food processor, combine the peanuts, garlic, lemon juice, oil, and cayenne and grind till the peanuts are finely chopped but not pureed. In a bowl, combine the crabmeat, scallions, salt and pepper, and mayonnaise, add the peanut mixture, and stir till well blended.

3. Spread 1 tablespoon of the mixture on each piece of toast, arrange the toasts on a baking sheet, and bake till lightly browned on top, about 10 minutes. Transfer the toasts to a serving tray, sprinkle parsley over the tops, and serve immediately.

Appetizers,
Canapés,
and Dips

Minced Clam, Black Olive, and Parmesan Canapés

Makes
18 canapés

The only precaution to take with these delectable canapés is not to overcook the clams, which toughens them. Remove them from the oven the second the cheese melts, and do try to serve them as hot as possible. I like to make these canapés with whole-grain bread, but any variety can be used so long as it has a fairly sturdy texture.

Two 6½-ounce cans minced clams, drained
12 to 14 black olives, pitted and minced
¼ cup minced red onion
2 tablespoons mayonnaise
6 slices whole-grain loaf bread (crusts removed), toasted
½ cup grated Parmesan cheese

1. Preheat the oven broiler.

2. In a bowl, combine the clams, olives, onion, and mayonnaise and mix till well blended. Spread equal amounts of the mixture on the toasts, cut each toast into thirds, and arrange them on a large baking sheet. Sprinkle cheese over the top of each and broil about 4 inches from the heat till the cheese is melted. Serve hot or warm.

Scandinavian Smoked Trout Canapés

Scandinavians grind all sorts of seafood to make small canapés or open-face sandwiches, and I find none so distinctive as smoked trout (or salmon) mixed with sour cream and spicy seasonings that is spread on rounds of pumpernickel and garnished with springs of fresh dill. Do notice that, for a toothy texture, part of the trout is simply chopped and added to the pureed mixture. It is also just as traditional to serve the mixture on thin rounds of cucumber instead of bread.

Makes 6 to 8 servings

> 1 pound smoked trout, skinned and boned
> ½ cup sour cream
> 2 tablespoons sunflower oil
> 2 tablespoons fresh lemon juice
> ½ teaspoon paprika
> Salt and cayenne pepper to taste
> Thin rounds of pumpernickel bread
> Fresh dill sprigs for garnish

1. Chop half the smoked trout and place it in a food processor. Add the sour cream, oil, lemon juice, paprika, and salt and cayenne, grind till the mixture is a thin puree, and scrape into a bowl. Finely chop the remaining trout, add to the puree, mix till well blended, cover with plastic wrap, and chill for 1 hour.

2. To serve, spread the mixture on the pumpernickel rounds and garnish each canapé with a small sprig of dill.

French Salt Cod Spread

Generally a smooth mixture of salt cod, garlic, olive oil, and cream, *brandade de morue* is found in households, restaurants, and cafés all over French Provence. Spread on fried or toasted croutons or just crusty French bread, the dish can be served with a green salad as a first course, as a canapé with cocktails or chilled rosé wine, or simply as a tasty snack. Some French cooks balk at making the spread with potatoes, others think nothing of adding lots of spices and herbs, and in Nîmes (where it supposedly originated), not so much as a trace of garlic is allowed. Personally, I like a heady, slightly chunky brandade (and often grind mine with a pestle in a large mortar instead of a food processor), but let your taste be your guide. Long, stiff sides of boneless salt cod (which must always be soaked in water before being cooked) can now be found in most fish markets and better grocery stores, and there is no substitute for this delectable spread.

Makes 4 to 6 servings as a main course; 8 to 12 as a party spread

1 pound boneless dried salt cod
1 cup milk
2 whole cloves
1 bay leaf
1 large potato, peeled and diced
1 garlic clove, peeled
Pinch of cayenne pepper
Freshly ground black pepper to taste
1 cup olive oil
½ cup heavy cream
Toasted French bread croutons

1. Place the salt cod in a pan or pot with enough cold water to cover and let soak for 8 to 10 hours, changing the water twice.

2. When ready to cook, break up the cod in a large saucepan with enough water to almost cover and add the milk, cloves, and bay leaf. Bring to a boil, reduce the heat to low, and let simmer till flaky, 10 to 15 minutes.

3. Meanwhile, place the diced potato in another saucepan with enough water to cover, bring to a boil, cook till very tender, 10 to 15 minutes, and drain.

4. Drain the cod and discard the cooking liquid, cloves, and bay leaf. Remove any bones or skin from the fish, flake it, and place it in a food processor. Add the garlic, potato, cayenne, black pepper, oil, and cream and reduce to a coarse puree. (If the spread is too stiff, add a little more oil and cream and puree till desired consistency.) Serve warm or at room temperature with the toasted French bread croutons.

Spread on fried or toasted croutons or just crusty French bread.

Potted Shrimp Spread

Authentic English potted shrimps are generally no more than diced cooked shrimp that are simply mixed with seasoned butter, placed in small pots or crocks and covered with additional melted butter, chilled till firm, and served as a first course. Delicious as it can be, the dish tends to be bland, so years ago I decided to transform the concept into this much more flavorful spread that never fails to be a big hit at cocktail receptions. If you'd like to serve it as an appetizer for 4 to 6 with toast or thin rye bread rectangles, double the recipe and divide the spread among small ramekins.

Makes about 1½ cups

6 tablespoons (¾ stick) butter, softened
2 scallions (part of green tops included), finely chopped
1 bay leaf
½ pound fresh shrimp, shelled and deveined
Salt and freshly ground black pepper to taste
3 tablespoons dry sherry
4 ounces cream cheese, softened
1 tablespoon fresh lemon juice
2 tablespoons minced fresh chives

1. In a large skillet, heat 1 tablespoon of the butter over moderate heat, add the scallions and bay leaf, and stir till soft. Add the shrimp and salt and pepper and stir till the shrimp are pink, about 3 minutes. Add the sherry, increase the heat, and boil till almost all the liquid is evaporated. Discard the bay leaf, transfer the shrimp to a cutting board, and finely dice.

2. In a bowl, combine the remaining 5 tablespoons butter and the cream cheese and stir till well blended and smooth. Add the shrimp, scallion mixture, lemon juice, and chives and stir till well blended. Scrape the spread into a 1½-cup crock and chill for at least 2 hours before serving with crackers or toast points.

Japanese Shrimp Spread with Sake

In Japan, sake, the country's national alcoholic beverage made from fermented rice, is generally used in the kitchen to make sauces and marinades, but today it's not unusual to find young chefs also incorporating the slightly sweet wine in all sorts of seafood canapés, loaves, dumplings, and stir-fries. Sake does have its own distinctive taste, but if you don't have a bottle, a semisweet sherry works just as well for this delectable spread. Do note that sake, once opened, keeps well in the refrigerator for no longer than about a month.

Makes about 2 cups

1 pound fresh shrimp
½ lemon
3 tablespoons sake
1 tablespoon minced scallion (white part only)
2 tablespoons fresh lemon juice
¼ teaspoon dry mustard
⅛ teaspoon grated nutmeg
8 tablespoons (1 stick) butter, softened
Salt and freshly ground black pepper to taste
Sesame crackers

1. Place the shrimp and lemon half in a large saucepan with enough water to cover, bring to a boil, remove from the heat, let stand for 1 minute, and drain. When cool enough to handle, peel, devein, and cut the shrimp in half.

2. In a blender or food processor, combine the shrimp, sake, scallion, lemon juice, mustard, and nutmeg and grind coarsely. Transfer the mixture to a large bowl, add the butter and salt and pepper, and mix till well blended. Pack the mixture into a crock, cover with plastic wrap, and chill for about 1 hour before serving with the sesame crackers.

Appetizers, Canapés, and Dips

Classic Smoked Salmon Spread

Makes about
2 cups

Rarely do you find velvety, expensive, sliced smoked salmon that doesn't have ragged, often discolored edges unsuitable for serving, and there is still no better way to utilize these tasty scraps than by grinding them into a puree and making a classic spread worthy of the most elegant receptions. This same recipe can also be used for leftover smoked sturgeon, trout, whitefish, or eel, though I do not recommend using any canned fish.

¼ pound smoked salmon, chopped
2 scallions (white parts only), chopped
2 tablespoons capers
1 tablespoon chopped fresh dill
Freshly ground black pepper to taste
8 ounces cream cheese
½ lemon

1. In a food processor, combine the smoked salmon, scallions, capers, dill, and pepper and grind to a puree.

2. Place the cream cheese in a bowl, squeeze the lemon half over the top, and whip till light and fluffy. Add the salmon mixture and mix till well blended and smooth. Scrape the mixture into a serving bowl or crock, cover with plastic wrap, and chill for about 30 minutes before serving on toast triangles or thinly sliced rye bread.

Charleston Shrimp Paste

Prepared ideally with tiny, sweet inlet shrimp and served at cocktail parties, afternoon teas, and on formal buffets, shrimp paste is one of Charleston, South Carolina's most glorious culinary legacies. Despite the fact that locals would disapprove, I sometimes add 2 to 3 tablespoons of semisweet sherry or gin to my mixture. Traditionally, the paste is spread on the area's distinctive benne (sesame) crackers, but if these are unavailable, it's just as good on toast points or thin water crackers. Note that the paste is best when served chilled, not cold.

Makes about
2 cups

1½ pounds fresh shrimp
½ lemon
1 tablespoon minced scallion (white part only)
2 tablespoons fresh lemon juice
¼ teaspoon dry mustard
⅛ teaspoon ground mace or grated nutmeg
Pinch of cayenne pepper
8 tablespoons (1 stick) butter, softened
Salt and freshly ground black pepper to taste
Chopped fresh parsley leaves for garnish

1. Place the shrimp and lemon half in a large saucepan with enough water to cover and bring to a boil. Remove from the heat, let stand for 1 minute, and drain. When cool enough to handle, peel, devein, and cut the shrimp in half.

2. In a blender or food processor, combine the shrimp, scallion, lemon juice, mustard, mace or nutmeg, and cayenne and grind just long enough to chop the shrimp coarsely. Transfer the

(continued)

Appetizers,
Canapés,
and Dips

mixture to a large bowl, add the butter and salt and pepper, and mix with a wooden spoon till the shrimp mixture and butter are well blended. Pack the mixture into a crock, cover with plastic wrap, and chill for at least 2 hours.

3. Remove from the refrigerator about 30 minutes before serving and sprinkle the parsley over the top.

Horseradish Shrimp Dip

Frankly, I don't know many chilled shrimp preparations that don't benefit from a little horseradish, and this smooth, tasty dip is a good example. Do experiment—within reason—with such other ingredients as minced hard-boiled eggs, cucumbers, olives, pimentos, bell peppers, and fresh tarragon.

Makes about
2 cups

¾ pound fresh shrimp
½ cup mayonnaise
½ cup sour cream
1 tablespoon prepared horseradish
2 tablespoons minced fresh chives
2 tablespoons minced fresh parsley leaves
2 tablespoons fresh lemon juice
Salt and freshly ground black pepper to taste

1. Place the shrimp in a saucepan with enough water to cover, bring to a boil, remove from the heat, and let stand for 2 minutes. Drain in a colander and, when cool enough to handle, peel, devein, and finely chop the shrimp.

2. In a bowl, combine the shrimp with the remaining ingredients and stir till well blended and smooth. Scrape the dip into another small bowl or crock, cover with plastic wrap, and chill for at least 30 minutes before serving with crackers or toasted bread rounds.

Boston Clam Dip

This basic recipe can also be used for minced or finely chopped oysters, fresh shredded crabmeat, and cooked finely chopped shrimp or lobster. In the case of either substitution, be sure to add about 3 tablespoons of bottled clam juice, and by all means feel free to experiment with the secondary ingredients and seasonings. Don't serve this dip too cold—merely chilled.

8 ounces cream cheese, softened
¼ cup sour cream
Two 6½-ounce cans minced clams, drained, 3 tablespoons of
    liquid reserved
½ small red bell pepper, seeded and finely chopped
2 tablespoons minced fresh parsley leaves
2 tablespoons minced fresh chives
1 teaspoon Worcestershire sauce
Tabasco sauce to taste
Salt and freshly ground black pepper to taste

In a bowl, whisk together the cream cheese and sour cream till well blended, add the clams plus the reserved liquor and all the remaining ingredients, and stir till well blended and smooth. Scrape the dip into a crock, cover with plastic wrap, and chill for about 30 minutes before serving with crackers or thick potato chips.

Mediterranean Sardine Dip

Since what you want in this elegant dip is a toothy paste and not a mushy puree, I do not recommend preparing it in a blender or food processor. Nor do I think any other bread or cracker has the same ideal texture of toasted pita for this particular dip. The dill adds an elusive flavor to the dip, but equally delicious are a few finely chopped capers.

Makes about
2 cups

Two 3¾-ounce cans skinless, boneless sardines packed in oil, drained
4 ounces cream cheese, softened
¼ cup sour cream
1 tablespoon fresh lemon juice
2 teaspoons Dijon mustard
2 tablespoons chopped fresh dill
Salt and freshly ground black pepper to taste
Toasted pita loaves, cracked into pieces

In a bowl, mash the sardines with a heavy fork till almost a paste; add the cream cheese, sour cream, lemon juice, mustard, dill, and salt and pepper, and stir till thoroughly blended. Transfer the dip to a serving bowl and serve with the cracked pita pieces.

Italian Hot Anchovy Dip

Makes about
2 cups (6 to 8
servings)

A specialty of Italy's Piedmont region, *bagna cauda* ("hot bath") is actually a warm sauce into which raw vegetables and bread are dipped and eaten as an appetizer. The ratio of oil to butter can differ radically, as can the number of garlic cloves and anchovies, but the one point on which every cook agrees is that the dip be prepared in an earthenware pot or chafing dish and kept as hot as possible over candle warmers at the table. Traditionally, this unusual appetizer would be followed by a sturdy meat or cheese frittata—or even pizza.

¾ cup extra-virgin olive oil
6 tablespoons (¾ stick) butter
4 garlic cloves, minced
10 oil-packed flat anchovy fillets, drained and finely chopped
Freshly ground black pepper to taste

In an ovenproof earthenware pot or chafing dish, heat the oil and butter over very low heat just till the butter begins to foam, add the garlic and stir till softened, about 2 minutes. Add the anchovies and stir till they dissolve into a paste, about 2 minutes. Add the pepper, stir well, and serve hot directly from the pot with crisp raw vegetables and morsels of sturdy country bread to dip into the mixture.

Soups and Salads

Italian Beef Dumpling Soup

**Makes
6 servings**

Italians love simple but rich flavors, and nothing exemplifies this truth more than the almost creamy meat dumplings used to enrich a soup such as this one, typically served before a plain roasted fish or perhaps pan-seared lamb or veal chops. Cooks are just as likely to use ground veal instead of the beef, and some might prefer equal quantities of chicken and beef broth to give the soup even more character. Since this is an appetizer soup, serve no more than a cup per person.

½ pound beef rump or round, trimmed of fat and
   cut into cubes
3 tablespoons butter, softened
2 tablespoons heavy cream
1 large egg
½ cup grated Parmesan cheese
¼ teaspoon grated nutmeg
Salt and freshly ground black pepper to taste
½ cup fine dry bread crumbs
6 cups chicken broth

1. In a food processor, combine the beef and butter, grind to a smooth paste, and scrape into a bowl. Add the cream, egg, cheese, nutmeg, salt and pepper, and bread crumbs and mix till well blended and firm. With your hands, form the mixture into dumplings about the size of small marbles.

2. In a large saucepan or pot, bring the broth to a boil, reduce the heat to a brisk simmer, add the dumplings, cover, and cook for 15 minutes, maintaining the broth at a steady simmer. Remove from the heat and let the soup stand for 3 to 4 minutes before serving.

Hungarian Goulash Soup

I've had delicious goulash soup in both Germany and Austria, but the first thing on my mind when I visit Budapest is where to go for an authentic Hungarian *gulyásleves* redolent of slightly fatty beef (including a little chopped beef heart), garlic, and caraway seeds and tangy with rose paprika. In a word, this is one of the most sublime soups ever devised, and if you happen to have any rich beef stock on hand to use instead of ordinary broth, so much the better. Here you must have quality Hungarian paprika for the right flavor, the ideal variety being semihot rose paprika available in finer markets.

Makes
6 servings

2 tablespoons bacon grease
1 pound boneless beef chuck or round, coarsely ground
3 medium onions, diced
2 garlic cloves, minced
3 tablespoons all-purpose flour
1 tablespoon Hungarian semihot paprika
2 tablespoons tomato puree
1 tablespoon red wine vinegar
6 cups beef broth
½ teaspoon caraway seeds
½ teaspoon dried marjoram
Salt and freshly ground black pepper to taste
3 medium potatoes, diced

1. In a large pot or casserole, heat the bacon grease over moderate heat, add the beef, and stir till lightly browned, about 10 minutes. Add the onions and garlic and stir till softened, about 10 minutes. Sprinkle the flour and paprika over the top and stir for 1 minute. Add the tomato puree and vinegar and stir 1 minute

(continued)

longer. Add the broth, caraway seeds, marjoram, and salt and pepper, bring to a simmer, cover, and cook for 45 minutes.

2. Add the potatoes, return the soup to a simmer, and cook till the potatoes are very tender, 20 to 30 minutes.

3. Serve hot.

In a word, this is one of the most sublime soups ever devised.

Southern Hamburger Soup

I don't think hamburger soup exists anywhere but in the American South, no doubt originally an economic means to feed a large family using a minimal amount of meat. Carelessly prepared, hamburger soup can be a wretched concoction, but when attention is paid to the quality of ingredients and the cooking method, nothing tastes better or warms the soul more on a cold winter day.

Makes
6 servings

1 pound ground beef chuck
1 medium onion, chopped
1 small green bell pepper, seeded and chopped
2 carrots, scraped and chopped
1 cup beef broth
1 cup tomato juice (or, preferably, V8 juice)
1 medium potato, diced
2 tablespoons chopped fresh parsley leaves
4 cups milk
⅓ cup all-purpose flour
Salt and freshly ground black pepper to taste

1. In a large saucepan or pot, stir the beef over moderate heat till nicely browned, about 10 minutes, and drain off all but about 1 tablespoon of fat. Add the onion, bell pepper, and carrots and stir till the vegetables soften, about 7 minutes. Add the broth and tomato juice, bring to a simmer, cover, and cook for about 10 minutes. Add the potato and parsley, cover, and simmer 15 minutes longer. In a small bowl, whisk together 1 cup of the milk and the flour till well blended, add to the soup, increase the heat slightly, and cook till the soup is thickened and bubbly. Add the remaining 3 cups milk and the salt and pepper, stir well, and simmer about 10 minutes longer.

2. Serve hot.

Viennese Liver Dumpling Consommé

Makes 6 to 8 servings

Long considered one of the hallmarks of Viennese cuisine, this consommé is served even in the city's most sophisticated restaurants as a prelude to juicy roasted meats or light, crispy schnitzels. I know of no better way to introduce liver to those who think they hate it, and personally, I could easily make a whole meal of this soup with slices of cured ham, ripe cheeses, and crusty rolls. When making the dumplings, add just enough of the flour to bind the liver mixture; if you use too much, the dumplings will be lumpy when simmered in the broth.

¼ pound calf's liver, trimmed and cut into pieces

1 small onion, chopped

1 egg yolk

2 tablespoons chopped fresh parsley leaves

½ teaspoon dried thyme

¼ teaspoon grated nutmeg

2 slices white loaf bread (crusts removed), soaked in milk and squeezed dry

Salt and freshly ground black pepper to taste

½ cup all-purpose flour, as needed

2 quarts beef broth

¼ cup minced fresh chives

1. In a food processor, combine the liver and onion and grind to a puree. Add the egg yolk, parsley, thyme, nutmeg, bread, and salt and pepper and process till the mixture is completely smooth. Scrape the mixture into a bowl and stir in enough flour to make a soft dough.

2. In a large saucepan, bring the broth to a boil, then reduce to a brisk simmer. Dip a teaspoon into the broth, fill it with liver batter, form into a dumpling with your fingers, and drop the dumpling into the broth. Repeat with the remaining batter, maintaining the broth at a steady simmer. Cover the pot and cook for 10 to 15 minutes.

3. Ladle the soup into soup bowls, garnish the tops with chives, and serve hot.

Cantonese Spiced Pork Meatball and Watercress Soup

**Makes
6 servings**

Chinese chefs grind far more pork than any other meat for various dumplings, savory cakes, meatballs, and stuffed vegetables, and the meatballs bound with rice, egg, and watercress for this spicy Cantonese soup have to be some of the most delectable ever conceived. Experiment with any number of spices to season the broth, if you like, and note that the ground meat of chicken legs makes just as good meatballs as the pork. Ground pork, chicken, and even turkey can be found packaged in many grocery stores, but if any does not look impeccably fresh, I buy parts and grind them myself.

2 tablespoons peanut oil
1 medium onion, finely chopped
1 garlic clove, minced
2 quarts beef broth
½ cup tomato puree
1 teaspoon ground allspice
½ teaspoon grated nutmeg
1½ pounds ground lean pork
½ cup halfway-cooked long-grain rice
1 large egg, beaten
2 tablespoons minced watercress
Salt and freshly ground black pepper to taste

1. In a large saucepan or pot, heat the oil over moderate heat, add the onion and garlic, and stir till softened, about 5 minutes. Add the broth, tomato puree, allspice, and nutmeg, bring to a boil, reduce the heat to low, cover, and simmer for about 20 minutes.

2. Meanwhile, combine the pork, rice, egg, watercress, and salt and pepper in a large bowl, mix thoroughly with your hands till well blended, and beat vigorously with a wooden spoon till the mixture is fluffy. To shape the meatballs, roll the mixture into balls about ½ inch in diameter.

3. Drop the meatballs into the simmering broth and stir gently to keep them from sticking to one another. Cover the pan and simmer the soup about 30 minutes longer.

4. Serve piping hot in wide soup bowls.

Farmhouse Chicken, Bacon, and Ham Hock Soup

Makes
6 servings

What is so special about this old-fashioned country soup is not only the blend of chicken and pork but also the wonderful, aromatic fresh stock derived from a long simmering of ingredients. When my Georgia grandfather made the soup, he would use the entire chicken; my mother preferred only the breast; and I like just the drumsticks and thighs. For the right texture, everything in the soup should be either diced or shredded, and when it comes to adding extra water, just remember that this is a soup and not a stew. Serve it piping hot with a tossed salad and corn sticks or sturdy crackers; in old country tradition, the perfect occasion is Sunday night supper.

6 slices bacon, chopped
2 chicken legs, disjointed
1 small meaty ham hock
1 large onion, studded with 3 whole cloves
3 celery ribs (leaves included), diced
1 medium red bell pepper, seeded and diced
½ teaspoon dried thyme, crumbled
½ teaspoon dried sage, crumbled
Salt and freshly ground black pepper to taste
3 quarts water
2 medium potatoes, diced

1. In a large, heavy skillet, fry the bacon over moderate heat till cooked but not crisp, and drain on paper towels. Add the chicken pieces to the fat and brown on all sides. Meanwhile, in a large, heavy pot, combine the ham hock, onion, celery, bell pepper, thyme, sage, salt and pepper, and water and bring to a boil. When the chicken has browned, add it to the pot along with the bacon, return the mixture to a boil, reduce the heat to low, cover, and simmer for 1 hour. With a slotted spoon, transfer the chicken to a plate and continue simmering the stock for about 45 minutes.

2. When cool enough to handle, skin the chicken pieces, remove the meat from the bones, and shred. Transfer the ham hock to a cutting board, strain the stock through a sieve into another large pot, and discard all the solids in the sieve. Shred the ham finely and add to the stock. Add the potatoes and, if the soup is too thick, more water. Bring to a simmer over moderate heat and cook till the potatoes are just tender, about 10 minutes. Add the chicken, stir well, and taste for salt and pepper.

3. Serve hot in wide soup bowls.

Greek Avgolemono Soup with Lamb and Rice Balls

Technically, avgolemono is a Greek egg-lemon sauce used to enhance everything from stuffed grape leaves to cabbage rolls to pastas, but never is the culinary concept more sublime than when it's applied to a soup made with either orzo pasta or small rice balls. Having a paternal Greek grandfather, I grew up eating avgolemono soup in one form or another, and a real treat was when Papa or my mother would add ground lamb to the rice balls and serve the soup as a main course with no more than chunks of tangy feta cheese, briny black olives, and endless loaves of pita bread. When making the sauce, just be very careful when adding the hot broth to the eggs to ensure that the mixture doesn't curdle—whisk constantly and vigorously.

Makes 4 to 6 servings

1 pound ground lean lamb leg or shoulder
1 medium onion, finely chopped
2 garlic cloves, minced
⅓ cup long-grain rice
3 tablespoons finely chopped fresh parsley leaves
1 tablespoon finely chopped fresh dill
1 teaspoon dried oregano
1 large egg yolk
Salt and freshly ground black pepper to taste
Chicken broth as needed
3 tablespoons olive oil
3 large eggs
Juice of 1 large lemon

1. In a bowl, combine the lamb, onion, garlic, rice, parsley, dill and oregano and stir. Add the egg yolk and salt and pepper, knead well till the mixture is well blended, and, with your hands, form balls about 1 inch in diameter. Place the balls in a large pot or casserole, add just enough broth to cover the balls, add the oil, and bring to a boil. Reduce the heat to low, cover, and simmer till the balls are tender, about 40 minutes, adding more broth if necessary to keep the balls covered.

2. Meanwhile, shortly before the balls are finished cooking, make the avgolemono sauce by whisking together the eggs and lemon juice in a bowl till frothy. Whisking vigorously, ladle about 1 cup of the hot broth into the egg mixture. Remove the pot from the heat and, whisking, add the egg mixture to the broth. Return the pot to the heat and stir well, but do not allow the soup to boil.

3. Serve immediately in soup bowls.

Having a paternal Greek grandfather, I grew up eating avgolemono soup in one form or another.

Tex-Mex Chicken and Bean Soup

Makes
4 servings

Talk about a quick, easy soup that needs no more than a basket of hot corn sticks and mugs of beer for a simple winter lunch. I think about this soup every time I see boned chicken legs on sale, and what's nice about the recipe is that ground pork loin or shoulder is just as good. If you don't mind boning a large turkey leg, often available at holiday time, this too can be substituted for the chicken, with even more flavorful results.

2 tablespoons corn oil
1 large onion, chopped
1 medium green bell pepper, seeded and chopped
1 garlic clove, minced
½ pound skinless, boneless chicken legs, ground
2 cups chicken broth
One 16-ounce can refried beans with liquid
¼ teaspoon chili powder
¼ teaspoon ground cumin
Salt and freshly ground black pepper to taste
6 taco shells, heated and crushed, for garnish
½ cup grated Monterey Jack cheese for garnish

1. In a large saucepan, heat the oil over moderate heat, add the onion, bell pepper, and garlic, and stir for 2 minutes. Add the chicken and stir till slightly browned, about 5 minutes. Add the broth, beans, chili powder, cumin, and salt and pepper, bring to a boil, reduce the heat to low, and simmer for 10 to 15 minutes, stirring occasionally.

2. Ladle the hot soup into soup crocks and garnish the tops with the crushed taco shells and grated cheese.

Shanghai Chicken Congee

Different versions of the potage known as congee are found in various provinces of China, but perhaps the most delectable is this Shanghai classic made with shredded chicken. Typically, the rice is cooked with the chicken and seasonings almost to a gruel, and what gives the dish much of its distinction is the pungent flavor of fresh coriander (cilantro or "Chinese parsley") leaves. Do note that the nature of the fresh leaves is altogether different from the dried seeds and that the latter should never be substituted. Congee is traditionally served with containers of soy sauce, sesame oil, and slivered scallions on the side.

Makes at least 6 servings

One 3-pound chicken, disjointed
1 cup long-grain rice
4 scallions (part of green tops included), finely chopped
4 thin slivers fresh ginger
¼ cup finely chopped fresh cilantro
1 teaspoon salt
Freshly ground black pepper to taste
1 tablespoon peanut oil
3 quarts water

1. Place all the chicken pieces in a large pot with enough water to cover, bring to a boil, and cook for about 5 minutes. Drain, add cold water to cover, drain again, transfer the chicken to a plate, and rinse out the pot.

2. Place all the remaining ingredients in the pot, bring to a boil, reduce the heat to low, cover, and simmer for about 10 minutes.

(continued)

Add the chicken pieces, return to a simmer, cover, and cook for 1 hour.

3. Remove the chicken legs, thighs, and breast, leaving in the remaining pieces of the carcass, and continue simmering, covered, 1 hour longer. Meanwhile, remove the skin and bones from the legs, thighs, and breast and shred the meat finely.

4. With a slotted spoon, remove and discard the chicken skin and bones in the pot, add the shredded meat, heat for about 5 minutes, and ladle the congee into individual serving bowls.

Indian Curried Fish Chowder

I call this Indian soup a chowder only by virtue of its thick texture and the potato that's used. In India, the chowder would be made with such exotic fish as pomfret, rahu, and singhara, but given their unavailability outside the region, striped bass, haddock, and cod make very good substitutions. As always, feel free to adjust the amount of curry powder to your taste, and, while saffron threads are expensive, a little goes a long way and provides just the right pungent savor.

Makes
6 servings

3 tablespoons peanut oil
3 scallions (part of green tops included), finely chopped
1 celery rib, finely chopped
1 garlic clove, minced
2 tablespoons curry powder
3 tablespoons all-purpose flour
1 large ripe tomato, peeled, seeded, and chopped
1½ quarts bottled clam juice
⅛ teaspoon chopped saffron threads
1 medium potato, peeled, boiled, and mashed
Salt and freshly ground black pepper to taste
1½ pounds fresh striped bass, haddock, or cod fillets, coarsely ground
1 cup heavy cream

In a large saucepan, heat the oil over moderate heat, add the scallions, celery, and garlic, and stir till softened, about 2 minutes. Add the curry powder and flour, stir well, and continue cooking about 2 minutes longer, stirring. Add the tomato, broth, saffron, potato, and salt and pepper and stir till the liquid is thickened. Bring to a boil, reduce the heat to low, and simmer 15 minutes longer. Add the fish, stir well, and simmer about 15 minutes longer. Stir in the cream, bring the chowder almost to a boil, and serve hot in wide soup plates.

Soups and
Salads

65

Russian Salmon
Solianka

Makes 4 to 6
servings

In rural Russian towns (as well as in Russian communities in the American upper Midwest), *solianka* is still most often made with ground beef, but when immigrants arrived in the Pacific Northwest about a century ago, it didn't take long to transform the soup completely by using the region's bountiful supply of fresh salmon. Since nothing makes a richer stock than the salmon's oily carcass, be sure to have the fishmonger save the head and bones if he cleans the fish for you, and since the soup's texture should be fairly coarse, I strongly recommend grinding the fillets in a meat grinder instead of a food processor. By no means leave out the dill pickles, which give the soup much of its distinction.

One 3- to 3½-pound fresh salmon
1 small onion, peeled and studded with 2 whole cloves
1 celery rib, cracked into thirds
6 black peppercorns
Salt to taste
1½ quarts water
4 tablespoons (½ stick) butter
1 medium onion, chopped
3 large ripe tomatoes, chopped
2 tablespoons chopped green olives
4 medium dill pickles, chopped
2 teaspoons capers, drained
1 bay leaf
Freshly ground black pepper to taste

1. Either dress the salmon yourself or have the fishmonger do it, reserving the head and bones and coarsely grinding the fillets. Place the fish head and bones in a large pot and add the studded onion, celery, peppercorns, salt, and water. Bring to a boil, skimming the froth, then reduce the heat to a low simmer, cover, and cook for 1½ hours. Strain the broth through cheesecloth into a bowl and reserve, discarding the solids. Wash out the pot.

2. Heat the butter in the pot over moderate heat, add the chopped onion and tomatoes, and cook to reduce the tomato juices slightly, about 10 minutes. Add the ground salmon, olives, pickles, capers, bay leaf, pepper, and just enough of the reserved stock to cover the ingredients. Bring to a low simmer, cover, and cook for about 15 minutes. Remove the bay leaf, taste for salt, and serve the soup hot in soup bowls or plates.

Atlantic Shrimp Bisque

Makes
6 servings

Historically, a bisque is a thick, rich soup consisting mainly of pureed seafood and cream and most often associated with classic French cuisine. When, however, the soup migrated around America (New England lobster bisque, Creole crawfish bisque, San Francisco crab bisque), the concept underwent radical regional changes, one of the most unusual and delicious being this East Coast version featuring Atlantic blue shrimp and enriched with diced potatoes, grated cheddar, and various seasonings. The ingredients for this bisque can indeed be pureed in a food processor to produce an appetizer soup that's as smooth and elegant as silk, but I prefer a bisque with more body that qualifies as a main course with maybe small ham biscuits or hot onion corn sticks.

6 tablespoons (¾ stick) butter
4 medium onions, finely chopped
3 medium potatoes, peeled and diced
2 cups water
3 cups milk
½ pound extra-sharp cheddar cheese, grated
1 pound fresh shrimp, peeled, deveined, and finely diced
Salt and freshly ground black pepper to taste
1 tablespoon dry sherry
½ cup chopped fresh parsley leaves

1. In a large saucepan, melt the butter over low heat, add the onions, and stir till fully softened, 5 to 7 minutes. Add the potatoes and water, increase the heat to moderate, and cook till the potatoes are tender, about 10 minutes.

2. In a small saucepan, combine the milk and cheese over low heat and stir till the cheese is melted. Add to the onions and potatoes and stir well. Add the shrimp, salt and pepper, and sherry, stir, and simmer gently over moderately low heat for 10 minutes.

3. To serve, sprinkle a little chopped parsley on the bottom of each soup bowl and fill with hot bisque.

I prefer a bisque with more body that qualifies as a main course with maybe small ham biscuits or hot onion corn sticks.

Neapolitan Meatball and Pasta Salad

Makes 4 to 6 servings

Neapolitan chefs don't make many composed salads, but when they do, it's with the same flair and demand for rich flavor as for most other dishes. For the right smooth meatball texture, be sure to include the ¼ pound of ground pork; and here's another time when freshly grated genuine Parmesan cheese makes all the difference. The shape and size of rotelle pasta are ideal for this particular salad, but if it's not available, fusilli, farfalle, or even penne is a sensible substitution. I like to serve this robust salad with large Italian bread sticks and a medium-bodied red wine such as Valpolicella or Bardolino.

1 pound ground beef round

¼ pound ground pork loin

1 cup grated Parmesan cheese

¼ cup fine dry bread crumbs

1 large egg, beaten

Salt and freshly ground black pepper to taste

3 tablespoons olive oil

1 medium onion, chopped

1 small green bell pepper, seeded and chopped

1 garlic clove, minced

1¼ cups beef broth

⅓ cup sour cream

1 pound dried rotelle

1. In a large bowl, combine the beef, pork, cheese, bread crumbs, egg, and salt and pepper, mix with your hands till well blended, and form rounded teaspoons of the mixture into meatballs.

2. In a large, heavy skillet, heat the oil over moderate heat, add the meatballs in batches, brown them lightly on all sides, and drain on paper towels. Add the onion, bell pepper, and garlic to the skillet and stir till lightly browned, about 10 minutes. Stir in the broth, bring to a boil, return the meatballs to the pan, reduce the heat to low, and simmer till cooked through, about 10 minutes. Stir in the sour cream, remove the pan from the heat, and let cool.

3. Bring a large pot of salted water to a boil. Cook the rotelle according to package directions till al dente; drain and transfer to a large serving bowl. Add the meatball mixture, toss till well blended, cover with plastic wrap, and chill for about 30 minutes. Serve at room temperature.

Swiss Dried Sausage and Gruyère Salad Vinaigrette

Makes
4 servings

Cervelat (or *cervelas*), now available in some markets, is a cured, cooked, and dried pork and/or beef sausage seasoned with garlic, herbs, and spices, and I don't think there's a town or village in Germany, Austria, and German-speaking Switzerland that doesn't have its own version of *wurstsalat* featuring the thinly sliced, diced, chopped, or even ground sausage. In Switzerland, the salad almost always includes the country's luscious Gruyère cheese, and, unlike the Germans and Austrians, the Swiss like to add a few chopped gherkins.

1 pound *cervelat* or kielbasa sausage
¼ pound Gruyère cheese, cubed
2 scallions (part of green tops included), chopped
2 medium ripe tomatoes, peeled, seeded, cut in half, and sliced
2 gherkins, chopped
1 large hard-boiled egg, sliced
3 tablespoons red wine vinegar
1 tablespoon Dijon mustard
1 tablespoon mayonnaise
6 tablespoons olive oil
Salt and freshly ground black pepper to taste
Chopped fresh chives for garnish

1. Remove any skin or casing from the sausage, chop the meat coarsely, and place in a salad bowl. Add the cheese, scallions, tomatoes, gherkins, and egg, toss well, and chill for 30 minutes.

2. In a small bowl, combine the vinegar, mustard, and mayonnaise and whisk till well blended and frothy. Add the oil and salt and pepper and whisk till the dressing is well blended.

3. When ready to serve, pour the dressing over the salad, toss well, and sprinkle chopped chives over the top.

Congealed Ham and Beet Salad

The American South has always been known for the great array of congealed salads that appear on birthday, wedding, graduation, and bereavement buffets, and I've always perceived this shredded ham and beet example to be one of the most elegant, colorful, and unusual. While there does seem to be a natural affinity between smoked ham and beets, cooked calf's tongue makes a delicious substitute so long as it's finely ground. Also feel free to try different herbs and spices in this salad.

Makes 8 to 10 servings

Two 1-pound cans whole beets
2 envelopes unflavored powdered gelatin
3 tablespoons sugar
½ cup orange juice
1 cup shredded or ground smoked ham
1 celery rib, finely chopped
¼ teaspoon powdered sage
¼ teaspoon grated nutmeg
Salt and freshly ground black pepper to taste
Romaine lettuce leaves for serving

1. Grease a 1½- to 2-quart ring mold and set aside.

2. Drain the juice from the beets into a saucepan and, if necessary, add enough water to measure 1½ cups of liquid. Sprinkle the gelatin over the liquid and let soak for 5 minutes. Heat the mixture till just warm, stir till the gelatin is completely dissolved, and pour into a large bowl to cool. Meanwhile, shred the beets into another bowl and set aside.

3. Add the sugar and orange juice to the gelatin mixture and stir till well blended. Add the shredded beets, ham, celery, sage,

(continued)

nutmeg, and salt and pepper and stir till well blended. Pour the mixture into the prepared mold, cover with plastic wrap, and chill till firm, at least 3 hours.

4. To serve, arrange lettuce leaves around the sides of a large serving platter and unmold the salad in the center.

Italian Tongue, Carrot, and Goat Cheese Salad

A specialty of Italy's Piedmont region, this substantial salad would typically be served as a luncheon main course with no more than chewy focaccia bread sprinkled with coarse salt (or the fat bread sticks called *grissini*) and bottles of Dolcetto or Barbaresco wine. A premium dry goat cheese is ideal for the salad, but for even more assertive flavor, you might look for a Toma cheese from the area that's well-aged enough to crumble. When dealing with the tongue, do be careful to peel off every trace of skin and to remove any bones or gristle before shredding the meat.

**Makes
6 servings**

One 2-pound veal tongue
1 small onion, peeled and studded with 3 whole cloves
1 celery rib, cut in half
½ lemon
2 bay leaves
4 medium carrots, scraped and shredded
½ pound dry goat cheese, crumbled
½ cup extra-virgin olive oil
3 tablespoons white vinegar
1 tablespoon balsamic vinegar
1 tablespoon minced fresh basil leaves
Salt and freshly ground black pepper to taste

1. To poach the tongue, place in a large enameled or stainless steel pot or casserole, add the onion, celery, lemon, and bay leaves, and add enough salted water to cover. Bring to a boil, skim the froth, reduce the heat to low, cover, and simmer till very tender, about 2½ hours. Remove the tongue, let cool, peel off the skin, and cut away the root, any small bones, and gristle.

(continued)

For even
more
assertive
flavor, you
might look
for a Toma
cheese
from the
area that's
well-aged
enough to
crumble.

2. Shred the meat coarsely, place in a large salad bowl, add the carrots and goat cheese, and toss well. In a small bowl, whisk together the oil, both vinegars, basil, and salt and pepper till well blended, pour over the salad, and toss well. Cover with plastic wrap, chill for about 30 minutes, and serve on salad plates.

Chicken Waldorf Salad with Honey-Sour Cream Dressing

The Waldorf salad created at New York's Waldorf Hotel in the late nineteenth century contained only diced apples, celery, maybe chopped walnuts, and mayonnaise, and, to be honest, I've always found the original to be the dullest salad on earth. Add, on the other hand, a few cups of diced, chopped, or shredded poached chicken or turkey breast, and substitute a slightly tangy honey-sour cream dressing for the mayonnaise, and you have something to boast about. The salad is traditionally served in lettuce cups, but if you want to be a bit classier, try a bed of either avocado or papaya slices.

Makes
6 servings

3 cups diced cooked chicken breasts
2 cups unpeeled, cored, and diced red apples
1 cup diced celery
¾ cup chopped walnuts
½ cup seedless golden raisins
3 tablespoons minced fresh chives
Salt and freshly ground black pepper to taste
½ cup sour cream
1 tablespoon cider vinegar
2 tablespoons mayonnaise
1 tablespoon honey
Boston lettuce leaves for cups

1. In a bowl, combine the chicken, apples, celery, walnuts, raisins, chives, and salt and pepper and toss well. In a small bowl, whisk together the sour cream, vinegar, mayonnaise, and honey till well blended and smooth, pour over the salad, and toss to coat all the ingredients. Cover with plastic wrap and chill for 2 hours.

2. To serve, arrange the lettuce cups on salad plates and fill with equal amounts of the salad.

Asian Chicken and Cashew Nuts in Lettuce Cups

Makes
4 servings

In some respects, this sumptuous salad is related to the better-known Chinese sesame noodles with peanut sauce served chilled or at room temperature in lettuce cups, the big difference being the wheat-flour noodles used for the more popular dish versus the thin, translucent rice-flour ones in this salad. Rice noodles can be found in Asian markets and some grocery stores, and they're usually sold in coiled nests packaged in cellophane. By no means overcook these delicate noodles, and when time comes to compose the salad, toss them very gently with the chicken mixture.

3 ounces rice noodles
2 teaspoons sesame oil
1 medium red onion, diced
1 medium green bell pepper, seeded and diced
¾ pound skinless, boneless chicken breasts, ground
½ cucumber, peeled and diced
3 tablespoons fresh lemon juice
3 tablespoons soy sauce
1 teaspoon sugar
3 tablespoons minced fresh cilantro
Salt and freshly ground black pepper to taste
½ cup coarsely chopped cashews
4 iceberg lettuce leaves for cups

1. In a saucepan, boil the noodles according to package directions. Drain and cut into 3-inch lengths.

2. In a large skillet, heat the oil over moderate heat, add the onion and bell pepper, and stir till softened, about 2 minutes. Add the chicken and stir till golden, 6 to 7 minutes. Add the cucumber and stir for 1 minute. Add the lemon juice, soy sauce, sugar, cilantro, and salt and pepper, and stir 2 to 3 minutes longer. Remove from the heat, add the cashews, and stir till well blended. In a bowl, combine the noodles and chicken mixture and toss gently till well blended.

3. To serve, arrange the lettuce cups on salad plates, fill the cups with equal amounts of the chicken-noodle salad, and serve at room temperature.

Hawaiian Curried Turkey, Rice, and Pineapple Salad

**Makes
6 servings**

This exotic main-course salad has not only an explosion of disparate flavors but also a textural consistency that couldn't be more beguiling. I suppose you could substitute a 14-ounce can of crushed pineapple (drained), but since the fresh is now so widely available year-round, it's really a crime not to use it. I like only a subtle curry flavor in my curried salads, but if your taste is more demanding, by all means adjust the amount of curry powder up to a full tablespoon—no more.

2 cups diced cooked turkey breast
2 cups diced fresh pineapple
2 celery ribs, chopped
1 small green bell pepper, seeded and chopped
2 tablespoons chopped pimentos
1 cup cooked long-grain rice
Salt and freshly ground black pepper to taste
½ cup mayonnaise
¼ cup sour cream
1 tablespoon fresh lime juice
1 teaspoon curry powder
Chopped ripe black olives for garnish

1. In a large salad bowl, combine the turkey, pineapple, celery, bell pepper, pimentos, rice, and salt and pepper, and toss lightly till well blended. In a small bowl, combine the mayonnaise, sour cream, lime juice, and curry powder and stir till well blended. Pour the dressing over the salad, toss lightly to coat all the ingredients, cover with plastic wrap, and chill for about 1 hour before serving.

2. Serve the salad with the chopped black olives sprinkled over the top.

Catalan Shredded Seafood Salad

Go into one of Barcelona's many seafood restaurants or simply plop down at a seaside café anywhere along Spain's Costa Brava, and the array of exotic seafood salads prepared with everything from hake to sea bream to squid to fat *gambas* (shrimp) is staggering. For this particular salad with a typical creamy dressing flavored with both sherry wine vinegar and dry sherry, I use whatever fresh firm fish is most available. Any fish such as mullet, fresh tuna, or grouper goes well in the salad so long as it can be shredded or flaked, and you might even want to add a few tiny boiled shrimp or chopped steamed clams. For authentic Catalan flavor, however, don't tamper too much with this dressing.

1 pound fresh red snapper fillets
1 pound fresh monkfish fillets
½ lemon
2 medium ripe tomatoes, peeled, seeded, and finely diced
3 scallions (part of green tops included), finely diced
½ cup half-and-half
2 tablespoons sherry vinegar
1 tablespoon dry sherry
Salt and freshly ground black pepper to taste
1 medium red onion, thinly sliced
1 medium cucumber, peeled and thinly sliced

1. Place the red snapper and monkfish in a large skillet and squeeze the lemon over the top. Add enough water to cover the fish, bring to a boil, reduce the heat to low, and simmer till the fish flakes easily, about 15 minutes. Drain the fish on paper

(continued)

Makes 4 to 6 servings

towels, press out as much liquid as possible with your fingers, shred it finely, and place in a large bowl.

2. In a glass or stainless steel bowl, combine the tomatoes, scallions, half-and-half, vinegar, sherry, and salt and pepper, and stir till well blended. Add the dressing to the fish, toss well, cover with plastic wrap, and chill for 2 hours.

3. When ready to serve, arrange a bed of red onions and cucumbers on salad plates and mound equal amounts of salad on the beds.

California Lobster and Avocado Salad in Radicchio Cups

What really sparks this classy salad is the hazelnut oil, an idea I got from the iconic California chef Jeremiah Tower. Exceptionally fragrant, the oil is so full-bodied that it really needs to be tamed with less robust virgin olive oil, especially considering the richness of the lobster and avocado. Note also that hazelnut oil turns rancid quickly and thus should always be stored in the refrigerator. If fresh Dungeness crab is available, it is equally delicious boiled, diced, or shredded and substituted for the lobster in this salad.

Makes
4 servings

2½ cups diced cooked lobster meat (from a 1½-pound boiled or steamed lobster)
2 cups diced ripe avocado
¼ cup minced fresh chives
1 tablespoon minced fresh tarragon
1 tablespoon prepared horseradish
2 tablespoons hazelnut oil
2 tablespoons virgin olive oil
2 tablespoons fresh lemon juice
Salt and freshly ground black pepper to taste
4 radicchio leaves for cups

1. In a large salad bowl, combine the lobster, avocado, chives, tarragon, and horseradish and toss gently. In a small bowl, whisk together both oils, lemon juice, and salt and pepper till frothy; pour over the salad, and toss gently to coat the ingredients. Cover with plastic wrap and chill for at least 1 hour before serving.

2. To serve, arrange the radicchio cups on salad plates and mound equal amounts of salad in each cup.

Soups and Salads

Portuguese Salt Cod, Tomato, and Chickpea Salad

**Makes
4 servings**

It was the Portuguese who first fished the Grand Banks of Newfoundland for cod and learned to salt and dry it for long preservation, and today it's said that Portuguese cooks know different ways to prepare *bacalhau* for each day of the year. Equally popular throughout that country are buff-colored, mild, nutty-flavored chickpeas (garbanzos), and when the two are combined with chopped tomatoes and other vegetables (and often pine nuts, raisins, and chopped hard-boiled eggs), moistened with fragrant olive oil, and seasoned with cayenne to make a main-course salad, the result is wondrous. You can go to the trouble of soaking and simmering dried chickpeas, but I find the canned product to be just as good. Serve the salad with rough country bread or bread sticks, and the ideal wine is a simple, crisp Portuguese *vinho verde*.

1 pound salt cod
2 medium ripe tomatoes, peeled, seeded, and chopped
1 medium onion, finely chopped
1 small green bell pepper, seeded and finely chopped
8 ounces canned chickpeas, drained
1 garlic clove, minced
2 tablespoons chopped fresh parsley leaves
¼ cup extra-virgin olive oil
2 tablespoons fresh lemon juice
Freshly ground black pepper to taste
Cayenne pepper to taste

1. Soak the cod in water for at least 10 hours, changing the water twice. Skin the fish and remove any bones, place in a saucepan with enough fresh water to cover, bring to a simmer, and cook till tender, about 20 minutes.

2. Drain the cod, flake finely, and place in a large salad bowl. Add the tomatoes, onion, bell pepper, chickpeas, garlic, and parsley and toss till well blended. In a small bowl, whisk together the oil, lemon juice, black pepper, and cayenne till well blended, pour over the salad, and toss to coat all the ingredients. Cover with plastic wrap and chill for about 30 minutes before serving.

Swedish Creamed Herring, Corned Beef, and Beet Salad

Makes 4 to 6 servings

Nobody grinds, minces, and chops foods as much as Scandinavians do, and never is the practice more obvious than on the elaborate smorgasbords of Sweden, Denmark, and Norway (open-face sandwiches, meatballs, loaves and pâtés, salads, and so on). Likewise, every country has its own version of creamed herring, potato, beet, and meat salad (always served with hard-boiled egg slices or wedges and chopped parsley), and this hearty Swedish example is the one my own Swedish grandmother loved to prepare for weekend suppers—served with her inimitable limpa bread. While you can go to the trouble of soaking and cooking salt herring the way Mama did, I find the herring marketed in jars to be fully acceptable for this salad.

One 5-ounce jar herring, drained and diced
1 cup diced cooked corned beef
1 cup diced boiled potatoes
1 cup diced pickled beets
½ cup peeled, cored, and diced apples
⅓ cup diced onion
¼ cup diced gherkins
3 tablespoons white vinegar
1 teaspoon grainy Dijon mustard
1 teaspoon sugar
Salt and freshly ground black pepper to taste
½ cup heavy cream
¼ cup sour cream
2 large hard-boiled eggs, sliced, for garnish
Chopped parsley leaves for garnish

1. In a large bowl, combine the herring, corned beef, potatoes, beets, apples, onion, and gherkins and toss gently. In a small bowl, whisk together the vinegar, mustard, sugar, and salt and pepper till well blended; pour over the salad, and toss gently. In another small bowl, whip together the heavy cream and sour cream, add to the salad, and toss gently to coat the ingredients. Pack the salad into a lightly greased, round, 2-quart mold, cover with plastic wrap, and chill till firm, about 2 hours.

2. To serve, unmold the salad onto a serving plate and garnish with the eggs and parsley.

I find the herring marketed in jars to be fully acceptable for this salad.

Sandwiches and Turnovers

English Potted Meat Tea Sandwiches

Makes 16 tea
sandwiches

In England, the filling for these tasty tea sandwiches would typically be made with tough but succulent beef shin (shank), simmered slowly in a double boiler for at least 3 hours before being finely ground and enriched with melted butter. Since this cut of meat virtually doesn't exist in U.S. markets, I've discovered that the best substitute is beef chuck (center cut), which is just as flavorful and requires half the cooking time. You can add all the butter while grinding the meat, but "potting" the mixture with a little melted butter on top not only keeps the mixture moist while it's being chilled but also allows you to spread a little butter on the bread before adding the filling. If you don't plan to serve these sandwiches immediately, be sure to cover them with plastic wrap so that they don't dry out.

1 pound boneless beef chuck, trimmed of excess fat
½ cup Madeira or sherry
1 teaspoon grated nutmeg
1 teaspoon salt
1 teaspoon freshly ground black pepper
8 tablespoons (1 stick) butter, melted and cooled
8 thin slices white loaf bread, crusts removed
8 thin slices whole-wheat loaf bread, crusts removed
Tiny parsley sprigs for garnish

1. Preheat the oven to 325°F.

2. Cut the beef into cubes and place in a small, heavy casserole. Add the Madeira or sherry, nutmeg, salt, pepper, and enough water to just cover the meat, cover, and bake till the meat is fork-tender, about 1½ hours. Let cool.

3. Transfer the meat to a food processor and grind to a fine puree, adding a little of the cooking liquid if necessary to produce a smooth texture. With the machine running, gradually add about three-quarters of the melted butter till the mixture is a smooth paste.

4. Scrape the filling into a crock, spoon the remaining butter over the top, and chill for at least 1 hour. When ready to make sandwiches, remove the filling from the refrigerator and allow to return to room temperature.

5. Cut both types of bread slices in half, spread filling over the white halves, and top with the whole-wheat halves. Stick a parsley sprig into the top of each sandwich.

Steak Tartare Sandwiches

Steak tartare, of course, is delicious by itself as a main course, but when the ground beef is transformed into a filling for tea or luncheon sandwiches, the result is not only unusual but also stunning. My formula for the mixture is pretty basic, so do feel free to experiment with these and other ingredients according to your taste. I do highly recommend that you grind the beef twice in a meat grinder for just the right texture (the risk of over-grinding in a food processor is high), and I urge you to use genuine French Cognac in this recipe. If you want to be truly extravagant, spoon about a teaspoon of salmon caviar instead of the chopped egg over the beef on each sandwich.

1 pound lean beef sirloin, ground twice in a meat grinder
1 small onion, finely chopped
2 garlic cloves, minced
1 large egg yolk
2 tablespoons finely chopped fresh parsley leaves
1 tablespoon Worcestershire sauce
1 tablespoon Cognac
Salt and freshly ground black pepper to taste
8 to 10 thin slices rye bread
Butter, softened, for spreading
1 large hard-boiled egg, finely chopped

In a large bowl, combine the beef, onion, garlic, egg yolk, parsley, Worcestershire, Cognac, and salt and pepper and mix with a wooden spoon till well blended and smooth. Spread one side of each slice of bread with butter and spread equal amounts of the steak tartare on the buttered sides of half of the bread slices. Sprinkle chopped egg over the tops, cover with the remaining bread slices, buttered sides down, and cut the sandwiches in half on the diagonal.

Makes 4 or 5 full sandwiches or 8 to 10 tea sandwiches

Tex-Mex Sloppy Joes

Also called "skillet burgers" in some parts of the United States, Sloppy Joes most likely originated in the Southwest during the 1950s or early '60s and were made with nothing but ground beef; chopped onion, celery, and bell pepper; and ketchup. This Tex-Mex version that I've eaten over and over in the Lone Star State might well be called "chili on a bun." It's appropriately messy but delicious; served with maybe some corn chips and ice-cold beer, it requires nothing more than a huge stack of napkins and a hearty appetite.

Makes 4 to 6 sandwiches

2 tablespoons corn oil
1 pound ground beef round
1 large onion, diced
1 medium green bell pepper, seeded and diced
One 14½-ounce can crushed tomatoes, drained
1 teaspoon chili powder
½ teaspoon ground cumin
¼ teaspoon dried oregano
1 tablespoon light brown sugar
2 teaspoons Worcestershire sauce
Salt and freshly ground black pepper to taste
4 to 6 hamburger buns, split and lightly toasted

1. In a large skillet, heat the oil over moderate heat, add the beef, and stir till lightly browned, 8 to 10 minutes. Add the onion and bell pepper and stir till well softened, about 5 minutes. Add the tomatoes, chili powder, cumin, oregano, brown sugar, Worcestershire, and salt and pepper, stir well, and cook till the mixture is thick, 10 to 12 minutes.

2. To serve, pile equal amounts of the mixture on the bottom halves of the buns, top with the other halves, and serve immediately with plenty of napkins.

Sandwiches and Turnovers

Coney Island Dogs

Makes
4 servings

What you're most likely to find today at the amusement park on Coney Island, New York, are ordinary hot dogs topped with ballpark mustard, sauerkraut, and maybe a little pickle relish, but half a century ago, a genuine Coney Island Dog (or simply "a Coney Island") was a long bun overflowing with a mixture of sumptuous different chopped ingredients—frankfurters included. I know because I was there as a youngster with my relatives and ate my share of these wondrous dogs. My re-creation of the original formula might not be perfect, but it comes mighty close to what my taste buds remember. (P.S. Ask anybody in Cincinnati what a "Coney" is, and you'll be regaled with details about a hot dog topped with chili and fluorescent yellow shredded cheese. I know nothing about the history of this conceit.)

4 slices lean bacon, finely chopped
1 medium onion, finely chopped
½ pound sauerkraut, rinsed, squeezed dry, and chopped
½ cup chicken broth
4 all-beef hot dogs, boiled and diced
2 large hard-boiled eggs, finely chopped
1 small dill pickle, finely chopped
1 tablespoon prepared mustard
Salt and freshly ground black pepper to taste
4 hot dog rolls (preferably extra-long), heated

1. In a large skillet, fry the bacon till crisp and drain on paper towels. Add the onion to the fat and stir till softened, about 2 minutes. Add the sauerkraut and stir well. Add the broth, bring to a boil, reduce the heat to low, cover, and simmer for 15 minutes.

2. Uncover the pan, increase the heat to high, and, stirring constantly, reduce the liquid till the sauerkraut is dry and almost sticks to the pan. Transfer the sauerkraut to a bowl, add the bacon, hot dogs, eggs, and pickle, and stir till well blended. Add the mustard and salt and pepper and mix till well blended.

3. To serve, spoon equal amounts of the mixture into the hot dog buns.

Ask anybody in Cincinnati what a "Coney" is, and you'll be regaled with details about a hot dog topped with chili and fluorescent yellow shredded cheese.

Black Forest Ham Biscuits with Mustard-Clove Butter

Makes about
10 biscuits

The cured, smoky hams produced in the mountains of Germany's Black Forest are some of the most prized on earth, and I'd return to the majestic Brenners Park-Hotel & Spa in Baden-Baden if for no other reason than to savor the creamy, ground ham biscuits with a mustardy clove butter served both at lunch in the grill and with afternoon tea in the Edwardian lounge. Actually, as I recall, the biscuits at the hotel are smaller and thinner than the ones featured here, but since I like my biscuits soft and fluffy, I take a few liberties with the size. In any case, serve the biscuits with any soup or at teatime, and if you want to gild the lily as I often do, mix a tablespoon or so of cream with the ham before stuffing the biscuit halves. Genuine Black Forest ham is now available in some fine delis, but if you can't find it, substitute any well-aged, mellow country ham.

1½ cups all-purpose flour
2 teaspoons baking powder
½ teaspoon salt
½ cup heavy cream
Milk for brushing
4 tablespoons (½ stick) butter, softened
1 tablespoon grainy mustard
⅛ teaspoon ground cloves
½ pound Black Forest or other cured ham, coarsely ground

1. Preheat the oven to 450°F.

2. In a bowl, combine the flour, baking powder, and salt and whisk till well blended. Add the cream and stir the mixture just till it forms a dough. On a lightly floured surface, pat the dough out about ½ inch thick, cut out rounds with a 2-inch biscuit cutter, and arrange on a baking sheet about 1 inch apart. Pat out the scraps of dough and cut out more rounds. Brush the tops of the rounds with milk and bake till the biscuits are golden brown, 12 to 15 minutes.

3. Meanwhile, combine the butter, mustard, and cloves in a small bowl and mix till well blended.

4. Split the biscuits in half and spread the interiors with the butter. Sandwich equal amounts of the ham in between the biscuit halves and serve hot or at room temperature.

Authentic French
Croques Monsieur

Contrary to what some snobs might think, a perfect French *croque monsieur* is a culinary masterpiece, but not even in Paris do you still find many examples of the authentic sandwich made with ground ham and Gruyère cheese between thin, dense slices of *pain de mie* that is dipped in béchamel sauce or egg batter and slowly browned in butter to a golden finish. A genuine *croque monsieur* is not an open-face sandwich of sliced ham and cheese that's quickly run under a broiler, which is what, more often than not, you find today in even the most reputable cafés. The tricky part of making these sandwiches is dipping them in the egg batter, a procedure that almost requires the deft use of tongs. Although many bakeries in the United States now bake some version of *pain de mie*, Pepperidge Farm's extra-thin white sliced bread has just about the right texture for these glorious sandwiches.

**Makes
4 sandwiches**

2 large eggs
Dijon mustard for spreading
8 slices thin, dense white loaf bread, crusts removed
¾ pound cooked ham, coarsely ground
¾ pound Gruyère cheese, coarsely ground
4 tablespoons (½ stick) butter

1. In a bowl, whisk the eggs well and pour into a wide, deep plate.

2. Spread mustard on one side of each slice of bread. Divide the ham and cheese evenly over the dressed sides of 4 slices of bread, top with the remaining 4 slices, dressed sides down, and press down with your hand to compact the filling.

3. In a large, heavy skillet, melt half of the butter over low heat. Using tongs, carefully and quickly dip both sides of two sandwiches in the egg, place in the skillet, and brown on one side, about 5 minutes. Turn the sandwiches over and brown the other sides, about 5 minutes. Repeat with the remaining butter and sandwiches.

4. Serve hot or warm.

Italian Sausage and Cheese Crostini

Makes 24 small
open-face
sandwiches

In Italy, the small open-face sandwiches known as crostini are made with everything from chopped onions and tomatoes to ground chicken livers to shredded leftover roast suckling pig (*porchetta*), but I've encountered none so delicious as these, made with spicy ground sausage and three different cheeses. The sandwiches are typically served with apéritifs, as a first-course appetizer, or alongside soups and salads, and what's nice is they can be prepared in advance with all but the Fontina cheese and then baked at the last minute. Any cheeses that have a good melting consistency are appropriate for the crostini—including a robust, elegant Gorgonzola.

8 ounces ricotta cheese

3 tablespoons dry vermouth

½ teaspoon salt

⅓ cup freshly grated genuine Parmesan cheese

3 sweet Italian sausages (about ½ pound)

6 tablespoons olive oil

4 tablespoons (½ stick) butter

12 slices Italian bread, crusts removed

¼ pound Fontina cheese, thinly sliced

1. In a bowl, combine the ricotta, vermouth, salt, and Parmesan; stir till well blended and smooth, and set aside.

2. Prick the sausages with a fork. In a skillet, heat 1 tablespoon of the oil, add the sausages, and cook, turning till browned on all sides, 12 to 15 minutes; drain on paper towels. Peel off and discard the casings, grind the meat in a food processor or chop it finely with a knife, add it to the cheese mixture, and stir till well blended.

3. Preheat the oven to 325°F. Grease a large baking sheet and set aside.

4. In a large, heavy skillet, heat the remaining 5 tablespoons oil and the butter over moderate heat. Cut the bread slices in half, add to the skillet in batches, fry them briefly on one side, and drain on paper towels.

5. Spread equal amounts of the sausage mixture on the fried sides of the bread, place the slices on the prepared baking sheet, and bake for 5 minutes. Top each sandwich with the Fontina, bake till the cheese melts, about 2 minutes, and serve hot.

Curried Chicken and Almond Sandwiches

Makes
6 sandwiches

Don't ask me why chicken and almonds are so compatible (in soups, salads, casseroles, and certainly sandwiches) or why, when ground or slivered, enhanced by just a teaspoon of curry powder, and bound with creamy mayonnaise, they make one of the most delightful fillings imaginable for sandwiches. Furthermore, don't ask why I can't imagine making these sandwiches with anything but chicken breast (preferably poached) and thin slices of pumpernickel bread. They're ideal, of course, for a simple lunch, but remember also that they can be cut into narrow rectangles and served at cocktail receptions and afternoon teas.

1 cup ground cooked chicken breast
½ cup slivered almonds, lightly toasted
1 tablespoon minced fresh parsley leaves
1 teaspoon minced onion
Salt and freshly ground black pepper to taste
½ cup mayonnaise
1 tablespoon heavy cream
1 teaspoon curry powder
12 thin slices pumpernickel bread

1. In a bowl, combine the chicken, almonds, parsley, onion, and salt and pepper and toss till well blended. In a small bowl, combine the mayonnaise, cream, and curry powder; stir till well blended, add to the chicken mixture, and stir till the mixture is bound to a spreadable consistency.

2. Spread equal amounts of the mixture on half of the bread slices, top with the remaining halves, and cut the sandwiches in half on the diagonal.

Turkey Meatball Pita Sandwiches

What to do with that pound of ground turkey on sale at the grocery store besides making the same turkey burgers or meat loaf? Why not make small meatballs to stuff with shredded lettuce into pitas spread with a minty cucumber dressing, the way the Greeks do? The meatballs are just as good made with ground lamb, in which case you might want to reduce the amount of cucumber and increase the mint in the dressing. In any case, just remember that too much dressing will make the toasted pitas unpleasantly soggy. All you need to serve with these luncheon sandwiches are small bowls of cured black olives and wedges of tangy feta cheese.

4 slices bacon
1 pound ground turkey
1 small onion, minced
1 celery rib, minced
2 slices white loaf bread, finely chopped
1 large egg, beaten
2 teaspoons Worcestershire sauce
Salt and freshly ground black pepper to taste
3 tablespoons heavy cream
½ cup mayonnaise
½ cup sour cream
½ cucumber, peeled, seeded, and minced
2 tablespoons minced fresh mint leaves
4 pita breads (6 inches in diameter), lightly toasted
Shredded romaine lettuce leaves

1. In a skillet, fry the bacon over moderate heat till crisp; drain on paper towels and crumble.

(continued)

**Makes
4 sandwiches**

2. Preheat the oven to 425°F. Grease a large baking pan.

3. In a large bowl, combine the bacon, turkey, onion, celery, white bread, egg, Worcestershire, salt and pepper, and heavy cream. Mix with your hands till well blended, and form into meatballs about the size of small marbles. Arrange on the prepared baking pan and bake till cooked through, 15 to 20 minutes.

4. Meanwhile, combine the mayonnaise, sour cream, cucumber, and mint in a small bowl and stir till well blended.

5. To make the sandwiches, slice a large pocket along one edge of the pitas, spread equal amounts of the cucumber dressing over the interiors, and fill the pockets with meatballs and the shredded lettuce.

Shrimp, Cream Cheese, and Caper Sandwiches

The inspiration for these easy, tasty sandwiches is the local specialty of Charleston, South Carolina, known as shrimp paste, which is traditionally spread on benne (sesame) crackers or toast points and served at all sorts of cocktail parties and receptions. The big difference is that shrimp paste is made with lots of softened butter, whereas my version, intended for more substantial luncheon sandwiches, calls for cream cheese to give the spread an altogether different texture. For even more beguiling flavor, you might also want to add a tablespoon or so of sherry, rum, or gin. Do note that this spread is not ground to a puree and should have a slightly dense, toothy texture. It's also good made with ground steamed clams or mussels.

Makes
6 sandwiches

½ pound fresh shrimp
8 ounces cream cheese, softened and cut into chunks
2 tablespoons minced fresh chives
2 tablespoons minced fresh dill
1 tablespoon capers
1 garlic clove, minced
Salt and freshly ground black pepper to taste
Mayonnaise for spreading
12 slices whole-grain loaf bread

1. Place the shrimp in a saucepan with enough water to cover, bring to a boil, remove from the heat, and let stand for about 2 minutes. Transfer to a colander and, when cool enough to handle, shell and devein the shrimp.

(continued)

2. In a food processor, combine the shrimp, cream cheese, chives, dill, capers, garlic, and salt and pepper; reduce to a coarse paste and scrape into a bowl.

3. Spread mayonnaise on one side of each slice of bread, spread equal amounts of the shrimp mixture over half of the bread slices, and top with the remaining slices, mayonnaise side down. To serve, cut the sandwiches in half on the diagonal.

Irish Deviled Salmon and Watercress Sandwiches

The Irish, like the English, love to "devil" all sorts of meat and seafood dishes with hot mustard, spicy peppers, tangy bottled sauces, and the like, and serious pubs all over Dublin seem to try to outdo one another with assortments of robust sandwiches that go so well with the sturdy beers and ales. Also typical are the unusual flavored butters (tomato, caper, onion, citrus, alcohol) used to complement the various fillings. The ideal bread for these sandwiches would be what is simply called "brown bread," our closest approximation being thin slices of whole wheat or multigrain. I do not recommend trying to use canned salmon, which never has the delicate flavor and flaky texture of fresh. Serve these sandwiches at any type of reception, and, since they disappear fast, always make plenty of them.

Makes 20 to 24 small sandwiches

8 tablespoons (1 stick) butter, softened
½ cup canned tomato puree
¼ teaspoon grated nutmeg
½ teaspoon light brown sugar
2 teaspoons dry sherry
2 cups finely flaked cooked salmon
2 tablespoons heavy cream
1 tablespoon Worcestershire sauce
1 tablespoon fresh lemon juice
1 teaspoon dry mustard
Salt and freshly ground black pepper to taste
20 to 24 thin slices whole-wheat loaf bread, crusts removed
1 cup chopped watercress

(continued)

1. In a food processor, combine the butter, tomato puree, nutmeg, brown sugar, and sherry; reduce to a fine puree, scrape into a bowl, and set aside. Rinse and dry the work bowl of the processor.

2. In the processor, combine the salmon, cream, Worcestershire, lemon juice, mustard, and salt and pepper and reduce to a spreadable paste.

3. Spread 10 to 12 slices of bread with the reserved tomato butter, spread equal amounts of the salmon paste over the top, sprinkle with the watercress, and add the top slices of bread. Serve the sandwiches cut in half on the diagonal.

Long Island Lobster Rolls with Tarragon-Brandy Mayonnaise

Rich lobster rolls are popular all along the New England coast, but at seaside restaurants and shacks on the eastern end of Long Island, they take on a sophistication rarely seen farther north and are often preferred even to a cooked whole lobster or ordinary lobster salad. Diced leftover meat from a 3½- to 4-pound steamed or boiled lobster is ideal for these rolls, but if you need to start fresh, just remember that a 2½-pound cooked lobster yields about 1 pound of meat. Though frozen lobster tails, which are widely available but expensive, can also be used, I find canned lobster meat to be religiously overcooked and tough.

Makes
6 servings

1 cup mayonnaise
3 tablespoons minced fresh tarragon leaves
1 tablespoon brandy
Salt and freshly ground black pepper to taste
1 pound cooked lobster meat, diced
2 celery ribs, diced
2 tablespoons capers
6 half-split hot dog rolls
4 tablespoons (½ stick) butter, melted

1. In a small bowl, combine the mayonnaise, tarragon, brandy, and salt and pepper and stir till well blended.

2. In another bowl, combine the lobster, celery, and capers, add the mayonnaise, and toss till the ingredients are well coated.

3. Toast the hot dog rolls, brush the interiors generously with butter, and spoon equal amounts of the lobster mixture into the rolls.

Sandwiches
and Turnovers

Cornish Beef Pasties

**Makes
6 pasties**

Pasties are to Cornwall in southwestern England what empanadas are to most South American countries, and there's not a pub or tavern in the region that doesn't pride itself on at least one style of the flaky, rich turnovers. Ground or diced beef and potato pasties are the most popular, but the endless variety of fillings includes everything from minced roast pork and turnips to finely flaked cooked mackerel and onions to ground leftover lamb and herbs. Eaten with the hands like a sandwich, an authentic pasty is practically a meal in itself, washed down, of course, with plenty of full-bodied beer or ale. An old rhyme in Cornwall goes as follows: "Pastry rolled out like a plate/Piled with turnip, tates, and mate/Doubled up and baked like fate/That's a Cornish pasty."

For the pastry:
   2 cups all-purpose flour
   ½ teaspoon salt
   1 cup chilled lard
   6 to 7 tablespoons cold water

For the filling:
   1 pound beef round, finely diced
   1 large onion, finely diced
   1 large potato, finely diced
   ½ teaspoon dried thyme, crumbled
   Salt and freshly ground black pepper to taste
   6 tablespoons (¾ stick) butter
   ¼ cup finely chopped fresh parsley leaves
   1 large egg yolk beaten with 1 tablespoon water
   ¾ cup heavy cream

1. To make the pastry, combine the flour and salt in a large bowl and cut in the lard with a pastry cutter till mealy. Gradually sprinkle the water over the surface, mixing briskly with a fork just till the dough holds together. Form the dough into a large ball, wrap in plastic wrap, and chill for at least 1 hour.

2. Preheat the oven to 350°F. Grease a large baking sheet and set aside.

3. To make the filling, combine the beef, onion, potato, thyme, and salt and pepper in a large bowl and mix till well blended. On a lightly floured surface, roll out the dough ⅛ inch thick and cut into six 5-inch rounds. Spoon 3 tablespoons of filling onto one side of each round, dot each with 1 tablespoon of the butter, and sprinkle with 1 tablespoon of the parsley. Moisten the edges of the pastry with water and fold them over the turnovers, crimping the edges with a fork. Prick the tops of the turnovers with the fork and brush with the egg wash.

4. Arrange the pasties on the prepared baking sheet and bake till lightly browned, 45 minutes to 1 hour. Fifteen minutes before the pasties are done, make a small slit in the top of each and spoon 2 tablespoons of the cream into the slits.

5. Serve the pasties hot or warm.

Shredded Pork Tacos

Makes 6 to 8
servings

I've never particularly cared for most tacos in the United States, often made with fried and greasy tortillas, but in Mexico (and parts of California), where softer, much more pliable tortillas (corn and wheat) are commonly used, the "sandwiches" can be memorable. While fillings include ground or diced cooked chicken, beef, chorizo sausage, and even goat, as well as guacamole, refried beans, and various grated cheeses, I find nothing more delectable than these slightly moist shredded pork tacos spiked with chipotle chiles and a little oregano. When two per person are served as a main course, the only other things needed are a basket of corn chips, perhaps an onion and tomato salad, and ice-cold beer.

1 tablespoon corn oil
1 small onion, chopped
4 garlic cloves, minced
1 cup water
½ cup tomato puree or ketchup
2 tablespoons chopped canned chipotle chiles in adobo
2 teaspoons dried oregano
Salt and freshly ground black pepper to taste
One 2- to 2½-pound boneless pork loin, trimmed of fat
12 to 16 corn tortillas (7 inches in diameter), lightly toasted

1. Preheat the oven to 350°F.

2. In a heavy casserole, heat the oil over moderate heat, add the onion and garlic, and stir for about 3 minutes. Add the water, tomato puree or ketchup, chiles, oregano, and salt and pepper and stir till well blended. Cut the pork into large chunks, add to the casserole, and turn to coat the meat well. Cover, bring the liquid to a boil, transfer the casserole to the oven, and cook till the pork is fork-tender, about 2½ hours.

3. Transfer the pork to a large bowl and shred with two large, heavy forks, moistening it with a little of the cooking liquid. Taste for salt and pepper, wrap equal amounts of the mixture in the tortillas, and serve immediately.

Mexican Fried Pork Burritos

Makes
6 servings

These spicy burritos can also be made with ground or finely diced beef, chicken, or chorizo sausage, but whichever filling you use, the main thing to remember is to fry the turnovers just till they are crisp to avoid greasiness—usually no more than about 2 minutes. Also, don't fail to add the vinegar to the filling, a special touch that not only counteracts the heavy texture of the refried beans but also gives the burritos a special tang. Serve the burritos with a favorite salsa as a main course.

2 tablespoons lard
1½ pounds ground lean pork
1 medium onion, finely chopped
1 garlic clove, minced
1 cup tomato sauce
2 tablespoons cider vinegar
1 teaspoon chili powder
½ teaspoon ground cumin
Salt and freshly ground black pepper to taste
12 wheat tortillas (7 inches in diameter)
1½ cups canned refried beans, heated and mashed
Corn oil for frying

1. In a large skillet, melt the lard over moderate heat, add the pork, and stir till browned, about 5 minutes. Add the onion and garlic and stir 5 minutes longer. Add the tomato sauce, vinegar, chili powder, cumin, and salt and pepper, stir well, bring to a simmer, and continue cooking about 15 minutes longer.

2. Spread each tortilla with about 1 tablespoon of the refried beans. Spoon a heaping tablespoon of the pork mixture on half the tortilla, fold the other half over the top, and then, starting with the meat-filled ends, roll up the tortilla.

3. Wipe out the skillet, heat about 1 inch of oil over moderate heat, and, placing each burrito in the oil with the open flap on the bottom, fry till crisp, about 2 minutes. Drain on paper towels and serve hot.

Ham and Cheddar Turnovers

**Makes about
18 turnovers**

Flexibility is the rule for these standard turnovers, which are as appropriate for cocktail receptions and buffets as they are for casual lunches. Ground ends of cured country ham are even more delicious than ordinary smoked ham; any number of assertive cheeses might be substituted for the cheddar; and all sorts of seasonings (minced bell or jalapeño peppers, finely diced sweet pickle, spicy mustard, and any variety of herbs) can be added to enhance the filling. What's also nice is that the unbaked turnovers freeze beautifully, reason enough to make them in quantity for last-minute emergencies. To save time and effort, commercial frozen pie pastry is always an option, but don't expect the turnovers to have the same luscious taste and texture.

For the pastry:
2 cups all-purpose flour
1 teaspoon baking powder
½ teaspoon salt
1 cup vegetable shortening
3 to 4 tablespoons cold water

For the filling:
2 tablespoons butter
2 tablespoons all-purpose flour
1 cup hot milk
1 pound cooked ham, ground
¼ pound extra-sharp cheddar cheese, ground or grated
1 small onion, minced
Salt and freshly ground black pepper to taste

1. To make the pastry, combine the flour, baking powder, salt, and shortening in a food processor and start processing while adding just enough water to make a firm dough. Shape the dough into a ball, wrap in plastic wrap, and chill till ready to use.

2. To make the filling, melt the butter in a saucepan over moderate heat, add the flour, and stir for 1 minute. Stirring constantly, gradually add the milk till the mixture thickens, about 5 minutes. Add the ham, cheese, onion, and salt and pepper, stir till well blended, and remove from the heat.

3. Preheat the oven to 375°F.

4. On a lightly floured surface, roll out the dough about ¼ inch thick and cut it into 3-inch squares. Place a full tablespoon of filling in the center of each square, fold each into a triangle, and pinch the edges together. Arrange the turnovers on a large baking sheet, bake till golden brown, 20 to 25 minutes, and serve hot.

Ground ends of cured country ham are even more delicious than ordinary smoked ham.

Main-Course Russian Beef and Pickle *Piroshki*

Makes about
10 *piroshki*

Traditionally, Russian *piroshki* are small turnovers filled with ground meats, seafood, cheeses, or mushrooms and served either as an hors d'oeuvre or as an accompaniment to soups and salads. Double or triple the size, however, and you have a luscious and unusual main course that requires nothing more than knives and forks, perhaps marinated cucumber slices or a tart tossed green salad, and a sturdy dry red wine. Do note that this rich pastry needs to be chilled overnight to develop the right texture, and remember that the pastry can always be cut into 2- to 3-inch squares if you prefer to serve the turnovers as finger appetizers. In either case, the unbaked *piroshki* freeze well in airtight containers or wrapped snugly in foil.

For the pastry:
2 cups all-purpose flour
½ teaspoon salt
8 tablespoons (1 stick) chilled butter, cut into pieces
4 ounces cream cheese

For the filling:
1½ cups minced cooked beef
2 tablespoons minced sweet pickle
1 tablespoon minced onion
1 tablespoon ketchup
Salt and freshly ground black pepper to taste

4 tablespoons (½ stick) butter, melted

1. To make the pastry, combine the flour, salt, butter, and cream cheese in a food processor and process till a firm dough forms. Form the dough into a ball, wrap in plastic wrap, and chill overnight.

2. Preheat the oven to 400°F.

3. To make the filling, combine the beef, pickle, onion, ketchup, and salt and pepper in a bowl and stir till well blended.

4. On a lightly floured surface, roll out the dough about ⅛ inch thick and cut out 6-inch squares. Re-roll the scraps of dough and cut out more squares. Spoon equal amounts of the beef filling onto half of each square, fold the other halves over the tops, and pinch the edges together with your fingers. Arrange the *piroshki* on two large baking sheets, brush each with the melted butter, and bake till golden brown, 20 to 25 minutes.

South American Ham, Egg, and Olive Empanadas

Popular in all South American countries and sold in pastry and sandwich shops of even the largest and most sophisticated cities, these savory turnovers, made with any number of ground fillings, range in size from the huge *empanada gallega* (large enough to feed an entire family) to tiny, ravioli-size *empanaditas*. The turnovers are a perfect way to use up any leftover cooked meats, poultry, and seafood, as well as a good excuse to experiment with various vegetables and seasonings. The ones here are intended as a main course for an informal lunch or supper and will feed 5 to 8 people, depending on appetites and what else is served. To make about 20 appetizer portions, cut the pastry into rounds with a 3-inch biscuit cutter and fill as for the larger rounds.

For the pastry:
   2 cups all-purpose flour
   1 teaspoon salt
   1 cup chilled lard
   4 to 5 tablespoons cold water

For the filling:
   2 tablespoons olive oil
   1 large onion, minced
   2 garlic cloves, minced
   2 medium fresh chile peppers, seeded and minced
   ½ pound cooked ham, ground or finely diced
   2 large hard-boiled eggs, finely chopped
   2 tablespoons grated Parmesan cheese
   10 pimento-stuffed olives, cut in half

1. To make the pastry, combine the flour, salt, and lard in a food processor and process till mealy. With the machine running, gradually add enough of the water to make a slightly sticky dough, form the dough into a ball, and set aside.

2. Preheat the oven to 375°F.

3. To make the filling, heat the oil over moderate heat in a large skillet, add the onion, garlic, and chiles, stir till fully softened, about 3 minutes, and scrape into a bowl. Add the ham, eggs, and cheese to the mixture and stir till well blended.

4. With a floured rolling pin, roll out the reserved dough on a lightly floured surface about ⅛ inch thick and cut into rounds about 6 inches in diameter. Re-roll the scraps of dough and cut out more rounds. Spoon equal amounts of the ham filling and two olive halves onto one half of each round and fold the other half of the pastry over the top. Press the edges together with your fingers or the tines of a fork, arrange on two large baking sheets, and bake till golden brown, about 25 minutes.

Gingered Turkey and Pecan Turnovers

Makes about 18 turnovers

Served with perhaps a mushroom or creamed vegetable sauce, these turnovers with a delightfully contrasting soft-crunchy texture are one of the best and most unusual ways I know to deal with leftover holiday turkey. They will serve 4 to 6 people at an informal supper, and since they're fairly rich, nothing goes better with them than a congealed salad. If you love ginger as much as I do, you might want to increase the amount slightly, remembering all the while that no spice can be more overpowering when used carelessly. The unbaked turnovers can also be frozen in airtight containers and served, when needed, at receptions.

For the pastry:
2 cups all-purpose flour
½ teaspoon salt
1 cup vegetable shortening
3 to 4 tablespoons cold water

For the filling:
3 tablespoons butter
1 small onion, minced
½ celery rib, minced
3 tablespoons all-purpose flour
⅛ teaspoon ground ginger
Salt and freshly ground black pepper to taste
1 cup half-and-half
2 cups ground or minced cooked turkey
½ cup finely chopped pecans

1. To make the pastry, combine the flour, salt, and shortening in a food processor and start processing while adding just enough water to make a firm dough. Form the dough into a ball, wrap in plastic wrap, and refrigerate till ready to use.

2. To make the filling, melt the butter in a heavy saucepan over moderate heat, add the onion, celery, and flour, and stir for 2 minutes. Add the ginger and salt and pepper and stir. Gradually add the half-and-half, stirring constantly till the mixture thickens slightly, about 5 minutes. Add the turkey and pecans, stir till well blended, and let cool.

3. Preheat the oven to 375°F.

4. On a lightly floured surface, roll out the dough ⅛ inch thick and cut into rounds with a 3-inch biscuit cutter or small juice glass. Place a rounded tablespoon of the turkey mixture over one half of each pastry round and fold the other half over the filling, pressing the edges together with your fingers. Arrange the turnovers on a large baking sheet and bake till golden brown, 20 to 25 minutes.

If you love ginger as much as I do, you might want to increase the amount slightly.

Mexican Duck Quesadillas

Makes
8 quesadillas

A specialty of Mexico's Oaxaca region, these succulent turnovers are traditionally made with wheat tortillas stuffed with shredded cooked duck or turkey, strips of poblano chiles, stringy Oaxaca cheese, and either the pungent herb epazote or cilantro. The quesadillas can be simply toasted under a broiler till the cheese melts, but I much prefer the authentic method of "frying" them in a hot skillet till they brown nicely on both sides—watching carefully so they don't burn. These turnovers will serve 4 people as a main course, but if you'd like to serve them as an appetizer, cut them into strips.

¼ cup lard
2 medium red onions, thinly sliced
2 tablespoons sugar
Salt and freshly ground black pepper to taste
2 tablespoons cider vinegar
8 wheat tortillas (7 inches in diameter)
½ pound Monterey Jack or Muenster cheese, grated
1 cup shredded cooked duck meat
2 tablespoons chopped fresh cilantro

1. In a large skillet, melt the lard over moderate heat, add the onions, and stir till softened, 9 to 10 minutes. Sprinkle the sugar and salt and pepper over the top and stir 3 to 5 minutes longer to caramelize the onions. Drizzle the vinegar over the top, stir 2 minutes longer, and remove from the heat.

2. Place 4 tortillas on a work surface, sprinkle half the cheese over the tops, divide the duck evenly over the cheese, divide the onions evenly over the duck, and sprinkle the remaining cheese and the cilantro evenly over the top. Place the remaining tortillas on the tops and press the quesadillas down with the palm of your hand.

3. Preheat the oven to 250°F.

4. Wipe the skillet with paper towels and place over moderate heat till hot. Place a quesadilla in the skillet and press down with a spatula till lightly browned, about 3 minutes. Turn it over, press down till lightly browned and the cheese melts, and transfer to the oven on a plate to keep warm. Repeat with the remaining quesadillas.

5. Cut each quesadilla in half or quarters and serve hot.

Brazilian Shrimp, Cashew, and Hearts of Palm *Empadinhas*

Makes about
10 *empadinhas*

Given the fact that the delicate, tender, ivory-colored shoots of palm trees are available fresh year-round in Brazil, and that cashew nuts were being cultivated there long before the Spanish and Portuguese arrived, it's no wonder that the two delicacies are generously used in numerous soups, salads, casseroles, and stuffed dishes. Curiously, the pastry for Brazilian *empadinhas* tends to be a little thicker and richer than that for empanadas in other South American countries, and the fillings have a toothier texture, as with these made with finely chopped shrimp (or other shellfish). In the United States, fresh hearts of palm are available only in Florida, but the canned ones packed in water are delectable—and equally expensive. Do note that, once opened, the hearts should be stored with their liquid in a non-metal container for up to a week in the refrigerator.

For the pastry:
2 cups all-purpose flour
1 teaspoon salt
8 ounces (2 sticks) chilled butter, cut into pieces
3 to 4 tablespoons cold water

For the filling:
2 tablespoons safflower oil
6 scallions (part of green tops included), minced
1 tablespoon all-purpose flour
1 cup milk
1 cup finely chopped cooked shrimp (or other shellfish)
1 cup finely chopped hearts of palm
½ cup finely chopped cashews
2 large hard-boiled eggs, finely chopped

2 tablespoons minced fresh parsley leaves
½ teaspoon paprika
Salt and freshly ground black pepper to taste

1. To make the pastry, combine the flour, salt, and butter in a food processor and process till mealy. With the machine running, gradually add enough of the water to make a firm dough. Form the dough into a ball and set aside.

2. Preheat the oven to 375°F.

3. To make the filling, heat the oil over moderate heat in a large, heavy saucepan, add the scallions, and stir till softened, about 3 minutes. Sprinkle the flour over the top and stir 2 minutes longer. Add the milk and stir till the mixture thickens slightly. Remove from the heat, add the shrimp, hearts of palm, cashews, eggs, parsley, paprika, and salt and pepper, and stir till well blended.

4. On a lightly floured surface, roll out the dough ⅛ to ¼ inch thick and cut out 6-inch rounds. Re-roll the scraps of dough and cut out more rounds. Spoon equal amounts of the filling onto one half of each round and fold the other half of the pastry over the tops. Press the edges together with your fingers or the tines of a fork, arrange on two large baking sheets, and bake till golden brown, 20 to 25 minutes.

Patties, Balls, and Dumplings

The Perfect American Hamburger

Since the all-American hamburger (and chopped steak) is the ultimate ground meat dish, why do we encounter so many bad ones? Here, basically, are the cardinal rules for producing a perfect burger: 1) Use only ground beef chuck that contains about 20 percent fat. 2) Allow about ½ pound of meat per burger. 3) For light, juicy burgers, the meat must be coarsely ground and handled as little as possible. 4) Cook the burgers over moderate heat on a charcoal grill or in a cast-iron skillet. 5) For rare burgers, cook for 4 to 5 minutes on each side; for medium-rare, 5 to 6 minutes; for medium, 6 to 7 minutes. 6) Use yeasty buns with rich texture, and always lightly toast and butter the buns. 7) Never press down on a burger, which releases precious juices. Traditional garnishes are mayonnaise (or mustard), ripe tomato slices, leaves of lettuce (only iceberg), and slices of raw onion. Special regional garnishes include avocado slices and Thousand Island dressing (California), chili (the South), barbecue sauce (Texas and the Southwest), bacon (the Northeast), and numerous varieties of cheese slices.

**Makes
4 hamburgers**

One 2-pound beef chuck roast, untrimmed
Salt and freshly ground black pepper to taste
4 tablespoons (½ stick) butter
4 split hamburger buns

1. Cut the beef into pieces and either grind coarsely (once) in a meat grinder or grind in a food processor just till the meat still has a coarse texture. Place in a bowl, add the salt and pepper, and gently form into 4 patties about 4 inches in diameter, handling the meat as little as possible and not flattening it down.

2. In a large cast-iron skillet, melt 2 tablespoons of the butter over moderate heat, add the patties, and cook for 5 minutes on each side for medium-rare.

3. Meanwhile, lightly toast the buns and spread the remaining 2 tablespoons of butter over the insides of each. Place a patty on the bottom half of each bun and top with selected garnishes and the other bun halves.

For light, juicy burgers, the meat must be coarsely ground and handled as little as possible.

Salisbury Steaks with Wild Mushroom Gravy

**Makes
4 servings**

Named for the nineteenth-century English doctor J. H. Salisbury, who advocated eating beef three times a day for sound health, Salisbury steak is considered to be the ancestor of the hamburger. Abused over the decades with soup mixes, bouillon cubes, and gloppy canned mushroom gravy, the steak is sublime when prepared with care and imagination and becomes testimony to the glory of ground meat. Treat it with the same respect you would a perfect burger. If you have fresh beef stock on hand for the gravy, so much the better, and do feel free to experiment with various types of wild mushrooms.

2 slices bacon, cut into small pieces
1½ pounds ground beef round or sirloin
1 small onion, minced
1 tablespoon Worcestershire sauce
Salt and freshly ground black pepper to taste
2 tablespoons butter
10 small shiitake mushrooms, chopped
2 tablespoons all-purpose flour
2 cups beef broth

1. In a large skillet, fry the bacon over moderate heat till almost crisp. Drain on paper towels, and remove the pan from the heat, leaving the fat in the skillet.

2. In a large bowl, combine the beef, bacon, onion, Worcestershire, and salt and pepper and mix lightly with your hands till well blended. Form the mixture into 4 oval steaks about 1 inch thick. Return the pan to the heat, add the steaks, and cook in the bacon fat for about 6 minutes on each side. Transfer the steaks to a heated platter and cover with foil to keep warm.

3. Melt the butter in the skillet, add the mushrooms, and stir till tender, about 5 minutes. Sprinkle the flour over the top, season with salt and pepper, and stir 2 minutes longer. Add the broth, increase the heat slightly, and stir till the gravy thickens, 3 to 5 minutes.

4. Serve the steaks with equal amounts of the gravy spooned over the tops.

Meat Loaf Burgers

Makes
4 servings

If you like ordinary meat loaf, you'll love these burgers, which have the advantage of being moist and succulent on the inside, with slightly crusty surfaces. For even more flavorful burgers, reduce the ground pork to ¼ pound and substitute about ¼ pound of bulk pork sausage. The burgers are equally delicious served on top of toasted hamburger bun halves.

1 pound ground beef chuck
½ pound ground pork
1 small onion, minced
1 celery rib, minced
½ small green bell pepper, seeded and minced
2 tablespoons minced fresh parsley leaves
1 large egg, beaten
¼ cup dry bread crumbs
2 tablespoons heavy cream
2 teaspoons Worcestershire sauce
Salt and freshly ground black pepper to taste
½ cup ketchup
2 teaspoons cider vinegar
2 teaspoons light brown sugar
½ teaspoon ground cloves

1. Preheat the oven to 400°F.

2. In a large bowl, combine the beef, pork, onion, celery, bell pepper, and parsley and mix with your hands till blended. Add the egg, bread crumbs, cream, Worcestershire, and salt and pepper and continue mixing just till well blended.

3. Gently form the mixture into 4 patties about 1 inch thick, arrange the patties on a large slotted baking pan, and bake for about 10 minutes. Turn the patties over and bake till cooked through and crusty, about 10 minutes longer.

4. Meanwhile, combine the ketchup, vinegar, brown sugar, and cloves in a small saucepan and simmer over low heat, stirring, for about 5 minutes.

5. Serve the burgers hot with equal amounts of the sauce spooned over the tops.

Southern Cracklin' Pork Burgers

**Makes
4 burgers**

In the American South, the crunchy rendered morsels of pork fat known as cracklings (or cracklin's) are used to enhance everything from salads to stews to breads, but never are they more relished than when added to ground pork for both flavor and textural contrast in these luscious burgers smothered with caramelized onions. If you're grinding your own meat, the best cut of pork for burgers is shoulder, and, as with beef, just make sure that the texture of the ground meat is coarse—not fine or mushy. Note also that most Southerners prefer their buns soft, not toasted.

2 tablespoons butter
2 medium onions, thinly sliced
2 slices white loaf bread, torn into small bits
¼ cup milk
¼ pound lean salt pork (rind removed), chopped
1½ pounds ground pork
1 garlic clove, minced
1 tablespoon Worcestershire sauce
Salt and freshly ground black pepper to taste
1½ cups fine dry bread crumbs
Mustard for spreading
4 split hamburger buns, wrapped in foil and heated

1. In a medium skillet, melt the butter over low heat, add the onions, and cook slowly, stirring, till caramelized, about 20 minutes. Transfer to a plate and keep warm.

2. Meanwhile, combine the bread and milk in a bowl and let soak. In a large skillet, fry the salt pork over moderate heat till crisp, stirring, and drain the cracklin's on paper towels. Remove the skillet from the heat and reserve the fat.

3. In a bowl, combine the ground pork, garlic, Worcestershire, salt and pepper, soaked bread, and the cracklin's, and mix with your hands till well blended. Form the mixture into 4 patties of equal size and coat the patties with the bread crumbs. Reheat the fat in the skillet over moderate heat, add the patties, and cook till nicely browned, about 7 minutes on each side.

4. To serve, spread mustard over the inside surfaces of the buns, place a burger on each bottom half, spoon caramelized onions generously over each burger, and cover with the bun tops.

Swedish Beef Lindström

In Sweden and the other Scandinavian countries, Beef Lindström is one of the most beloved classic dishes, and in restaurants, the ground steak is often served topped with a fried egg. Typically, the large patties are made with prime cuts of meat, the texture is much finer and tighter than that of other burgers, and almost always the steaks are flattened slightly and cooked till medium done and lightly browned. Because of the other ingredients, the steaks are neither dry nor tough—especially with a soft fried egg on top. For just the right texture, be sure to chill the meat mixture before forming it into patties.

1½ pounds finely ground beef sirloin or top round
1 medium onion, minced
½ cup mashed potatoes
½ cup minced cooked beets or pickled beets
3 tablespoons minced capers
2 large egg yolks
3 tablespoons half-and-half
Salt and freshly ground black pepper to taste
3 tablespoons butter

1. In a large bowl, combine the beef, onion, potatoes, beets, capers, egg yolks, half-and-half, and salt and pepper, and mix with your hands till well blended. Cover with plastic wrap and chill for at least 1 hour.

2. Form the mixture into 4 large patties and flatten slightly. In a large skillet, melt the butter over moderate heat, add the patties, and cook till lightly browned on the bottoms, 6 to 7 minutes. Turn the patties over and cook the other sides till lightly browned, 6 to 7 minutes.

3. Serve hot.

French Hamburgers with Herb-Cream Sauce

Leave it to the French to elevate the humble hamburger to noble heights by grinding only the most prime cuts of beef and crowning the patty with a suave cream sauce. An authentic *haché à la crème* is never light and juicy, it is never cooked more than medium-rare, and it is never served on a bun. For the right texture, the meat mixture must be stirred vigorously with a wooden spoon till it is very compact, and for a slightly crusty finish, the patties must be dusted in a little flour.

**Makes
6 servings**

6 tablespoons (¾ stick) butter
1 medium onion, minced
2 pounds finely ground lean beef sirloin or round
1 large egg, beaten
Salt and freshly ground black pepper to taste
½ cup all-purpose flour
1 tablespoon olive oil
¼ cup beef broth
½ cup heavy cream
1 tablespoon minced fresh parsley leaves
1 teaspoon dried thyme, crumbled
1 teaspoon dried tarragon, crumbled

1. In a small skillet, melt 2 tablespoons of the butter over moderate heat, add the onion, stir till very soft, about 5 minutes, and transfer to a large bowl. Add the beef, egg, and salt and pepper and stir vigorously till well blended and smooth. With your hands, form the mixture into 6 patties about 1 inch thick, and dust each patty all over in the flour.

2. In a large, heavy skillet, heat the oil and 2 tablespoons of the remaining butter over moderately high heat, add 3 patties, cook
(continued)

*An authentic
haché à la
crème is
never light
and juicy,
it is never
cooked
more than
medium-
rare, and
it is never
served on
a bun.*

for 4 to 5 minutes on each side for medium-rare, and keep warm on a heated plate. Repeat with the remaining 3 patties.

3. Pour off any fat from the skillet, add the broth, and cook till it is reduced almost to a syrup, scraping bits and pieces from the bottom of the pan. Add the cream, parsley, thyme, tarragon, and salt and pepper to taste and cook till the sauce thickens slightly. Remove the pan from the heat and swirl in the remaining 2 tablespoons butter till it is well incorporated in the sauce.

4. Serve the hamburgers hot with the sauce spooned over the tops.

Turkish Lamb Burgers

Both Turkish and Greek cooks know how to deal with ground lamb like nobody else (burgers, balls, fritters, small pies, and more), and where their dishes differ is mainly in the choice of spices and other seasonings. The best cut of lamb for these aromatic ground steaks is shoulder, since it has sufficient fat to produce juicy flavor and texture, and if you want your burgers to taste like the ones found in the restaurants of Istanbul, you'll grind the lamb twice and cook the ovals just till they're lightly browned all over.

Makes
4 servings

1½ pounds ground lamb shoulder
2 tablespoons heavy cream
2 large eggs, beaten
¼ teaspoon ground cinnamon
⅛ teaspoon ground aniseed
Salt and freshly ground black pepper to taste
½ cup fine dry bread crumbs
2 tablespoons olive oil
½ cup plain yogurt
2 scallions (part of green tops included), chopped

1. In a bowl, combine the lamb, cream, eggs, cinnamon, anise, salt and pepper, and bread crumbs; mix with your hands till well blended, and form the mixture into four 1-inch-thick oval patties.

2. In a large, heavy skillet, heat the oil over moderate heat, add the patties, and cook till the bottoms are lightly browned, 4 to 5 minutes. Turn the patties, cook till the other sides are lightly browned, 4 to 5 minutes, and drain on paper towels.

3. Arrange the burgers on serving plates, spoon equal amounts of the yogurt over the tops, and sprinkle each with the scallions.

Moroccan Spiced Turkey Patties

Makes
4 servings

While one of the glories of Moroccan cooking is an 8-pound turkey that is stuffed with almonds, raisins, rice, and spices and slowly braised in an earthenware casserole, a similar and much easier result can be attained with these spicy patties topped with a smooth yogurt sauce. Unlike the ubiquitous *kefta* dishes of finely ground, almost pasty beef or lamb found along the streets of Rabat, Fez, and other major cities, the turkey (or chicken) patties made with dark meat are more likely to be prepared in private homes and tend to have a coarser and juicier texture. If you relish sweet dishes as much as the Moroccans do, you can add about a tablespoon of honey to the sauce.

1½ pounds ground turkey (preferably dark meat)
¼ cup seedless dark raisins
1 tablespoon tomato paste
⅛ teaspoon ground cinnamon
⅛ teaspoon ground ginger
Salt and freshly ground black pepper to taste
2 tablespoons olive oil
½ cup plain yogurt
2 teaspoons fresh lemon juice
⅛ teaspoon ground cumin
⅛ teaspoon cayenne pepper

1. In a bowl, combine the turkey, raisins, tomato paste, cinnamon, ginger, and salt and pepper, and mix with your hands till well blended (do not overmix). Gently form the mixture into 4 patties about 1 inch thick.

2. In a large skillet, heat the oil over moderate heat, add the patties, and cook for about 6 minutes. Turn the patties over and cook the other sides till lightly browned, 5 to 6 minutes.

3. Meanwhile, in a bowl, combine the yogurt, lemon juice, cumin, and cayenne, and mix till well blended.

4. Serve the patties hot with equal amounts of the sauce spooned over the tops.

Greek Chopped Lamb Steaks

These chopped lamb steaks are typical of the style of dishes I was accustomed to eating on occasion when my Greek grandfather was alive, and you're just as likely to find steaks like these in the restaurants of Athens as on Greek-American tables. Greeks, of course, are notorious for cooking all lamb dishes till the meat is fork-tender, by explanation of why the steaks are broiled for a full 8 minutes on each side. To counteract any possible dryness, however, the patties are not only moistened with yogurt but also always topped with a moist, well-flavored garnish such as these marinated cucumbers, black olives, and scallions. The end result is sublime.

Makes
4 servings

¼ cup Greek olive oil
3 tablespoons white wine vinegar
3 tablespoons fresh lemon juice
1 teaspoon dried oregano, crumbled
1 garlic clove, minced
Salt and freshly ground black pepper to taste
2 Kirby cucumbers, peeled and coarsely chopped
8 to 10 Greek black olives, pitted and coarsely chopped
2 scallions (part of green tops included), finely chopped
1½ pounds ground lamb shoulder
1 small onion, minced
2 mint leaves, minced
1 cup plain yogurt

1. In a bowl, combine the oil, vinegar, and lemon juice and whisk till well blended. Add the oregano, garlic, and salt and pepper and stir till well blended. Add the cucumbers, olives, and scallions, stir well, cover with plastic wrap, and let marinate for about 1 hour.

2. Preheat the oven broiler.

3. In a bowl, combine the lamb, onion, mint, and yogurt, and mix with your hands till well blended. Form the mixture into 4 thick oval patties, place on the rack of a broiler pan, and broil about 4 inches from the heat till cooked through, about 8 minutes on each side.

4. Drain the cucumber mixture and serve the burgers hot with a little of the mixture spooned over the tops.

Scandinavian Meatballs with Dilled Sour Cream Sauce

The art of making and cooking meatballs (*frikadeller*) reaches a zenith in all the Scandinavian countries, and to eat these moist, spicy wonders over buttered noodles with lingonberry or red currant jelly on the side is a gustatory experience rarely encountered elsewhere. The very finest meatballs are made with at least three different meats that are finely ground or diced for the smoothest possible texture, but so long as the sauce in which the balls are tossed is full-flavored, the dish can be made exclusively with only one meat, if necessary. Typically, a small ramekin of jelly is provided for each person, a speck of which is dabbed on each meatball as it is eaten.

Makes 6 to 8 servings

1 pound finely ground beef chuck
½ pound finely ground pork
½ pound finely ground veal
2 slices bacon, finely diced
2 scallions (white parts only), minced
2 garlic cloves, minced
2 cups dry bread crumbs
½ cup milk
2 large eggs, beaten
¼ teaspoon ground allspice
Salt and freshly ground black pepper to taste
3 tablespoons butter
3 tablespoons all-purpose flour
1 cup beef broth
½ cup sour cream
½ teaspoon fresh lemon juice
2 tablespoons minced fresh dill
Cayenne pepper to taste
Chopped fresh parsley leaves for garnish

1. Preheat the oven to 425°F.

2. In a large bowl, combine the beef, pork, veal, bacon, scallions, garlic, bread crumbs, milk, eggs, allspice, and salt and pepper, and mix with your hands till well blended. Using a rounded tablespoon, form the mixture into balls, arrange the balls on a large rimmed baking pan, and bake till lightly browned, 15 to 20 minutes.

3. Meanwhile, melt the butter in a saucepan over moderate heat, add the flour, and whisk for 1 minute. Whisking, add the broth, sour cream, and lemon juice; bring to a boil, reduce the heat to moderate, and simmer till the sauce is slightly thickened, about 3 minutes.

4. Transfer the sauce to a large bowl, add the meatballs, dill, and cayenne, toss gently to coat, and serve hot sprinkled with the chopped parsley.

The very finest meatballs are made with at least three different meats that are finely ground or diced for the smoothest possible texture.

Greek Minted Meatballs

Makes 6 to 8
servings

It's debatable whether Greek *keftedes* are the most beguiling meatballs on earth, but it's for sure that none is more delicious than the ones I knew as a child growing up in a part-Greek household—especially when served with moist, buttery orzo pasta and a vinegary Greek salad. Genuine *keftedes* are always made with a combination of ground beef and lamb, but of course, what gives the balls their real distinction are the cinnamon and mint, both of which should be adjusted according to taste. The meatballs are never served with any type of sauce and are almost as good at room temperature as they are hot.

1 cup fine fresh bread crumbs
1½ cups half-and-half
8 tablespoons (1 stick) butter
2 medium onions, minced
2 garlic cloves, minced
1 pound ground beef round
1 pound ground lamb shoulder
2 large eggs, beaten
2 teaspoons ground cinnamon
¼ cup finely chopped fresh mint leaves
Salt and freshly ground black pepper to taste
2 cups all-purpose flour
3 tablespoons olive oil

1. In a small bowl, combine the bread crumbs and 1 cup of the half-and-half and let soak for 5 minutes.

2. Meanwhile, in a skillet, melt 4 tablespoons of the butter over moderate heat, add the onions and garlic, and stir till softened, about 8 minutes. Transfer the onions and garlic to a large bowl, add the soaked bread crumbs plus the two meats, and mix with your hands till well blended. Add the remaining ½ cup half-and-half, the eggs, cinnamon, half of the mint, and salt and pepper, and continue mixing till well blended. Form the mixture into balls about 1 inch in diameter and dust them lightly in the flour.

3. Preheat the oven to 200°F.

4. In a large skillet, melt the remaining 4 tablespoons butter over moderate heat and add the oil. Add the meatballs in batches and brown on all sides, about 10 minutes. Drain on paper towels, transfer to a platter, and keep hot in the oven till ready to serve in a heated bowl topped with the remaining chopped mint.

Meatballs Stroganoff

Named after the nineteenth-century Russian diplomat Count Paul Stroganoff, beef Stroganoff is usually thin slices of premium beef, onions, and mushrooms cooked with an elegant sour cream sauce and served with rice pilaf. When and why this noble classic evolved partly as a more humble meatball dish served with buttered noodles remains a mystery, but, as with so many ground meat dishes, it was most likely due to economic measures taken by cooks after the Russian Revolution in the early twentieth century. Whatever the reason, there can be no doubt that this is still another example of a modified dish being just as succulent as the original when prepared correctly.

Makes 4 to 6 servings

1 slice white loaf bread, finely shredded
¼ cup milk
1½ pounds ground beef round
1 small onion, minced
1 large egg, beaten
1 tablespoon paprika
1 teaspoon Dijon mustard
¼ teaspoon grated nutmeg
Salt and freshly ground black pepper to taste
3 tablespoons butter
¼ pound mushrooms, thinly sliced
¼ cup beef broth
2 tablespoons red wine
1 cup sour cream
3 tablespoons finely chopped fresh parsley leaves

1. In a small bowl, soak the bread in the milk for about 5 minutes, then transfer to a large bowl. Add the beef, onion, egg, paprika, mustard, nutmeg, and salt and pepper, mix with your hands till well blended, and form the mixture into balls about 1½ inches in diameter.

2. In a large, heavy skillet, melt the butter over moderate heat, add the meatballs, and brown lightly on all sides. Add the mushrooms, shake the skillet to distribute them evenly around the meatballs, cover, and cook for about 5 minutes. Add the broth and wine, stir, and cook till the liquid is slightly reduced, about 5 minutes. Add the sour cream, stir, and bring almost to a boil.

3. Serve hot sprinkled with the parsley.

Shanghai Lion's Head

**Makes
4 servings**

Peking, Canton, and other Chinese provinces have their own versions of these large, exotic meatballs, but perhaps the most sophisticated Lion's Head (so-called because the irregularly shaped balls resemble a lion's head and the shredded greens his mane) hails from Shanghai. On home territory, the dish might well be made with spicy, air-cured, finely diced Chinese bacon (or pig belly), and the meat mixture would no doubt contain a few local diced black mushrooms (available in some of our Chinese markets). Bok choy is the preferred green for this dish, but if you can't find any, use napa cabbage, spinach, or regular cabbage. Be sure to serve the Lion's Head piping hot.

1¼ pounds ground pork
2 scallions (part of green tops included), minced
1 garlic clove, minced
20 water chestnuts, finely diced
1 teaspoon finely minced fresh ginger
3 tablespoons soy sauce
1 tablespoon dry sherry
¼ teaspoon sesame oil
Salt and freshly ground black pepper to taste
1 large egg, beaten
2 to 3 tablespoons cornstarch
2 tablespoons peanut oil
1½ cups chicken broth
1 pound bok choy or napa cabbage, chopped

1. In a large bowl, combine the pork, scallions, garlic, water chestnuts, ginger, 1 tablespoon of the soy sauce, the sesame oil, salt and pepper, and egg, and mix with your hands till well blended. Add enough of the cornstarch to bind the mixture, still mixing with your hands (the mixture should not be too wet). Form the mixture into 4 large, irregularly shaped meatballs.

2. In a large skillet, heat the peanut oil over moderate heat, add the meatballs, and cook till nicely browned on one side, about 7 minutes. Turn and cook till the other sides are browned, about 7 minutes longer, and remove from the heat.

3. In an ovenproof casserole large enough to hold the meatballs, combine the broth and remaining 2 tablespoons soy sauce and bring to a boil. Add the meatballs, reduce the heat to low, cover, and simmer for 15 minutes. Scatter the bok choy over the top of the meatballs, cover, and continue simmering till the meatballs are cooked through and the bok choy is steamed, about 10 minutes.

4. To serve, arrange a meatball in each of 4 wide soup bowls surrounded by some of the bok choy, and spoon a little of the broth over each.

Catalonian Lamb Meatballs

**Makes
6 servings**

Today, many of the Spanish restaurants of Barcelona that once prided themselves on regional Catalonian food have fallen victim to the fusion cuisine epidemic, but move up into the Pyrenees and you'll have no problem finding plenty of no-nonsense retreats serving authentic specialties like these spicy *albondigas* made with the area's superior lamb. Unless you have an amenable butcher, buy either lamb shoulder (usually marketed as meat for lamb stew) or lean rib chops and grind it yourself. Do feel free to experiment with various herbs and spices for these meatballs. When formed in a smaller size and served with toothpicks, they also make an unusual and delectable party appetizer.

1 cup fresh bread crumbs
¼ cup dry red wine
2 pounds ground lamb
2 large eggs, beaten
2 garlic cloves, minced
¼ cup chopped fresh parsley leaves
½ teaspoon dried thyme, crumbled
⅛ teaspoon grated nutmeg
⅛ teaspoon ground cumin
Salt and freshly ground black pepper to taste
3 tablespoons olive oil
1 medium onion, chopped
1 cup beef broth
3 tablespoons tomato sauce
2 tablespoons sherry

1. In a small bowl, combine the bread crumbs and wine and let soak for about 5 minutes. In a large bowl, combine the lamb, eggs, garlic, parsley, thyme, nutmeg, cumin, and salt and pepper, and mix with your hands till well blended. Add the soaked bread crumbs and mix till smooth. Using a rounded tablespoon, form and roll the mixture into 24 to 30 meatballs and place on a platter.

2. In a large ovenproof casserole, heat the oil over moderate heat, and brown the meatballs on all sides. Add the onion and stir gently till it is softened, about 5 minutes. Add the broth, tomato sauce, and sherry, and stir well. Bring to a low boil, reduce the heat to low, cover, and simmer for about 40 minutes.

3. Serve hot.

Do feel free to experiment with various herbs and spices for these meatballs.

Portuguese Gingered Codfish Balls

Makes
4 servings

Ground or minced salt cod is used to make spreads, fritters, turnovers, and small cakes from one end of Portugal to the next, but without question, the most popular specialty is the spicy balls (*os bolinhos de bacalhau*) served everywhere from bars to fancy restaurants to picnics. Since cod is a relatively bland fish, it lends itself to endless flavorings, and none does greater wonders and adds just the right tang than grated fresh ginger—so long, that is, as it's not overplayed. Do notice that the balls need to be chilled briefly to maintain a firm texture when fried, and while I prefer mine as hot as possible, the custom in Portugal is to serve them at room temperature with lots of shoestring potatoes and black olives. Rolled about an inch in diameter and fried no more than 2 or 3 minutes, the balls also make a delightful cocktail appetizer.

½ pound dried salt cod
1 cup mashed potatoes
1 small onion, minced
1 garlic clove, minced
2 tablespoons minced fresh parsley leaves
¼ teaspoon grated fresh ginger
Freshly ground black pepper to taste
1 large egg, beaten
Vegetable oil for frying

1. Place the cod in a bowl with enough water to cover and soak for 8 to 10 hours, changing the water twice.

2. Drain the fish well, discard any skin and bones, mince finely, and place in a large bowl. Add the potatoes, onion, garlic, parsley, ginger, pepper, and egg, and mix till well blended and smooth. Form the mixture into 2-inch balls, place on a plate, cover with plastic wrap, and chill for about 1 hour.

3. Heat about 2 inches of oil in a large, heavy skillet over moderately high heat, add the balls (in batches, if necessary), fry till golden brown, 3 to 5 minutes, and drain on paper towels.

4. Serve the balls hot or at room temperature.

Jewish Gefilte Fish

If gefilte fish often gets a bad rap, it's usually because the balls are so full of matzo meal that they're doughy and tough, or because cooks don't go to the trouble of making a broth that jells properly around the balls when chilled. The truth is that gefilte fish can be a delicious and almost elegant dish when it's prepared with care. I personally see no need for any thickening agent in the fish mixture if a light texture is what you're aiming for, but if you prefer a more compact body to the balls, by all means add about ¼ cup of matzo meal—no more. For this classic dish, there is no substitute for grated fresh horseradish as a garnish. Do note that the dish must chill overnight.

Makes 4 or 5 servings

1 pound *each* fresh whole carp, pike, and white fish, filleted and heads, bones, and skins reserved
2 medium onions, quartered
2 garlic cloves, peeled and smashed
1 large parsley sprig
Salt and freshly ground black pepper to taste
2 large eggs, beaten
3 tablespoons water
1 carrot, scraped and cut in julienne
Grated fresh horseradish for garnish
Dill pickles for garnish

1. Rinse the fish heads, bones, and skins and place in a large pot. Add one of the onions, one of the garlic cloves, the parsley sprig, salt and pepper, and enough water to just cover. Bring to a boil, reduce the heat to low, cover, and simmer for at least 1 hour. Strain the broth into a bowl, discard the solids, and reserve the broth.

2. In a food processor, combine the fish fillets and the remaining onion and garlic clove, process to a fine paste, and scrape into a bowl. Add the eggs, water, and salt and pepper to taste, and stir till the texture is fine and smooth. Form the mixture into about 10 balls of equal size and place on a platter.

3. In a large skillet, bring the reserved broth to a brisk simmer, add the fish balls to the broth, cover, and simmer gently for 1 hour. Add the carrot and simmer 30 to 45 minutes longer. Transfer the contents of the pan to a large bowl, let cool, cover with plastic wrap, and chill overnight.

4. Serve the gefilte fish in its jellied broth with the grated horse-radish and pickles on the side.

Hungarian Meat Dumplings

Makes
4 servings

I've always said that the test of any reputable restaurant in Budapest is the ubiquitous beef consommé with either ground meat or calf's liver dumplings, and I'd return to one (Gundel) just for the meat dumplings and bacon served over buttery noodles as a main course. For just the right texture, these dumplings really must be made with a little semolina (the same coarsely ground durum wheat flour used in fine pastas), so plan accordingly if you want them to turn out right. The dumplings can be made with either the indicated ground meats or the same amount of trimmed calf's liver, and they are delicious in any clear broth or served on top of buttered egg noodles.

½ pound finely ground beef round
¼ pound finely ground pork
2 large potatoes, peeled and grated
1 large egg, beaten
1 tablespoon all-purpose flour
1 tablespoon semolina
Salt and freshly ground black pepper to taste
1 quart water
1 teaspoon salt

1. In a large bowl, combine the beef, pork, potatoes, egg, flour, semolina, and salt and pepper, and mix with your hands till well blended and smooth. Form the mixture into oval dumplings about the size of a walnut and place on a plate.

2. In a large saucepan or pot, combine the water and salt and bring to a boil. Reduce the heat, add the dumplings, and simmer over very low heat till the dumplings are cooked through, 20 to 25 minutes. Drain the dumplings and serve in a soup or over buttered noodles.

Siberian Lamb Dumplings

Eaten in soups or served separately with melted butter or sour cream all over Russia, pelmeni are most often made with lesser cuts of ground beef or minced cabbage or mushrooms. In Siberia (and also Armenia), however, the filling for the succulent dumplings is almost always ground or minced lamb (or a combination of ground meats), and they are either simmered in broth or fried in butter and served traditionally with borsch. Pelmeni differ from other such stuffed envelopes or ravioli in that the pastry must be rolled paper-thin, a tricky procedure that may take a little practice. Fried, the dumplings can be delectable, but if you decide to do this style, it's still a good idea to pre-boil them for about 3 minutes in broth or water to firm up the pastry.

Makes about 6 servings

3 cups all-purpose flour
4 large eggs
¾ pound ground lamb shoulder
1 small onion, minced
½ teaspoon salt
¼ teaspoon freshly ground black pepper
4 cups beef broth
1 large egg white, beaten

1. Mound the flour on a work surface and make a depression in the center. Break the eggs into the depression and, with your hands, mix the flour and eggs till a firm dough forms. Knead the dough till it is smooth and elastic, cover with a towel, and let stand for about 1 hour.

(continued)

2. Meanwhile, combine the lamb, onion, salt, pepper, and 2 table-spoons of the broth in a bowl and mix with your hands till well blended.

3. Roll out the dough till it is paper-thin and cut into circles with a 3-inch biscuit cutter. Re-roll the scraps and cut out more circles. Spoon 1 teaspoon of the lamb mixture in the center of each circle, moisten the edges with the egg white, fold the edges over to form a crescent, and pinch the edges securely together with your fingers.

4. Bring the remaining broth to a boil in a large pot, add the dumplings in batches, and cook for about 15 minutes. Transfer the dumplings with a slotted spoon to a heated platter or pot and keep warm.

Bavarian Liver and Bacon Dumplings

Various soups with liver dumplings are as popular all over Germany as in Austria and Hungary, but what makes the *leberknödel* in Bavaria so distinctive is the addition of pungent double-smoked bacon to the meat mixture. (The bacon is now available in most U.S. markets.) Although canned beef consommé or broth can be used in this recipe, the dumplings really are much more delicious if you can make a fresh, light, strained beef stock in which to simmer and serve them. Dropped by the teaspoon and simmered for 3 to 4 minutes, the dumplings can also be used to transform ordinary homemade vegetable soup into a special treat.

Makes 4 to 6 servings

½ to ¾ pound calf's liver, trimmed
3 slices double-smoked bacon, finely chopped
1 tablespoon vegetable oil
1 medium onion, finely chopped
1 garlic clove, minced
2 cups fresh bread crumbs, soaked in ½ cup milk
2 large eggs, beaten
2 tablespoons minced fresh parsley leaves
¼ teaspoon dried marjoram
Salt and freshly ground black pepper to taste
Dry bread crumbs for thickening
2 quarts beef consommé or broth

1. Place the liver in a saucepan with enough water to cover, bring to a simmer, cook for about 5 minutes, and drain.

2. In a food processor or meat grinder, combine the liver and bacon, grind to a fine consistency, and scrape the mixture into a large bowl. In a small skillet, heat the oil over moderate heat, add the
(continued)

onion and garlic, stir for about 5 minutes, and add to the meat mixture. Add the soaked bread crumbs, eggs, parsley, marjoram, and salt and pepper, and mix till well blended and smooth, adding just enough dry bread crumbs to make the mixture firm. Form the mixture into 4 to 6 balls.

3. In a large saucepan or pot, bring the consommé to a boil, add half the balls, reduce the heat to moderately low, and simmer till the dumplings are cooked through, 10 to 12 minutes. Transfer the dumplings to a plate and repeat with the remaining balls.

4. To serve, float one dumpling in each soup bowl of hot consommé or broth.

French Seafood Quenelles

One of the masterpieces of classic French cuisine involving ground seafood, these light, delicate quenelles are usually served with a rich lobster, Parmesan cheese, or mushroom sauce. I also love them baked with a cheese sauce as a gratin—and the more pungent the cheese, the better. Ideally, the quenelles should be poached in a fresh fish stock, but given that impracticality, water and bottled clam juice work almost as well for a poaching liquid. Don't overcook these dumplings, and for smooth, even ovals, be sure to keep the teaspoons wet as you work. As for seasoning, all you want is a pinch of grated nutmeg—no more or the spice will overwhelm the dish.

**Makes
4 servings**

½ to ¾ pound fresh lean fish fillets (such as pike, whitefish, or snapper), cut into pieces
½ pound fresh shrimp, peeled, deveined, and cut in half
1 large egg white
1 cup heavy cream
½ teaspoon fresh lemon juice
1 teaspoon salt
Ground white pepper to taste
Grated nutmeg to taste
1 quart water
1 cup bottled clam juice

1. In a meat grinder or food processor, grind the fish and shrimp together to a paste, scrape into a large bowl, cover with plastic wrap, and chill for 1 hour.

2. Add the egg white to the seafood and beat with a wooden spoon till the mixture thickens, about 3 minutes. Gradually add the

(continued)

cream, beating constantly till the mixture holds its shape. Add the lemon juice, salt, pepper, and nutmeg and stir till well blended and firm.

3. Preheat the oven to 200°F.

4. Pour the water and clam juice into a large stainless steel or enameled skillet and bring the liquid to a very gentle simmer. Using two wet teaspoons, form the seafood mixture into egg-size ovals, slide half the ovals into the liquid, and poach till just firm, about 5 minutes. Remove the quenelles with a slotted spoon, drain on paper towels, place on a plate, and keep warm in the oven while poaching the remaining quenelles.

Loaves, Croquettes, and Cakes

American Meat Loaf Deluxe

**Makes
8 servings**

Suffice it to say that after experimenting with all-American meat loaves for most of a lifetime, I've concluded that this is not only the ultimate moist, full-flavored, crusty loaf but also unquestionably the supreme tribute to not one but four ground meats. Tamper with the ingredients at your own risk, and do remember that if you overmix them, you'll probably end up with a tough loaf. Meat loaf baked in a loaf pan will be crusty on top but soft on the sides, while one baked free-form (my preference) will have overall crustiness. As for gravy, there is no gravy. Great meat loaf requires no gravy. Do not serve gravy with this meat loaf.

5 tablespoons butter
½ pound large mushrooms, stems finely chopped and
    caps reserved
1 large onion, finely chopped
½ medium green bell pepper, seeded and finely chopped
2 celery ribs, finely chopped
3 garlic cloves, minced
½ teaspoon dried thyme, crumbled
½ teaspoon dried rosemary, crumbled
1 pound ground beef round or rump
1 pound ground pork
1 pound ground veal
½ pound bulk pork sausage
1 tablespoon Dijon mustard
½ cup ketchup
3 tablespoons Worcestershire sauce
½ teaspoon Tabasco sauce
Salt and freshly ground black pepper to taste
3 large eggs, beaten

1 cup fresh bread crumbs, soaked in ½ cup heavy cream
3 slices bacon
Pimento-stuffed green olives, cut in half

1. In a medium skillet, melt 3 tablespoons of the butter over moderate heat, add the mushroom stems, and stir for about 5 minutes or till most of their liquid has evaporated. Add the onion, bell pepper, celery, garlic, thyme, and rosemary; reduce the heat to low, cover, and simmer for about 15 minutes or till the vegetables are soft and the liquid has evaporated.

2. Preheat the oven to 350°F.

3. Place the meats in a large bowl, add the cooked vegetables, and mix lightly. Add the mustard, ketchup, Worcestershire, Tabasco, salt and pepper, eggs, and bread crumbs and mix with your hands till blended thoroughly. Shape the mixture into a firm oval loaf, place in a shallow baking or gratin dish, drape the bacon over the top, and bake for 1 hour in the upper third of the oven. Remove the bacon strips and continue baking 15 to 20 minutes longer, depending on how thick the loaf is and how crusty you want the exterior to be.

4. Shortly before the meat loaf is removed from the oven, melt the remaining 2 tablespoons butter in a small skillet over moderate heat, add the reserved mushroom caps, and stir till nicely glazed, about 2 minutes. Transfer the meat loaf to a large, heated platter, arrange the olives over the top, and garnish the edges with the mushroom caps.

Chicken and Sweet Potato Loaf

Makes 4 to 6
servings

Ground chicken or turkey (especially dark meat) makes a very respectable loaf, so long, that is, as enough secondary ingredients are added to guarantee succulent flavor and moistness. What makes this particular loaf distinctive is the sweet potato, but if you don't have one on hand, substitute about a cup of finely diced carrots. The bacon, of course, adds both savor and moistness, but if you want the top to be crusty, remove the strips during the final 15 minutes of baking.

2 tablespoons vegetable oil
1 medium sweet potato, peeled and finely diced
1 medium onion, finely diced
1 celery rib, finely diced
½ green bell pepper, seeded and finely diced
1½ pounds ground chicken
1 slice white loaf bread, soaked in ¼ cup milk
¼ cup ketchup
2 tablespoons Worcestershire sauce
1 large egg, beaten
Salt and freshly ground black pepper to taste
3 slices lean bacon

1. Preheat the oven to 350°F. Grease a 9 by 5 by 3-inch loaf pan and set aside.

2. In a large skillet, heat the oil over moderate heat, add the sweet potato, onion, celery, and bell pepper, and stir till the vegetables are well softened but not browned, 6 to 8 minutes. Transfer to a large bowl, add the chicken, bread, ketchup, Worcestershire, egg, and salt and pepper, and mix with your hands till well blended. Transfer the mixture to the prepared loaf pan, smooth the top, arrange the bacon slices over the top, and bake for 1 hour.

3. Allow the loaf to cool for about 10 minutes before serving in slices.

Smoked Ham and Olive Loaf

Unlike so many people, I'm never at a loss at coming up with ways to use up leftover baked ham, this delectable loaf being just one of many examples. Why ham and olives are so compatible I don't know, but equally delicious with smoked ham are finely chopped capers or sweet pickles. So that this loaf will slice easily and evenly, be sure that the ham is finely ground in a meat grinder or food processor. While I generally like to eat it with only Dijon mustard on the side, serving it with a good fruit chutney makes the loaf delightfully unusual.

Makes 4 to 6 servings

1½ pounds finely ground smoked ham
2 cups fresh bread crumbs
½ cup finely chopped pimento-stuffed green olives
1 tablespoon light brown sugar
1 tablespoon Dijon mustard
Salt and freshly ground black pepper to taste
2 large eggs, beaten
1 cup milk
1 tablespoon cider vinegar

1. Preheat the oven to 375°F. Grease a 9 by 5 by 3-inch loaf pan or dish and set aside.

2. In a large bowl, combine all the ingredients, mix with your hands till well blended (do not overmix), transfer the mixture to the prepared pan, and bake till firm, about 1 hour. Let the loaf stand for about 10 minutes, and then transfer to a serving platter. Serve hot or warm in slices.

Loaves, Croquettes, and Cakes

Irish Pork, Ham, and Bacon Pub Loaf

Makes 4 to 6
servings

In pubs throughout Ireland, food can be as important as the staggering variety of heady lagers, ales, and stouts, and at the top of the list in popularity is the array of meat, poultry, and seafood loaves often displayed in elaborate polished wood and glass cases. A sturdy loaf such as this one would most surely be made with smoky, lean Irish bacon, so if you're unable to find this or English bacon in the market, look for the domestic artisanal equivalent. The loaf is delicious warm for lunch with a tart salad and preferably some soda bread, but in an Irish pub, it would typically be served slightly chilled or at room temperature.

1 pound ground cooked ham
½ pound lean ground pork
1 small onion, minced
2 tablespoons minced fresh parsley leaves
2 tablespoons minced sweet pickle
1¼ cups crushed cracker crumbs
¾ cup milk
1 large egg, beaten
1 teaspoon dry mustard
½ teaspoon dried sage, crumbled
Salt and freshly ground black pepper to taste
3 slices lean smoky bacon

1. Preheat the oven to 350°F. Grease a 9 by 5 by 3-inch loaf pan and set aside.

2. In a large bowl, combine the ham, pork, onion, parsley, pickle, and cracker crumbs and mix with your hands till well blended. In a small bowl, combine the milk, egg, mustard, sage, and salt and pepper; whisk till well blended, add to the meat mixture, and mix gently till well blended and smooth (do not overmix). Scrape the mixture into the prepared pan, arrange the bacon slices over the top, and bake, uncovered, for about 1 hour.

3. Loosen the loaf from the pan, transfer to a platter, and let stand for at least 15 minutes before serving in slices.

A sturdy loaf such as this one would most surely be made with smoky, lean Irish bacon.

Pork and Wild Mushroom Loaf

Unlike most meat loaves, which for a light texture contain chopped ingredients that should never be overmixed, this one is very compact—almost like a pâté—and easy to slice for a stylish buffet. It is also baked in a loaf pan placed in a water bath for slow, even, gentle cooking. Ideally, the vegetables should be ground in a food processor, but since the risk of reducing them to a paste or puree is high, my advice is simply to make sure they're finely diced. Ordinary mushrooms can be used, of course, but the loaf won't have the same luscious savor.

Makes 6 to 8
servings

2 tablespoons butter
2 medium onions, finely diced
2 celery ribs, finely diced
1 garlic clove, minced
1 pound shiitake or chanterelle mushrooms, finely diced
2 pounds finely ground pork
1 cup fine bread crumbs
1 cup finely chopped fresh parsley leaves
¼ teaspoon dried sage, crumbled
1 tablespoon Dijon mustard
2 large eggs, beaten
Salt and freshly ground black pepper to taste

1. Preheat the oven to 350°F. Grease a 9 by 5 by 3-inch loaf pan or dish and set aside.

2. In a large skillet, melt the butter over moderate heat, add the onions, celery, garlic, and mushrooms, stir till the vegetables are softened and the mushrooms release any of their liquid, 8 to 10 minutes, and remove from the heat.

3. Place the pork in a large bowl, add the vegetable mixture and all remaining ingredients, and stir till well blended. Transfer the mixture to the prepared loaf pan and smooth the top. Place the pan in a larger baking pan, pour enough boiling water to come about 1½ inches up the sides of the loaf pan, and bake till slightly crusty on top, 1¼ to 1½ hours.

4. Serve hot or at room temperature.

Scandinavian Jellied Veal Loaf

Jellied veal dishes are common on virtually all Scandinavian smorgasbords, and none is more succulent than a loaf such as this one, traditionally served with pickled beets. Serious Swedish or Danish chefs would never use commercial gelatin to make any jellied meat loaf, aware that perfect flavor and texture can be attained only by slowly simmering gelatinous veal shanks with the other ingredients. Occasionally you do find packaged veal shanks in the meat cases of grocery stores, but if not, any good butcher should be willing to cut one or two. Do notice that this loaf must be chilled overnight till it is fully firm.

Makes 6 to 8 servings

1 to 1½ pounds veal shanks
1 pound boneless veal shoulder
½ pound boneless pork loin
1 medium onion, quartered
2 whole allspice berries
2 bay leaves
1 tablespoon salt
1 teaspoon freshly ground black pepper
1 quart water
Lettuce leaves for serving

1. In a medium casserole or pot, combine the meats, onion, all-spice, bay leaves, salt, pepper, and water, and bring the liquid to a low boil, skimming any scum from the top. Reduce the heat to very low, cover, and simmer till the meats are very tender, 2 to 2½ hours.

2. Transfer the meats to a plate, strain the broth into another pot, bring to a low boil, and simmer, uncovered, till reduced to about 3½ cups. Let the broth cool, place in the refrigerator, chill for at least 2 hours, and skim every trace of fat from the top.

3. Meanwhile, remove the meat from the veal shanks and discard the bones. Cut all the meats into pieces, combine them in a food processor, and grind finely.

4. Return the ground meats to the skimmed broth, bring to a boil, and cook, uncovered, for about 3 minutes. Pour the mixture into a 1½- to 2-quart mold or loaf pan, cover with plastic wrap, and chill overnight till firm.

5. Unmold on a bed of lettuce leaves and serve in thin slices.

Mixed Meat and Spinach Loaf

This is not only an exceptionally succulent meat loaf but also, because of the slightly wet spinach, a very moist one. It really is preferable to use fresh spinach, but if the leaves are not bright green and crisp (or have any dark spots), use a 10-ounce package of frozen spinach. Since the texture of the loaf should be fairly coarse, handle the ingredients as little as possible when mixing. And, once again, if you prefer a crusty top, remove the bacon during the final 15 minutes of baking.

1 pound fresh spinach, rinsed and stems removed
½ pound ground beef rump or round
½ pound ground veal
½ pound ground pork
1 medium onion, finely chopped
1 celery rib, finely chopped
1 garlic clove, minced
¼ cup finely chopped fresh parsley leaves
¼ teaspoon grated nutmeg
Salt and freshly ground black pepper to taste
2 large eggs, beaten
¼ cup milk
½ cup fresh bread crumbs
3 slices bacon

1. Preheat the oven to 350°F.

2. Tear the wet spinach leaves into pieces, place in a large saucepan, cover, and cook over moderate heat for about 2 minutes, stirring once or twice. Drain in a colander, rinse with cold water, squeeze with your hands to extract most but not all moisture, and finely chop.

3. In a large bowl, combine the spinach, meats, onion, celery, garlic, parsley, nutmeg, salt and pepper, eggs, milk, and bread crumbs; mix with your hands till well blended, and form the mixture into an oval loaf. Place the loaf on a slotted baking pan, arrange the bacon slices over the top, and bake for 1 to 1¼ hours.

4. Allow the loaf to stand for about 15 minutes before serving in slices.

Pennsylvania Dutch Scrapple

Makes 8 servings

The name of this delicious age-old Pennsylvania Dutch specialty derives from the ground or finely chopped "scraps" of cooked pork and pork liver that were mixed with finely ground cornmeal, seasonings, and broth before being packed into loaf pans and chilled till firm. Traditionally, the loaf is cut into slices that are browned in butter and served for breakfast or brunch, much like sausage patties. Since pork liver is a bit too racy for most tastes, I substitute calf's, and even those who generally have an aversion to liver quickly become addicts once they've sampled a few slices—preferably with fried eggs.

2 to 2½ pounds pork neck bones or pigs' knuckles

½ pound calf's liver

1 quart water

2 teaspoons salt

1 cup finely ground cornmeal

1 medium onion, finely chopped

1 tablespoon finely chopped fresh sage leaves (or 1 teaspoon dried sage, crumbled)

1 teaspoon chopped fresh thyme leaves (or pinch of dried thyme)

1 small fresh red chile pepper, seeded and minced

Pinch of grated nutmeg

Salt and freshly ground black pepper to taste

All-purpose flour for dusting

4 tablespoons (½ stick) butter

1. In a kettle or large saucepan, combine the neck bones and liver and add the water and salt. Bring to a boil, reduce the heat to low, cover, and simmer till the pork almost falls off the bones, about 1½ hours. Transfer the meats to a plate, strain the cooking broth, and reserve.

2. Remove the pork meat from the bones (including skin if knuckles are used), place the pork and liver in a food processor, grind finely, and scrape the mixture into a bowl. Add 1 cup of the reserved broth and stir well.

3. In a large saucepan, combine the cornmeal with the remaining broth, stir till no longer lumpy, and simmer till thickened, stirring. Add the ground meats, onion, sage, thyme, chile pepper, nutmeg, and salt and pepper and stir till the mixture is well blended. Bring to a simmer, cover, and simmer for about 45 minutes, stirring often to prevent sticking and lumping. Pour the mixture into a large loaf pan, let cool, then refrigerate overnight.

4. When ready to serve, cut the loaf into ½-inch-thick slices and dust the slices lightly in flour. In a large skillet, melt the butter over moderate heat, add the slices, brown for about 3 minutes on each side, and drain on paper towels. Serve hot.

Traditionally, the loaf is cut into slices that are browned in butter and served for breakfast or brunch, much like sausage patties.

Loaves, Croquettes, and Cakes

Curried Chicken Croquettes

Makes 6 to 8
servings

Once served with a creamy mushroom or spicy tomato sauce at country clubs and department-store tearooms all over the country, chicken croquettes are now regaining respect in even the most sophisticated kitchens, partly because they lend themselves to an endless variety of flavorings and cooking techniques. Needless to say, croquettes are also the perfect way to use up ground leftover holiday turkey, goose, or duck, and when they are curried like in this recipe, they are worthy of even the most formal dining affairs and can easily stand on their own without a trace of any sauce.

3 tablespoons butter
1 small onion, minced
3 tablespoons all-purpose flour, plus more for dredging
½ cup chicken broth
½ cup whole milk
2 tablespoons dry sherry
3 cups coarsely ground cooked chicken
2 teaspoons curry powder
Salt and freshly ground black pepper to taste
2 large egg yolks
1½ cups fine bread crumbs
1 large egg white beaten with 3 tablespoons water
Vegetable oil for frying

1. In a large saucepan, melt the butter over moderate heat, add the onion, sprinkle on the 3 tablespoons flour, and whisk till softened, about 2 minutes. Whisking rapidly, add the broth, milk, and sherry and whisk till well blended. Add the chicken, curry powder, and salt and pepper and stir till well blended. Remove the pan from the heat, and, whisking constantly, add the egg yolks and whisk till well blended. Return the pan to the heat; cook, stirring, for about 2 minutes, and remove from the heat. Transfer the mixture to a bowl, let cool, then refrigerate for about 30 minutes.

2. Spread the flour and bread crumbs on two separate plates and the egg mixture in a shallow bowl. Shape the chicken mixture into 6 to 8 balls, roll lightly in the flour, and pat into oval patties. Dip the patties in the egg mixture, then in the bread crumbs. Place on a large plate, cover with plastic wrap, and chill for about 30 minutes.

3. In a large, heavy skillet, heat about 1 inch of oil over moderate heat till a little water flicked in with the fingers sputters. Add half the patties, fry till golden brown and crispy, about 3 minutes on each side, and drain on paper towels. Repeat with the remaining patties.

4. Serve hot.

Norwegian Venison Croquettes

Makes 4 to 6
servings

Since herds of reindeer roam all over central Norway, venison is one of the country's most popular meats, and while the prized rack and haunch are almost always roasted, meat from the shank, neck, and shoulder is either used for savory stews and casseroles or ground for sausage and all sorts of burgers, loaves, and croquettes. The problem with venison is that the lean meat tends to be dry; the solution being that, for ground dishes, a little ground fatty pork (or simply pork fat) must also be added for moistness. In this country, various cuts of federally inspected venison are generally found only in better butcher shops, so if you can't find any, substitute ground buffalo meat, which has much the same gamy flavor and texture and is increasingly available in our markets. Serve these croquettes with either lingonberry preserves or red currant jelly.

1 pound ground venison
½ pound ground fatty pork
1 small onion, minced
1 garlic clove, minced
1 tablespoon capers, minced
2 large egg yolks, beaten
2 teaspoons white vinegar
½ cup heavy cream
1 tablespoon red currant jelly
Salt and freshly ground black pepper to taste
Vegetable oil for deep frying

1. In a large bowl, combine the meats, onion, garlic, capers, egg yolks, vinegar, cream, jelly, and salt and pepper, and mix with your hands till well blended and smooth. Form the mixture into 4 to 6 oval croquettes and chill for 30 minutes.

2. In a large skillet, heat about 1 inch of oil over moderate heat, add the croquettes, fry till well done and crusty, 6 to 7 minutes on each side, and drain on paper towels.

3. Serve hot.

French Ham and Veal Croquettes

Makes 4 to 6
servings

Since the word *croquette* derives from the French *cro-quer* ("to crunch"), it's little wonder that these delectable cylinders with crunchy exteriors and soft interiors have always been an ideal way to use up leftover meats all over France. So that the croquettes hold their form and are easier to work with, just be sure to chill briefly not only the meat mixture but also the battered croquettes themselves before frying them. I love these croquettes plain, but they're also wonderful with any mustard sauce—or simply dabs of pungent Dijon mustard.

1 pound cooked ham, finely diced
¼ pound cooked veal, finely diced
1½ cups chicken broth
4 tablespoons (½ stick) butter
1 medium onion, finely diced
1 garlic clove, minced
½ teaspoon powdered sage
Salt and freshly ground black pepper to taste
1 cup all-purpose flour
1 large egg beaten with 1 tablespoon water
1 cup fine bread crumbs
Vegetable oil for deep frying

1. In a food processor, combine the ham, veal, and broth, grind to a puree, and set aside.

2. In a large skillet, melt the butter over moderate heat, add the onion, garlic, sage, and salt and pepper, and stir till softened, about 2 minutes. Sprinkle ½ cup of the flour over the top and stir about 2 minutes longer. Add the meat puree and stir till the mixture is thickened, about 2 minutes. Scrape the mixture into a bowl, chill for about 30 minutes, and wipe out the skillet.

3. Form the mixture into 4 to 6 oval croquettes. Roll them in the remaining ½ cup flour, dip into the egg mixture, roll in the crumbs, and chill for about 30 minutes.

4. Pour about 1 inch of oil into the skillet over moderate heat, add the croquettes, fry till nicely browned and crusty, about 4 minutes on each side, and drain on paper towels.

5. Serve hot.

I love these croquettes plain, but they're also wonderful with any mustard sauce.

Country Ham Croquettes with Mustard Sauce

Croquettes made with ordinary baked ham are classic and always good, but when leftover aged country ham is used and the croquettes served with a tangy mustard sauce, the result is truly memorable. As with most croquettes, feel free to experiment with a few olives, capers, sweet pickles, and the like if you want additional flavor sensations, and for ideal firm texture, it's a good idea not only to grind the ham as finely as possible (though not to a paste) but also to chill the mixture overnight before forming the cylinders. Since the ham will be salty, no salt is needed in this recipe.

For the sauce:
2 tablespoons butter
2 tablespoons all-purpose flour
1 cup whole milk
¼ cup Dijon mustard
1 teaspoon cider vinegar
Freshly ground black pepper to taste

For the croquettes:
4 tablespoons (½ stick) butter
3 scallions (white parts only), finely chopped
3 tablespoons all-purpose flour, plus more for dredging
1½ cups milk
4 cups finely ground cooked country ham
3 large egg yolks
¼ teaspoon powdered sage
Freshly ground black pepper to taste
1 large egg beaten with 2 tablespoons water
2 cups fine dry bread crumbs
Peanut oil for deep frying

1. To make the sauce, melt the butter in a small saucepan over moderately low heat, add the flour, and stir till a smooth paste forms. Gradually add the milk, stirring till thickened and smooth, 3 to 4 minutes. Add the mustard, vinegar, and pepper, stir vigorously till well blended, and keep the sauce warm over very low heat.

2. To make the croquettes, melt the butter in a saucepan over moderate heat, add the scallions and flour, and whisk till soft and well blended, about 2 minutes. Whisking rapidly, add the milk till well blended; add the ham, stir well, and remove from the heat. Whisking rapidly, add the egg yolks, return to the heat, add the sage and pepper, and whisk till well blended. Scrape the mixture into a dish, cover, and refrigerate overnight.

3. With your hands, divide the mixture into 6 balls and roll lightly in the extra flour. Pat the balls into smooth oval croquettes, dip briefly into the egg mixture, dredge in the bread crumbs, and place on a plate till ready to fry.

4. In a large, heavy skillet, heat about 1 inch of oil over moderately high heat for about 1 minute. Fry the croquettes till golden brown, about 3 minutes on each side, and drain briefly on paper towels.

5. Serve the croquettes hot with the mustard sauce on the side.

Spicy English *Rissoles*

**Makes
4 servings**

Often resembling either croquettes or turnovers, *rissoles* have origins that are as varied as the many different ingredients used to make them and the ways to form and cook them. The ones featured here are English classics, though depending on where you find them and who's cooking, the filling might be other ground meats, poultry, or seafood and the spices anything from cumin to cloves to curry powder. If leftover cooked meats are used in place of the fresh, just be warned that the *rissoles* can be distastefully dry if fried for more than 5 minutes on each side. In England, *rissoles* are traditionally served with mashed potatoes and some type of chutney.

½ pound beef round or rump, cut into pieces
½ pound lamb shoulder, cut into pieces
1 medium onion, minced
1 garlic clove, minced
¼ cup fresh bread crumbs
¼ cup minced fresh parsley leaves
1 large egg, beaten
¼ teaspoon ground cinnamon
¼ teaspoon ground ginger
⅛ teaspoon ground turmeric
Salt and freshly ground black pepper to taste
1 cup whole-wheat flour
2 tablespoons butter
1 tablespoon vegetable oil

1. In a food processor, combine the beef and lamb, grind finely (but not to a paste), and transfer to a bowl. Add the onion, garlic, bread crumbs, parsley, egg, cinnamon, ginger, turmeric, and salt and pepper, and mix with your hands till well blended. Form the mixture into 4 oval *rissoles*, coat all over with the flour, and chill for about 30 minutes.

2. In a large skillet, heat the butter and oil over moderate heat, add the *rissoles*, fry till golden brown, about 7 minutes on each side, and drain on paper towels.

3. Serve hot.

French Chicken Croquettes Pojarsky

**Makes
6 servings**

Created in the early nineteenth century by a Russian chef named Pozharsky, these buttery croquettes (made originally with minced partridge or grouse) were quickly adapted to the French repertoire and prepared with more readily accessible ground chicken or veal. (The croquettes were one of the first dishes I learned to make at La Varenne cooking school in Paris.) What makes the croquettes so sumptuous, of course, is all the butter, but if you have a phobia about consuming this much fat, the butter that is creamed with the chicken and bread crumbs could be reduced to as little as 8 tablespoons (with less succulent results). Traditionally, the croquettes are served with dilled fried potatoes and mushrooms stewed in sour cream, but any plain vegetable or tart salad goes well with this rich dish.

10 thin slices white loaf bread, crusts removed
½ cup heavy cream
½ pound plus 4 tablespoons (2½ sticks) butter, softened
2 pounds chicken cutlets or boned breasts, cut into pieces
2 teaspoons salt
¼ teaspoon freshly ground black pepper
1 cup all-purpose flour
1 large egg beaten with 1 tablespoon sunflower or canola oil
1½ cups fresh bread crumbs
½ cup sunflower or canola oil
Fresh lemon juice as needed

1. Tear the bread into a bowl, add the cream, and let soak. In a small, heavy saucepan, whisk 4 tablespoons of the butter over moderate heat till it turns a russet brown, and keep warm.

2. Grind the chicken twice in a meat grinder, or grind it in a food processor, till almost a paste but not a puree. In a large bowl, cream 1½ sticks of the remaining butter with an electric mixer and, with the mixer still running, gradually add the chicken till well blended. Gradually add the soaked bread pieces, then the salt and pepper, and continue beating till the mixture is homogeneous. With your hands, form the mixture into 12 small oval croquettes, dust each in the flour, dip briefly into the egg mixture, and coat lightly with the bread crumbs.

3. In a large, heavy skillet, heat the remaining 4 tablespoons butter plus the oil over moderately low heat, add the croquettes, and cook till golden, about 5 minutes on each side. Transfer to a warm serving platter, season with additional salt and pepper to taste, and drizzle the browned butter and a little lemon juice over the tops.

4. Serve immediately.

Russian Salmon Croquettes Pojarsky

**Makes
4 servings**

Unlike classic French chicken or veal croquettes Pojarsky, these authentic Russian ones made with salmon require less butter and no cream due to the oily richness of the fish. Truer to their Russian heritage, the croquettes are also spiked with a little vodka, and since most domestic vodka is virtually tasteless, be sure to use a good imported one. Russians like their croquettes browned to an almost crusty, nutty finish, which is why these are cooked exclusively in butter for up to 7 minutes on each side.

1½ pounds fresh salmon fillets, cut into pieces
3 slices white loaf bread, soaked in ¼ cup milk
1 small onion, grated
2 large eggs
6 tablespoons (¾ stick) butter, softened
⅛ teaspoon grated nutmeg
Salt and freshly ground black pepper to taste
2 tablespoons vodka
1 cup dry bread crumbs

1. In a food processor, combine the salmon and soaked bread, grind finely (but not to a paste), and transfer to a large bowl. Add the onion, eggs, 3 tablespoons of the butter, nutmeg, salt and pepper, and vodka, and beat with an electric mixer till well blended and very smooth, 2 to 3 minutes. Form the mixture into 8 oval croquettes, coat them with the bread crumbs, and chill for about 30 minutes

2. In a large, heavy skillet, melt the remaining 3 tablespoons butter over moderate heat, add the croquettes, and cook them till nicely browned, about 7 minutes on each side.

3. Serve piping hot.

Sherried Turkey Hash Cakes

Who says that leftover holiday turkey can't be turned into a simple but sophisticated dish guaranteed to impress both family and finicky guests? And for variety, you can use equal amounts of ground turkey and baked ham, flavor the cakes with hot mustard or a little curry powder, and even add a few ground toasted almonds or water chestnuts. I like to serve these cakes with red cabbage coleslaw, hot corn sticks, and either a fine California Chardonnay or a spicy Alsatian Riesling.

Makes 4 to 6 servings

2 medium boiling potatoes, peeled and diced
8 tablespoons (1 stick) butter, softened
1¼ to 1½ pounds cooked turkey, chopped (about 3 cups)
1 medium onion, chopped
1 medium celery rib, chopped
½ green bell pepper, seeded and chopped
3 large eggs, 2 beaten
½ cup heavy cream
2 tablespoons dry sherry
Salt and freshly ground black pepper to taste
1 cup all-purpose flour
2 cups very fine bread crumbs
¼ cup vegetable oil

1. Place the potatoes in a medium saucepan with enough water to cover, bring to a boil, reduce the heat slightly, and cook till the potatoes are very tender, about 15 minutes. Drain, transfer to a large bowl, and puree with a potato masher or heavy fork. Add half the butter in pieces and beat with an electric mixer or wooden spoon till light and fluffy.

(continued)

2. In a food processor, grind the turkey, onion, celery, and bell pepper to a medium texture and transfer to the bowl of potatoes. Add the unbeaten egg, cream, sherry, and salt and pepper, and beat till the mixture is smooth. Cover the bowl with plastic wrap and chill the mixture for about 30 minutes.

3. Shape the mixture into 4 to 6 oval cakes, dust each evenly in the flour, dip into the beaten eggs, roll evenly in the bread crumbs, cover again, and chill about 30 minutes longer.

4. In a large, heavy skillet, heat the remaining 4 tablespoons butter with the oil over moderate heat, add the cakes, and cook till golden brown and crusty, 4 to 5 minutes.

5. Serve hot.

Shanghai Fried Pork and Scallion Cakes

If these beguiling Chinese packets were smaller and not traditionally flattened before frying, they'd almost qualify more as turnovers than cakes. And in fact, nobody says you can't cut smaller pieces of dough, roll it into smaller circles, reduce the amount of filling, and serve the cakes as cocktail or first-course appetizers. Briny, dense oyster sauce is a miraculous seasoning for a multitude of Chinese dishes and is available in all Asian markets and many grocery stores. Just remember that if you use too much of the rich sauce, it will overwhelm the cakes.

Makes 4 to 6 servings

½ cup peanut oil
1 pound boneless pork shoulder, minced
4 scallions (part of green tops included), minced
2 garlic cloves, minced
1 tablespoon minced fresh ginger
1 tablespoon soy sauce
2 teaspoons oyster sauce
1 teaspoon salt
½ teaspoon freshly ground black pepper
2½ cups all-purpose flour
½ cup water

1. In a skillet, heat 2 tablespoons of the oil over moderate heat, add the pork, scallions, and garlic, and stir for 2 minutes. Add the ginger, soy sauce, oyster sauce, salt, and pepper, stir 1 minute longer, and set the filling aside.

2. In a bowl, combine the flour, water, and 2 tablespoons of the oil, and stir well till the dough comes together, adding more water if necessary. On a floured surface, knead the dough till very
(continued)

Loaves,
Croquettes,
and Cakes

197

smooth, 8 to 10 minutes, form into a ball, and roll into a 12-inch-long rope. Cut into 2-inch pieces of dough, roll the pieces into 8-inch circles, and spoon about 2 tablespoons of the filling into the center of each. Bring up the sides of each circle, pinch the edges together to encase the filling securely, and gently flatten each cake with your hands.

3. In a large, heavy skillet, heat half of the remaining oil (2 tablespoons) over moderate heat, add half the cakes, fry till golden brown, 3 to 4 minutes on each side, and drain on paper towels. Repeat with the remaining oil and cakes.

4. Serve hot.

Maryland Deviled Crab Cakes

Tangy deviled crab baked in crab shells is popular all along the eastern seaboard in the United States, but only in Maryland have I encountered the sublime mixture fried as crab cakes. For these cakes, the crabmeat is finely flaked for a compact texture, just enough bread crumbs to bind the mixture are added, and the mixture is lightened with egg white. The cakes are usually served as a main course with either tartar or mustard sauce, but if you prefer, feel free to pat the mixture into tiny rounds and fry them for cocktail receptions or buffets.

Makes
4 servings

½ cup whole milk

½ cup mayonnaise

1 large egg white

1½ teaspoons dry mustard

2 teaspoons Worcestershire sauce

2 teaspoons fresh lemon juice

Tabasco sauce to taste

2 scallions (part of green tops included), minced

1 small red bell pepper, seeded and minced

Salt and freshly ground black pepper to taste

1 pound fresh lump crabmeat, picked over for shells and cartilage and finely flaked

1 cup fine dry bread crumbs

1 tablespoon butter, melted

¼ cup peanut oil

2 tablespoons butter

1. In a bowl, whisk together the milk, mayonnaise, and egg white till well blended. Add the mustard, Worcestershire, lemon juice, Tabasco, scallions, bell pepper, and salt and pepper and stir till (continued)

Loaves,
Croquettes,
and Cakes

well blended. Gently fold in the crabmeat and ½ cup of the bread crumbs till well blended.

2. Form the mixture into 4 oval cakes. In a small bowl, combine the remaining ½ cup bread crumbs with the melted butter, mix well, and turn each cake in the mixture to coat lightly.

3. In a large, heavy skillet, heat the oil and the 2 tablespoons butter over moderate heat, add the crab cakes, and cook till lightly browned, 3 to 4 minutes on each side. Drain briefly on paper towels.

4. Serve immediately.

For these cakes, the crabmeat is finely flaked for a compact texture.

New England Codfish Cakes

Traditionally made with fresh (not salt) cod and mashed potatoes, New England codfish cakes tend to be heavy. When fine bread crumbs are substituted for the potatoes, however, the results are vastly improved, and when the cakes are browned to a crusty finish, they are utterly sublime and need nothing more than a few squeezes of fresh lemon juice. The texture of these cakes should be fairly coarse.

**Makes
4 servings**

1 to 1¼ pounds fresh skinless cod fillets, any bones removed
    and flesh cut into pieces
2 scallions (white parts only), minced
1 celery rib, minced
¼ cup minced fresh parsley leaves
2 cups fine bread crumbs
1 tablespoon Worcestershire sauce
Salt and freshly ground black pepper to taste
1 large egg, beaten
¼ cup vegetable oil
Fresh lemon wedges for serving

1. In a food processor, grind the cod coarsely and transfer to a large bowl. Add the scallions, celery, parsley, 1 cup of the bread crumbs, Worcestershire, salt and pepper, and egg, and stir till the mixture is well blended. Form the mixture into 4 cakes of equal size, coat with the remaining 1 cup bread crumbs, and chill for about 30 minutes.

2. In a large, heavy skillet, heat the oil over moderate heat, add the fish cakes, brown for 4 to 5 minutes on each side for a crusty exterior, and drain on paper towels.

3. Serve the cakes hot with the lemon wedges.

Spicy Cajun Catfish Cakes with Mushroom Sauce

**Makes
4 servings**

Catfish from the bayous and waterways are so highly regarded in southern Louisiana that the fish is honored at a catfish festival held annually in Des Allemands, and while nothing is more popular than plain fried catfish (whole, fritters, fingers), cooks also love to grind, chop, or mince the larger critters to make all types of cakes and croquettes, much as they do with crawfish. In Cajun country, they don't bat an eye at using canned soups to make sauces, and all I can say on that score is that the one time I tried to "improve" the mushroom sauce for these particular cakes by using fresh cream and celery, it was bland by comparison.

1 pound fresh catfish fillets, cut into pieces
2 cups mashed potatoes
3 scallions (part of green tops included), minced
½ small green bell pepper, seeded and minced
3 tablespoons minced fresh parsley leaves
1 garlic clove, minced
1 teaspoon cayenne pepper
Salt and freshly ground black pepper to taste
1 large egg, beaten
1 cup all-purpose flour
1 cup finely chopped mushrooms
1 cup dry white wine
One 10¾-ounce can cream of celery soup
¼ cup vegetable oil

1. In a food processor, grind the catfish finely and transfer to a large bowl. Add the potatoes, scallions, bell pepper, parsley, garlic, cayenne, salt and pepper, and egg, and mix till well blended and smooth. Form the mixture into 4 cakes of equal size, dust all over in the flour, and chill for about 30 minutes.

2. Meanwhile, combine the mushrooms and wine in a saucepan, bring to a boil, and cook for 2 minutes. Add the soup, stir well, bring to a simmer, and cook for about 3 minutes. Keep the sauce warm over very low heat.

3. In a large, heavy skillet, heat the oil over moderate heat, add the fish cakes, brown for 4 to 5 minutes on each side, and drain on paper towels.

4. Serve the cakes hot with sauce spooned over the tops.

Japanese Fish and Pork Cakes

**Makes
4 servings**

Japanese cooks are even more adept at combining seafood and pork than Portuguese ones, and never is the art more evident than when they grind or mince squid, octopus, eel, or various types of white fish with fatty pork to make all sorts of delectable patties, cakes, and turnovers. What really gives these particular cakes their distinction are the special spice powder and fresh ginger. If you can find the seven-spice powder known as *shichimi* in finer markets, all the better; if not, use any Japanese blended spice powder. And while simply grated raw ginger works fine, for a real flavor zing, try to squeeze a tablespoon of juice out of about ¼ cup of grated fresh ginger.

¾ pound fresh white fish fillets (sea bass, red snapper, or sole), cut into pieces
½ pound pork shoulder, cut into pieces
2 scallions (green tops only), finely minced
1 teaspoon grated fresh ginger
1 tablespoon cornstarch mixed with 1 tablespoon water
1 teaspoon sesame oil
Salt and freshly ground black pepper to taste
2 tablespoons sweet sherry
1 tablespoon soy sauce
¼ teaspoon Japanese blended spice powder
3 tablespoons peanut oil

1. In a food processor, combine the fish and pork, grind coarsely, and transfer to a bowl. Add the scallions, ginger, cornstarch, sesame oil, and salt and pepper, and stir till well blended. With your hands, form the mixture into 4 flat cakes of equal size and set aside.

2. In a small bowl, combine the sherry, soy sauce, and spice powder, stir till well blended, and set aside.

3. In a large skillet, heat the peanut oil over moderate heat, add the cakes, and cook till golden on the bottom, 4 to 5 minutes. Turn, cook till the other sides are golden brown, about 5 minutes, and drain on paper towels.

4. Serve the cakes hot with a little of the sauce spooned over the tops.

Pies, Quiches, and Soufflés

All-American Chicken Pot Pie

**Makes
6 servings**

Nothing is more wretched than a poorly made chicken pot pie with a heavy, gloppy sauce and tough, soggy pastry, but when this American classic is handled with care, it can be the most glorious dish on earth. This is one time when store-bought pastry can't compare with freshly made, and if you like lots of pastry in chicken pot pie, you might want to double the pastry recipe, roll out half the dough about ⅛ inch thick, cut it into 1-inch strips, and arrange the strips between two layers of filling. Also, if you prefer a really creamy sauce, decrease the number of cups of stock and add more cream. A whole chicken yields the most flavor, but 4 chicken breasts can be substituted for a more formal pie.

For the pastry:
2 cups all-purpose flour
¼ teaspoon salt
⅔ cup vegetable shortening
¼ cup ice water

For the filling:
One 3½-pound chicken, cut up
1 medium onion, quartered
2 celery ribs (leaves included), each broken into 3 pieces
Salt and freshly ground black pepper to taste
½ cup heavy cream
2 carrots, scraped, diced, and blanched for 5 minutes in boiling water
1 cup fresh or frozen green peas
2 tablespoons butter, melted

1. To make the pastry, combine the flour and salt in a bowl, add the shortening, and work with your fingertips till the mixture is mealy. Stirring with a spoon, gradually add the water till a ball of dough forms, wrap in plastic wrap, and chill till ready to use.

2. To make the filling, place the chicken pieces in a large pot and add the onion, celery, and salt and pepper. Add enough water to cover, bring to a boil, reduce the heat to low, cover, and simmer for 30 minutes. With a slotted spoon, transfer the chicken to a cutting board and, when cool enough to handle, skin and bone the pieces, cut the meat into large dice, and set aside. Strain 5 cups of the stock into a bowl, add the cream, stir to blend well, and set aside.

3. On a lightly floured surface, roll out half the pastry about ⅛ inch thick and line the bottom and sides of a 10 by 8-inch casserole or baking dish with it. Roll out the other half and reserve for the top of the pie.

4. Preheat the oven to 350°F.

5. Arrange half the diced chicken over the bottom of the casserole and arrange half the carrots and peas over the chicken. Make another layer with the remaining chicken and vegetables, season with salt and pepper to taste, and pour the reserved creamed stock over the top. Fit the remaining pastry over the top of the pie, pressing down the edges and trimming off the excess. Cut one or two vents in the pastry, brush the top with the melted butter, and bake till bubbly and the top is golden brown, 40 to 45 minutes.

6. Serve piping hot.

A whole chicken yields the most flavor, but 4 chicken breasts can be substituted for a more formal pie.

Greek Chicken and Feta Pie

Makes
6 servings

In Greece, this sumptuous pie subtly flavored with ouzo might just as easily be made with ground or minced beef, lamb, rabbit, or even goat, and it might well be served either at room temperature or cold, depending on how casual the occasion. Chicken legs provide more flavor than breasts and wings, and if the feta is not tangy enough (the best is Greek or Bulgarian cured in brine), add a little grated Romano or Parmesan.

1 pound ground or minced chicken

3 scallions (part of green tops included), chopped

2 celery ribs, chopped

3 tablespoons chopped fresh dill

1 teaspoon dried thyme, crumbled

½ teaspoon dried tarragon, crumbled

Salt and freshly ground black pepper to taste

½ pound full-flavored feta cheese, crumbled

2 large eggs, beaten

2 tablespoons Greek olive oil, plus more for brushing

½ teaspoon ouzo or other anise-flavored liqueur

1 pound phyllo pastry (fresh or frozen)

1 large egg yolk beaten with 1 tablespoon water

1. Preheat the oven to 350°F. Grease a 10-inch pie plate and set aside.

2. In a large bowl, combine the chicken, scallions, celery, dill, thyme, tarragon, and salt and pepper, and stir till well blended. Sprinkle the feta over the top and mix till well blended. Add the eggs, oil, and ouzo and toss till the ingredients are well coated.

3. Brushing each sheet of phyllo lightly with oil, line the bottom and sides of the prepared pie plate with half the pastry and spread the chicken mixture evenly over the pastry. Arrange the remaining sheets of phyllo over the top, brushing each one with oil; press the edges of the pastry together to seal and cut several vents in the top. Brush the top with the egg wash and bake till golden brown, 40 to 45 minutes.

4. To serve, allow the pie to cool slightly and cut into wedges.

Montezuma Pie

In Mexico and the American Southwest, there are as many styles of Montezuma pie as there are of picadillo, some made with ground beef or pork, others with a variety of spicy chiles, and still others with exotic cheeses. The main thing to remember about any Montezuma pie is that the tortillas will disintegrate if overcooked, resulting in a mushy pie with little appetizing texture. Watch carefully after about 20 minutes of baking to make sure they are still intact.

Corn oil
10 to 12 corn tortillas
1 pound ground chicken or turkey
1 large onion, chopped
1 garlic clove, minced
Two 4-ounce cans green chiles, drained and chopped
Two 28-ounce cans crushed tomatoes with juice
Salt and freshly ground black pepper to taste
1 cup sour cream
1 cup grated Monterey Jack cheese

1. Preheat the oven to 350°F.

2. In a small skillet, heat about ½ inch of oil, dip the tortillas into the oil just to soften, about 5 seconds, and drain on paper towels.

3. In another large skillet, heat about 2 tablespoons of oil over moderate heat, add the chicken, onion, garlic, and chiles, and stir till the chicken is slightly cooked and the vegetables softened, about 5 minutes. Add the tomatoes and their juice and salt and pepper, and stir about 10 minutes longer.

4. In a 1½- to 2-quart casserole or baking dish, layer about one-third of the tortillas, one-third of the chicken mixture, and one-third of the sour cream. Repeat the layering twice more, sprinkle the cheese over the top, and bake till bubbly and golden, 25 to 30 minutes.

5. Serve hot.

Moroccan Bisteeya

Bisteeya is one of the great hallmarks of Moroccan cooking, a pie that is often made with pigeons, that is traditionally eaten with the fingers as a first course, and that is as relished at royal feasts as on modest home tables. The problem for most outsiders (myself included), however, is that the intense spiciness and sweetness of the dish can be overwhelming. As a result—and with apologies to my expert friend Paula Wolfert—I've reduced slightly both the cinnamon and sugar in this recipe. Do not make *bisteeya* with less flavorful chicken breasts, and remember that leaves of strudel pastry (available frozen) work just as well as the phyllo. It's almost not worth going to the trouble to make a rich, complex, festive *bisteeya* unless you invite a crowd, and the most sensible dish to serve afterward is grilled fish.

Makes 10 to 12 servings

4 pounds chicken thighs and legs, excess fat removed
1 large onion, minced
3 cinnamon sticks, broken into pieces
1 teaspoon ground ginger
Pinch of pulverized saffron
¼ cup chopped fresh cilantro
¼ cup chopped fresh parsley leaves
12 tablespoons (1½ sticks) butter
3 cups water
1 teaspoon salt
1 teaspoon freshly ground black pepper
¼ cup fresh lemon juice
10 large eggs, beaten
1 pound blanched almonds
¼ cup confectioners' sugar
½ pound phyllo pastry (fresh or frozen)
8 tablespoons (1 stick) butter, melted
½ teaspoon ground cinnamon

1. In a large casserole, combine the chicken, onion, spices, herbs, 8 tablespoons of the butter, water, salt, and pepper. Bring to a boil, reduce the heat to low, cover, and simmer for 1½ hours. Remove the chicken parts and let cool; remove the meat from the bones, finely shred, and set aside.

2. Discard any bones and the cinnamon sticks from the casserole, bring the liquid to a boil, and reduce to about 1 cup. Reduce the heat to low, add the lemon juice and eggs, cook till the eggs set, and set aside.

3. In a skillet, melt 2 tablespoons of the remaining butter, add the almonds, brown lightly, and place in a food processor. Add the confectioners' sugar and remaining 2 tablespoons butter and process for a few seconds till well blended.

4. Preheat the oven to 425°F. Butter a 10-inch cake pan.

5. Layer 6 phyllo leaves in the prepared pan, brushing each with the melted butter. (The leaves should cover the bottom of the pan and extend up and over the sides.) Spread the shredded chicken over the bottom, cover with the eggs, and top with the almond mixture. Fold the extending layers of pastry over the filling to enclose completely and cover with 2 more layers of phyllo, brushing each sheet with butter. Tuck the phyllo edges underneath the pie to form a neat top and brush the entire surface with melted butter.

6. Bake till the top is golden, about 20 minutes. Loosen the edges with a spatula, invert onto a large, heavy baking sheet, and continue baking 15 minutes longer. Remove from the oven, tilt to pour off excess butter, transfer to a serving plate, and sprinkle the ground cinnamon over the top.

7. Serve piping hot.

It's almost not worth going to the trouble to make a rich, complex, festive bisteeya unless you invite a crowd.

Southern Beef Pot Pie with Cheese Biscuit Crust

Makes
4 servings

Talk about an easy, economical, and delicious dish to put together when ground beef is on sale and you want something substantial to serve a couple of close friends. The Southern touch, of course, is adding a little grated Parmesan to the biscuit mixture and simply mounding the dough on top of the pie for a loose, crunchy finish. If you don't care to make your own tomato sauce for this pie, however, this is one time you really should make every effort to find a top-quality bottled one. With this pot pie, I like to serve a congealed vegetable salad and a variety of sweet pickles.

2 tablespoons vegetable oil
1 medium onion, finely chopped
2 carrots, scraped and finely chopped
1 garlic clove, minced
1 pound ground beef round
2 cups tomato sauce (fresh or commercial)
Salt and freshly ground black pepper to taste
1 cup all-purpose flour
2 teaspoons baking powder
3 tablespoons grated Parmesan cheese
2 tablespoons vegetable shortening
½ cup milk

1. Preheat the oven to 400°F. Grease a 1-quart casserole or baking dish.

2. In a large skillet, heat the oil over moderate heat, add the onion, carrots, and garlic, and stir till the vegetables are tender, about 5 minutes. Add the beef and stir, breaking up with a spoon, till no longer pink, about 5 minutes. Add the tomato sauce and salt and pepper, bring to a boil, reduce the heat to low, and cook, stirring, till the mixture has thickened, about 10 minutes. Scrape the mixture into the prepared casserole.

3. In a bowl, whisk together the flour, baking powder, and cheese till well blended; add the shortening, and work with your fingertips till the mixture is mealy. Add the milk and stir just till the dough comes together. Mound the dough on top of the filling and bake till the pie is golden brown and slightly crunchy, 15 to 20 minutes.

4. Serve hot.

English Shepherd's Pie

Makes
4 servings

Originally created in England to use leftovers from the ubiquitous "Sunday roast," authentic shepherd's pie is traditionally a dish of cooked ground or minced lamb or mutton mixed with gravy and topped with crusty browned mashed potatoes. Today, however, ground beef is often used to make the pie, and it's not unusual to find a few green peas, diced carrots, or other chopped vegetables mixed in. No matter what meat you choose, it does make a difference in flavor and texture when you start the dish from scratch instead of simply using leftovers. Also, for the most delectable crust, mix plenty of butter with the potatoes and mash them as finely as possible—preferably with an electric mixer.

2 tablespoons butter
1 large onion, finely chopped
1 garlic clove, minced
1½ pounds ground lamb
¼ teaspoon dried thyme, crumbled
1 small bay leaf, crumbled
Salt and freshly ground black pepper to taste
1 tablespoon all-purpose flour
½ cup canned crushed tomatoes, drained
¼ cup water
3 tablespoons finely chopped fresh parsley leaves
3 cups hot buttered mashed potatoes

1. Preheat the oven to 400°F.

2. In a large skillet, melt the butter over moderate heat, add the onion and garlic, and stir till almost golden, about 5 minutes. Add the lamb, thyme, bay leaf, and salt and pepper and stir till the meat is lightly browned, about 10 minutes. Sprinkle the flour over the top and stir. Add the tomatoes, water, and parsley; bring to a simmer, cover the pan, and cook for 30 minutes.

3. Spoon the lamb mixture into a 1½-quart casserole or baking dish, spread the potatoes evenly over the top, and bake, uncovered, for about 20 minutes. Increase the heat and broil for 2 to 3 minutes to brown the top.

4. Serve hot.

Mexican Tamale Pie

In Mexico's Yucatán, tamale pie is usually made with a spicy chicken and pork mixture and cooked in a banana leaf; along the west coast, small shrimp are used; but almost everywhere else (including Texas), ground beef, or a mixture of beef and pork, along with corn, is the most popular filling. As with any tamale pie, it's important when cooking the cornmeal to add the meal slowly to the boiling water, stirring constantly, just till the mixture is a firm mush. This is a sturdy dish that needs no more than a tart green salad served with it.

1 quart water
3 teaspoons salt
1 cup yellow cornmeal
2 slices bacon
½ pound ground beef chuck
½ pound ground pork
1 medium onion, chopped
½ small green bell pepper, seeded and chopped
1 garlic clove, minced
1 cup corn kernels (fresh or frozen)
One 8-ounce can tomato sauce
1 tablespoon chili powder
¼ teaspoon ground cumin
¼ teaspoon dried oregano, crumbled
Freshly ground black pepper to taste
3 tablespoons grated Monterey Jack cheese

1. Preheat the oven to 350°F. Grease a 9-inch square baking pan and set aside.

2. In a large saucepan, bring the water and 2 teaspoons of the salt to a boil, gradually add the cornmeal in a stream, and stir steadily. Reduce the heat to low and continue stirring till the mixture thickens, about 5 minutes. Spread three-quarters of the mixture over the bottom of the prepared pan and set aside.

3. In a large, heavy skillet, fry the bacon over moderate heat till crisp, drain on paper towels, and crumble. Add the beef and pork to the skillet and brown lightly. Add the onion, bell pepper, and garlic and stir till the vegetables soften, about 5 minutes. Add the corn, tomato sauce, chili powder, cumin, oregano, black pepper, bacon, and the 1 teaspoon remaining salt, stir well, and let cook for about 5 minutes. Spoon the meat and vegetables over the cornmeal mush in the pan, spoon the remaining mush over the meat and vegetables, sprinkle the cheese over the top, and bake till golden, about 30 minutes.

4. Let the pie stand for about 10 minutes before cutting into squares.

Canadian Pork Pie

Although I've eaten *tourtière* in one form or another all over eastern Canada, the residents of Quebec province deem the earthy, spicy pork pie to be almost their national dish. While the ingredient variations can be as radical as the cooking techniques from one locale to the next, it's generally agreed that ground or chopped pork is the foundation of any authentic *tourtière*, even when chicken, rabbit, or wild game is added, and that the two essential spices are nutmeg and cloves. Today, you can usually find packaged ground pork in all better markets, but since I like the ratio of lean meat to fat in pork shoulder (or butt) for this pie, I grind or chop my own. Serve this hearty dish with only a tart green or endive salad and either gutsy red wine or sturdy dark ale.

Makes 4 to 6 servings

For the dough:
> 1¼ cups all-purpose flour
> 6 tablespoons (¾ stick) chilled butter, cut into bits
> 2 tablespoons chilled lard, cut into bits
> ¼ teaspoon salt
> 3 tablespoons ice water

For the pie:
> 3 tablespoons lard
> 3 thick slices Canadian bacon, minced
> 1 pound ground or minced lean pork
> 1 medium onion, chopped
> 1 garlic clove, minced
> ½ teaspoon salt
> Freshly ground black pepper to taste
> ¼ teaspoon grated nutmeg
> ¼ teaspoon ground cloves

¼ teaspoon celery seed
1½ teaspoons cornstarch
1 cup water
1 cup cubed boiled potatoes

1. To make the dough, combine the flour, butter, and lard in a bowl and blend with your fingertips till the mixture is mealy. Add the water, stir well, and form the dough into a ball. Place on a lightly floured surface and knead for about 30 seconds. Re-form into a ball, dust with flour, wrap in plastic wrap, and chill for 1 hour.

2. Meanwhile, to make the pie, melt the lard in a large, heavy saucepan over moderate heat, add the bacon, and stir for 2 minutes. Add the pork, onion, and garlic and cook with the bacon for 3 minutes, stirring. Add the seasonings, cornstarch, and water, bring the liquid to a boil, reduce the heat to low, cover, and simmer for 30 minutes. Uncover, add the potatoes, and cook for 5 minutes longer.

3. Preheat the oven to 425°F. Grease a 9-inch pie pan and set aside.

4. Divide the chilled dough in half and, on a lightly floured surface, roll out each half about ⅛ inch thick. Line the prepared pan with half the dough, scrape the pork and potato mixture into the pan, and cover with the remaining dough. Press the edges of the pie together and prick the top with a fork. Bake for 10 minutes, reduce the heat to 350°F, and bake till golden, about 30 minutes.

5. Serve hot in wedges.

Castilian Pork and Chorizo Pie

Scented with garlic and paprika, chorizo sausage is found all over Spain, but even jealous Spaniards admit that none is finer or plays a more important role in cooking than that produced in the province of Castille. Unlike Mexican and South American chorizo, which is made with fresh pork, the Spanish version uses smoked pork, and for a pie such as this one, it does pay off to try to find the genuine item. Remember when shopping for chorizo to get the less cured, softer sausage instead of the harder, drier style, which is most often simply eaten as a cold cut appetizer. Also typical of Castilian cooking are the pimentos and hard-boiled eggs often used to enhance the flavor of any meat pie.

For the pastry:
- 1 cup water
- 3 tablespoons butter
- 3 tablespoons olive oil
- ¼ teaspoon salt
- 2½ cups all-purpose flour
- 1 large egg, beaten

For the filling:
- 3 tablespoons olive oil
- 2 medium onions, chopped
- 2 garlic cloves, minced
- 1 pound ground lean pork
- ½ pound minced Spanish chorizo sausage
- 1 ripe tomato, chopped
- One 4-ounce jar sliced pimentos, drained
- Salt and freshly ground black pepper to taste
- 2 large hard-boiled eggs, chopped
- 3 tablespoons warm water
- 1 large egg beaten with 1 tablespoon water

1. To make the pastry, heat the water, butter, oil, and salt in a saucepan over moderate heat till the butter melts, and remove from the heat. Add the flour and whisk till well blended. Whisk in the egg till well blended. Transfer to a floured work surface and knead till the dough is elastic and no longer sticky. Cover with plastic wrap and let stand for about 30 minutes.

2. Meanwhile, to make the filling, heat the oil in a large skillet over moderate heat, add the onions and garlic, and stir till softened, about 5 minutes. Add the pork and chorizo and stir 5 minutes longer. Add the tomato, pimentos, and salt and pepper and cook about 10 minutes longer, stirring occasionally. Add the hard-boiled eggs, remove from the heat, and thin the filling with the water, stirring.

3. Preheat the oven to 350°F.

4. Divide the pastry into 2 balls and roll out each ball about ⅛ inch thick. Line the bottom and sides of a 10-inch pie plate with half the pastry, spread the filling evenly over the bottom, and cover with the remaining pastry. Press together the edges of the pastry to seal, cut several vents in the top, brush the top with the egg wash, and bake till golden brown, 40 to 45 minutes.

5. To serve, allow the pie to cool slightly, then cut into wedges.

Remember when shopping for chorizo to get the less cured, softer sausage instead of the harder, drier style.

Maryland Clam Pie

Like a superior chicken pot pie, a proper Maryland clam pie not only requires a little effort but also almost demands a freshly made pastry. The best live soft-shell clams to use for this pie are either large eastern chowder clams or smaller steamers, or Pacific razor clams, but since nothing toughens clams more than long cooking, I would never dream of using whole clams unless they were exceptionally small and I shucked them myself. Nor would any Maryland clam pie taste right without the subtle flavor of bacon.

**Makes
6 servings**

For the pastry:
2 cups all-purpose flour
¼ teaspoon salt
⅔ cup vegetable shortening
¼ cup ice water

For the filling:
2 slices bacon
1 scallion (white part only), chopped
1 garlic clove, minced
¼ pound mushrooms, diced
3 tablespoons all-purpose flour
1½ cups bottled clam juice
2 tablespoons dry sherry
¼ cup heavy cream
3 cups chopped fresh clams
¼ teaspoon dried tarragon
Salt and freshly ground black pepper to taste
1 large egg yolk, beaten
1 large egg beaten with 1 tablespoon water

1. To make the pastry, combine the flour and salt in a bowl, stir, and cut in the shortening with a pastry cutter till it resembles coarse meal. Stirring, gradually add the water till a firm ball of dough forms, wrap in plastic wrap, and chill for at least 30 minutes.

2. To make the filling, fry the bacon in a skillet over moderate heat till crisp, drain on paper towels, and crumble. Add the scallion, garlic, and mushrooms to the skillet and stir till the mushrooms render most of their liquid, 5 to 7 minutes. Sprinkle the flour over the top and stir about 1 minute longer. Add the clam juice and sherry, bring to a boil, and cook for about 1 minute. Add the cream and stir till the sauce is slightly reduced, about 8 minutes. Add the bacon, clams, tarragon, and salt and pepper and cook about 2 minutes longer. Remove the skillet from the heat, whisk a little of the hot sauce into the egg yolk, then stir the egg yolk mixture into the clam mixture.

3. Preheat the oven to 375°F.

4. Pour the clam mixture into a deep 10 by 9-inch baking dish. On a floured surface, roll out the pastry ¼ inch thick, fit it over the top of the pie, trim and crimp the edges, and cut a small vent in the center. Brush the pastry with the egg wash, place the dish on a heavy baking sheet, and bake till bubbly and golden, 45 to 50 minutes.

5. Serve hot.

Ham, Bacon, and Leek Quiche

I don't hesitate a second to use a commercial pie shell for this or any other quiche, since the pastry plays such a minor role in the overall flavor and texture of the dish. Ground or finely diced leftover pork, chicken, or turkey, as well as bulk pork sausage cooked with the bacon, can successfully be substituted for the ham, and if you prefer to make an all-vegetable quiche (finely chopped squash, zucchini, broccoli, spinach, and so on) with only the bacon for flavoring, this same recipe can be used. As with any quiche, it's always a good idea to spread a sheet of foil underneath the pan to catch any drips.

Makes 4 to 6 servings

1 commercial 9-inch pie shell
2 slices bacon
1 large leek (white part only), rinsed well and finely chopped
1 garlic clove, minced
½ pound cooked ham, finely diced
½ teaspoon powdered sage
Salt and freshly ground black pepper to taste
4 large eggs
1 cup half-and-half
¼ cup grated Parmesan cheese

1. Preheat the oven to 375°F.

2. Fit a sheet of foil snugly against the bottom and sides of the pastry in the pan, allowing for enough to cover the edges of the crust, and bake till slightly golden, about 20 minutes.

3. Meanwhile, fry the bacon in a large skillet over moderate heat till almost crisp, drain on paper towels, and chop. Add the leek and garlic to the skillet and stir till softened, about 3 minutes. Add the ham, sage, and salt and pepper, stir about 2 minutes longer, and remove the pan from the heat.

4. In a bowl, whisk together the eggs and half-and-half, pour into the leek and ham mixture, and stir in the bacon. Pour the mixture into the baked pie shell, sprinkle the cheese over the top, and bake till golden, about 40 minutes.

5. Let the quiche stand for about 10 minutes, then cut into wedges.

Santa Fe Ham, Jalapeño, and Pimento Quiche

Makes 4 to 6 servings

I identify this succulent quiche with Santa Fe only because a friend there once made it with the leftovers of an exceptional local ham that he had cured himself, partly with salt, pepper, and honey. Pimentos, in my opinion, enhance any style of smoked or cured ham, and the jalapeño and cilantro add just the right zing to balance the flavors. Cut into smaller wedges, the quiche can also be served hot or at room temperature at cocktail parties and receptions.

1 commercial 9-inch pie shell
1 cup finely chopped cooked ham
1 small fresh jalapeño chile pepper, seeded and finely chopped
One 4-ounce jar pimento slices, drained and chopped
1 cup grated Monterey Jack cheese
2 tablespoons minced fresh parsley leaves
2 tablespoons minced fresh cilantro
Salt and freshly ground back pepper to taste
3 large eggs
1¼ cups half-and-half

1. Preheat the oven to 375°F.

2. Fit a sheet of foil snugly against the bottom and sides of the pastry in the pan and bake till slightly golden, about 20 minutes.

3. In a bowl, toss together the ham, jalapeño, pimentos, cheese, parsley, cilantro, and salt and pepper, and spread the mixture over the inside of the baked shell. In another bowl, whisk together the eggs and half-and-half, pour over the filling, and bake till the quiche is golden and a knife inserted 1 inch from the pastry edge comes out clean, 40 to 45 minutes.

4. Allow the quiche to cool for about 10 minutes, then cut into wedges.

Italian Prosciutto and Spinach Frittata

A type of open-face omelette, Italian frittatas can be made with endless combinations of finely chopped cooked meats, poultry, and vegetables, and they always make a delightful brunch dish or main course served with cold cuts and plenty of crusty bread. Quickly browned under the broiler, frittatas are delicious served hot, but in Italy you're just as likely to find them at room temperature and even cold. If you're not satisfied with the quality of prosciutto in your market, by all means substitute finely chopped bacon that's only partially fried.

Makes 4 to 6 servings

3 tablespoons olive oil
1 medium onion, finely chopped
2 garlic cloves, minced
½ pound prosciutto, finely chopped
One 10-ounce package frozen spinach, thawed, squeezed dry, and finely chopped
⅛ teaspoon grated nutmeg
6 large eggs
Salt and freshly ground black pepper to taste

1. Preheat the oven broiler.

2. In a large, heavy skillet, heat the oil over moderate heat, add the onion and garlic, and stir for about 2 minutes. Add the prosciutto, spinach, and nutmeg and stir about 2 minutes longer. In a bowl, whisk the eggs with the salt and pepper, pour over the prosciutto and spinach mixture, reduce the heat to low, and cook till the eggs are just barely set.

3. Place the skillet under the boiler till the frittata is lightly browned, run a sharp knife around the edges to loosen it from the pan, slide it onto a serving plate, and cut into wedges.

4. Serve the frittata hot or at room temperature.

Alsatian Meat Quiche

Makes 4 to 6
servings

Overshadowed by the universally popular cheese quiche from its neighboring Lorraine province in France, Alsace's meat quiches are not only more robust but also lend themselves to endless variety with the region's wealth of pork, beef, lamb, and wild game products. Feel free to experiment with different meat combinations, wild mushrooms, and herbs in this recipe, and also don't disqualify the possibility of using the chopped meat from leftover baked short ribs of beef, pork spareribs, and roasted lamb or venison.

1 commercial 9-inch pie shell
½ pound ground lean pork
½ pound ground veal
Salt and freshly ground black pepper to taste
⅛ teaspoon powdered sage
⅛ teaspoon dried rosemary, crumbled
2 tablespoons butter
1 small onion, finely chopped
½ cup finely chopped mushrooms
1 large egg
1 large egg yolk
1 cup heavy cream

1. Preheat the oven to 375°F.

2. Fit a sheet of foil snugly against the bottom and sides of the pastry in the pan, allowing for enough to cover the edges of the crust, and bake till slightly golden, about 20 minutes. Meanwhile, season the pork and veal with salt and pepper, sage, and rosemary, and set aside.

3. In a large skillet, melt the butter over moderate heat, add the onion and mushrooms, and stir for about 5 minutes. Add the two meats, stir till most of the liquid in the pan has evaporated, and remove from the heat.

4. In a bowl, whisk together the egg, egg yolk, cream, and salt and pepper to taste till well blended, add to the meat and vegetables, and stir well. Pour the mixture into the baked shell, reduce the oven to 350°F, and bake till the quiche is set and golden, about 45 minutes.

5. Let stand for about 10 minutes, then cut into wedges.

Feel free to experiment with different meat combinations, wild mushrooms, and herbs in this recipe.

Shrimp Quiche

While there's nothing fancy or unusual about this quiche, you simply won't find an easier and tastier option when trying to come up with something to serve friends at a casual spring or summer lunch. Include a bowl of fresh fruit compote, maybe a few tiny ham biscuits, a bottle of Chardonnay, and some homemade cookies for dessert, and nobody could ask for a more satisfying meal. I actually prefer this quiche slightly chilled when the temperature outside soars.

Makes 4 to 6 servings

1 commercial 9-inch pie shell

4 slices bacon

2 scallions (white parts only), minced

½ pound fresh shrimp, shelled, deveined, and minced

1 cup grated Swiss cheese

2 tablespoons minced fresh parsley leaves

⅛ teaspoon grated nutmeg

Salt and freshly ground black pepper to taste

3 large eggs

1 cup heavy cream

½ cup bottled clam juice

1. Preheat the oven to 375°F.

2. Fit a sheet of foil snugly against the bottom and sides of the pastry in the pan and bake till slightly golden, about 20 minutes.

3. Meanwhile, fry the bacon in a skillet over moderate heat till crisp, drain on paper towels, and crumble. Pour off all but about 1 tablespoon of fat from the skillet, add the scallions, and stir till softened, about 3 minutes.

4. Sprinkle the bacon, scallions, shrimp, cheese, parsley, nutmeg, and salt and pepper over the inside of the baked shell. In a bowl, whisk together the eggs, cream, and clam juice till well blended, pour over the filling, and bake till the quiche is golden and a knife inserted 1 inch from the pastry edge comes out clean, 40 to 45 minutes.

5. Allow the quiche to cool for about 10 minutes, then cut into wedges.

Country Ham, Grits, and Cheese Soufflé

American Southerners learned centuries ago to grind or chop the leftover nubs of a cured country ham for all sorts of dishes, but perhaps the ultimate examples of this ingenuity are the elegant soufflés in which ham is combined with any number of other regional ingredients. Regular smoked ham or even ground cooked lean pork could also be used, but if ever there were reason to track down a bag of luscious stone-ground grits (and by no means try to make this soufflé with the instant or quick-cooking varieties), this dish justifies the effort.

1 cup bread crumbs
2 cups water
½ teaspoon salt
½ cup stone-ground or regular grits
½ cup grated Parmesan cheese
2 tablespoons butter
Freshly ground black pepper to taste
Tabasco sauce to taste
½ cup finely chopped cooked ham
1 garlic clove, minced
4 large eggs, beaten

1. Preheat the oven to 350°F. Butter a 1½-quart soufflé dish or casserole and sprinkle the bread crumbs over the bottom and sides.

2. In a heavy saucepan, combine the water and salt and bring to a boil. Gradually add the grits, stirring; reduce the heat to low, and cook for 15 to 20 minutes or till thick and creamy, stirring constantly. Remove the pan from the heat, add the cheese, butter, pepper, Tabasco, ham, and garlic, and stir till well blended. Add the eggs and stir till well blended. Scrape the mixture into the prepared dish and bake till golden brown, 30 to 35 minutes.

3. Serve hot.

Chicken Liver Soufflé Bocuse

I don't think I've ever dined at Paul Bocuse's Michelin three-star restaurant outside Lyon in France (and the occasions have been numerous over the years) without at least tasting this rich, memorable soufflé that's always served with a light, herby tomato sauce. Paul once told me that the dish was originally devised by Lyonnaise home cooks to use up leftover chicken livers, but I can assure you there's nothing homey about this sublime soufflé, which can be prepared either in one large dish or in individual ramekins. For the right texture, do not use a food processor to grind the liver mixture, but rather chop it by hand to the consistency of a paste just as directed. The soufflé can be served as either an appetizer (in small portions) or main luncheon dish with perhaps marinated cucumbers, some celery rémoulade, and toasted croutons.

Makes
4 servings

1 tablespoon butter
1 small onion, finely chopped
1 garlic clove, minced
2¼ cups crumbled stale bread
2 cups milk
¼ pound chicken livers, trimmed and finely chopped
2 tablespoons minced fresh parsley leaves
Salt and freshly ground black pepper to taste
4 large eggs, separated

1. Preheat the oven to 350°F. Butter a 1-quart soufflé dish and set aside.

2. In a small skillet, melt the butter over moderate heat, add the onion and garlic, stir till softened, about 2 minutes, and remove from the heat.

(continued)

3. In a bowl, combine the bread and milk, and when it has softened, crush it with a fork, pour off the excess milk, and transfer the bread to a cutting board. Add the onion and garlic, livers, parsley, and salt and pepper to the bread and chop the ingredients to a paste. Scrape into a bowl, add the egg yolks, and stir till well blended and smooth. In another bowl, whisk the egg whites till stiff, and fold them into the liver mixture. Scrape the mixture into the prepared soufflé dish and bake till puffy and golden, about 45 minutes.

4. Serve immediately.

Crabmeat and Mushroom Soufflé

For years, one of my standard dishes to serve at special luncheons has been Crab Imperial, prepared with a sherried white sauce or mayonnaise, sprinkled with grated Parmesan, and baked in shells or ramekins till golden brown. While this American classic remains a favorite, equally delicious but much less rich and cloying is this sublime soufflé, made with little more than shredded lump crabmeat, diced mushrooms, and a little fresh dill. Since the soufflé must be served the second it comes out of the oven, I make things easy on myself by already having on the table perhaps a congealed salad or chilled minted peas, small pickled peaches, and a big basket of sesame sticks.

Makes 4 to 6 servings

8 tablespoons (1 stick) butter
1 small onion, minced
6 large mushrooms, diced
6 tablespoons all-purpose flour
2 cups milk, heated just to a boil
8 large eggs, separated
½ teaspoon dry mustard
Salt to taste
Worcestershire sauce to taste
1½ cups shredded lump crabmeat
1 tablespoon minced fresh dill

1. In a small skillet, melt 2 tablespoons of the butter over moderate heat. Add the onion and mushrooms, stir for 2 to 3 minutes, and set aside.

2. Preheat the oven to 375°F. Butter a 2-quart soufflé dish and set aside.

(continued)

The soufflé
must be
served the
second it
comes out
of the oven.

3. In a large saucepan, melt the remaining 6 tablespoons butter over low heat, add the flour, and whisk till golden, 2 to 3 minutes. Remove the saucepan from the heat, add the milk all at once, and whisk till the mixture is thickened and smooth. Let cool slightly.

4. One at a time, beat the egg yolks into the flour mixture, then add the mustard, salt, and Worcestershire and stir till well blended. Add the mushroom mixture, crabmeat, and dill, blend well, and transfer the mixture to a large bowl.

5. Pour the egg whites into another large bowl and whisk till stiff peaks form. Gently fold the whites into the crabmeat mixture with a rubber spatula, scrape the mixture into the prepared soufflé dish, and bake till puffy and golden, 30 to 35 minutes.

6. Serve immediately.

French Salmon Soufflé

Leftover poached, baked, or grilled salmon can always be used to create delightful salads, but if you want to serve something a bit more elegant for lunch in the French style, flake the fish well and use it to make this relatively easy soufflé. As to whether you can substitute canned salmon for the fresh, the answer is yes, so long as it's a top-quality brand, drained well and finely flaked. The egg whites for this soufflé need to be whisked till really stiff, and to facilitate the process, add about ¼ teaspoon of cream of tartar before you start whisking.

Makes
4 servings

4 tablespoons (½ stick) butter
1 scallion (white part only), minced
¼ cup all-purpose flour
1 cup milk
Salt and freshly ground black pepper to taste
4 large eggs, separated
½ pound cooked salmon, finely flaked
1 tablespoon minced fresh parsley leaves
⅛ teaspoon grated nutmeg

1. In a saucepan, melt the butter over moderate heat, add the scallion, and stir for 2 minutes. Add the flour, stir well, then gradually add the milk, stirring till the sauce thickens, about 2 minutes. Add the salt and pepper and reduce the heat to low. In a small bowl, whisk the egg yolks till foamy, whisk in a little of the hot sauce, add the mixture to the pan, and stir for about 1 minute. Remove the pan from the heat, stir in the salmon, parsley, and nutmeg, fit a piece of wax paper over the top, and let cool.

2. Preheat the oven to 350°F. Butter a 1½-quart soufflé dish and set aside.

(continued)

3. In a bowl, whisk the egg whites till very stiff, stir half of them into the salmon mixture, then fold in the remainder with a rubber spatula. Scrape the mixture into the prepared soufflé dish and bake till puffy and golden brown, about 40 minutes.

4. Serve immediately.

Brazilian Salt Cod Soufflé

There is virtually nothing that serious Brazilian chefs have not learned to do with salt cod, including ways to make all types of spreads, puddings, pies, and soufflés. Although this particular main-course soufflé is remarkably light given the sturdy texture of the fish, don't expect it to rise over the edges of the dish the way other soufflés can do. When the soufflé is simply puffy and golden brown, it is ready to serve—preferably with a compote of tropical fruits and buttered croutons or toast.

Makes 4 to 6 servings

1 pound boneless salt cod
4 tablespoons (½ stick) butter
2 tablespoons all-purpose flour
2½ cups half-and-half
1 cup soft fresh bread crumbs
6 large eggs, separated
¼ cup finely chopped fresh parsley leaves
¼ teaspoon grated nutmeg
Salt and freshly ground black pepper to taste

1. Place the salt cod in a baking pan with enough water to cover and let soak for 8 to 10 hours, changing the water twice.

2. Change the water a third time, bring to a low boil, and simmer the cod for about 15 minutes. Drain, cut into chunks, and discard any skin and bones. Place the cod in a food processor and grind almost to a puree.

3. Preheat the oven to 350°F. Butter a 1½-quart soufflé dish and set aside.

4. In a large saucepan, melt the butter over moderate heat, add the flour, and whisk for about 1 minute. Add the half-and-half

(continued)

and continue whisking till the mixture thickens slightly, about 3 minutes. Add the bread crumbs and cod and stir about 3 minutes longer. In a small bowl, whisk the egg yolks till foamy and add to the cod mixture, whisking constantly. Add the parsley, nutmeg, and salt and pepper, stir well, remove the pan from the heat, and let cool slightly.

5. In another bowl, whisk the egg whites till they hold soft peaks, and gently fold them into the cod mixture with a rubber spatula. Scrape the mixture into the prepared soufflé dish and bake till puffy and golden, about 40 minutes.

6. Serve immediately.

Casseroles and Pastas

Ham, Cheese, and Broccoli Casserole

**Makes
6 servings**

This is a tried-and-true casserole that I've been making for years, and it's still one of the best and easiest ways I know to use up leftover ham. Served at the table to family and friends, the dish needs no more than a tart salad and hot buttery rolls, but double the recipe and use a larger casserole and you also have an ideal buffet dish intended to serve lots more people. Zucchini, yellow squash, or cauliflower, cut in bite-size pieces, can be substituted for the broccoli, and there's room here for lots of experimentation with various cheeses.

½ to ¾ pound fresh broccoli florets, cut in half
6 tablespoons (¾ stick) butter
¼ cup all-purpose flour
2 cups milk, heated
¾ cup grated Swiss cheese
¼ cup grated Parmesan cheese
Salt and freshly ground black pepper to taste
½ pound cooked ham, chopped
1 cup dry bread crumbs

1. Preheat the oven to 375°F. Butter a 1½-quart casserole and set aside.

2. Place the broccoli in a saucepan with about 1 inch of water and bring to a boil. Reduce the heat to moderate, cover, steam till crisp-tender, about 12 minutes, and drain.

3. In a saucepan, melt 4 tablespoons of the butter, add the flour, and stir for 2 minutes. Whisking the mixture, add the milk gradually and cook for about 5 minutes. Add the two cheeses and salt and pepper and stir till the cheeses melt. Remove the sauce from the heat.

4. Layer the broccoli and ham alternately in the prepared casserole and pour the cheese sauce over the top. Sprinkle the bread crumbs over the top, dot with the remaining 2 tablespoons butter cut into bits, and bake till bubbly and golden, about 30 minutes.

5. Serve hot.

Italian Beef, Wild Mushroom, and Orzo Casserole

Makes
6 servings

Italian cooks don't make that many casseroles, but when they do, the ingredients usually have a flair that couldn't be more enticing. Nothing is more delicious in this beef casserole, for example, than the orzo, an enlarged rice-shaped pasta that is not only more toothsome than rice but also absorbs flavors much better. By all means feel free to experiment with various ground meats or poultry, wild mushrooms, and assertive cheeses in this casserole.

½ pound dried orzo
2 tablespoons olive oil
1 large onion, finely chopped
1 garlic clove, minced
¾ pound ground beef round
¼ pound chanterelle or cep mushrooms, chopped
One 28-ounce can diced tomatoes with juice
½ teaspoon dried thyme, crumbled
½ teaspoon dried oregano, crumbled
Salt and freshly ground black pepper to taste
1 cup grated Parmesan cheese

1. In a large pot of salted boiling water, cook the orzo according to package directions, drain, and set aside.

2. Preheat the oven to 375°F. Grease a 2-quart casserole or baking dish and set aside.

3. In a large skillet, heat the oil over moderate heat, add the onion and garlic, and stir till softened, about 3 minutes. Add the beef and mushrooms and stir for about 5 minutes. Add the tomatoes, thyme, oregano, and salt and pepper and continue stirring till the mixture thickens, about 15 minutes. Add the orzo and stir till well blended.

4. Spoon about half the beef and orzo mixture into the prepared casserole, sprinkle half the cheese over the top, repeat with the remaining mixture and cheese, and bake till bubbly and golden, 25 to 30 minutes.

5. Serve piping hot.

Greek Moussaka

Moussaka, of course, can be made with ground beef, but, having been raised in a part-Greek family, I've always been accustomed to using lamb as my grandfather did and as most cooks in Greece do. If you do prefer beef, just be sure to buy only ground chuck for the best flavor, and if you have difficulty finding ground lamb shoulder and your butcher won't cooperate, either order a small boneless shoulder roast or buy shoulder chops and grind the meat yourself. Do be warned that if you over-broil the eggplant slices, they will fall apart while baking in the casserole. If you want to serve this popular dish to a crowd, it's easy enough to double the recipe and use a larger casserole.

Makes
6 servings

6 tablespoons olive oil
1 large onion, finely chopped
2 garlic cloves, minced
1 pound ground lamb shoulder
¼ teaspoon ground cinnamon
¼ teaspoon ground allspice
Salt and freshly ground black pepper to taste
One 28-ounce can crushed tomatoes with juice
Two 1-pound eggplants, peeled and thinly sliced crosswise
1 cup plain yogurt
½ cup sour cream
¼ pound feta cheese, finely crumbled
3 tablespoons grated Parmesan cheese

1. Preheat the oven broiler. Grease a 2-quart shallow casserole or baking dish and set aside.

2. In a large, heavy skillet, heat 2 tablespoons of the oil over moderate heat, add the onion and garlic, and stir till softened, about 2 minutes. Add the lamb and stir till it is no longer pink, about 5 minutes. Add the cinnamon, allspice, salt and pepper, and tomatoes and stir well. Bring to a simmer, cook till the sauce is slightly thickened, about 15 minutes, and remove from the heat.

3. Meanwhile, arrange the eggplant slices on a broiler rack, brush them with 2 tablespoons of the oil, and broil just till golden, 2 to 3 minutes. Turn the slices over, brush with the remaining 2 tablespoons oil, and broil till golden brown, about 3 minutes.

4. Reduce the oven to 375°F.

5. Arrange overlapping slices of eggplant in the prepared casserole, spoon the lamb sauce evenly over the top, and layer the remaining eggplant slices over the lamb. In a bowl, combine the yogurt, sour cream, feta, and Parmesan, stir till well blended, spoon the mixture evenly over the top, and bake till the moussaka is bubbly and golden, about 45 minutes.

6. Serve hot.

If you want to serve this popular dish to a crowd, it's easy enough to double the recipe and use a larger casserole.

Chicken Divan Parisienne

Makes
6 servings

Created and served with great flourish in the Divan Pa-
risienne Restaurant at New York's Chatham Hotel in the early
part of the twentieth century, this sumptuous casserole quickly
became an American classic in homes and on country club
buffets all over the country. Today, the variations of chicken
Divan are countless (poached slices or whole breasts used in
place of the diced chicken, Hollandaise sauce added to the
cheese sauce, other vegetables substituted for the broccoli,
and chopped nuts sprinkled over the layers), but, at least in
my opinion, there's still nothing more delicious than the original concept. The dish is as ideal for the buffet as for the dinner table.

One 2-pound head broccoli, stems removed
4 tablespoons (½ stick) butter
¼ cup all-purpose flour
1 cup chicken broth
1 cup milk
Salt and freshly ground black pepper to taste
⅛ teaspoon grated nutmeg
½ cup grated Parmesan cheese
3 tablespoons dry sherry
½ pound cooked chicken breast (or turkey breast), diced
½ cup heavy cream

1. Break the broccoli into florets and place them in a large sauce-pan with enough water to cover. Bring to a boil, reduce the heat to moderate, cook just till tender, about 10 minutes, and drain.

2. Preheat the oven to 350°F. Butter a shallow 2-quart casserole and set aside.

3. In a medium saucepan, melt the butter over moderate heat, add the flour, and stir for about 1 minute. Gradually add the broth and milk and stir till thickened. Add the salt and pepper, nut-meg, ¼ cup of the cheese, and the sherry, stir till the cheese melts, and remove from the heat.

4. Arrange the broccoli in the prepared casserole in a single layer, sprinkle the remaining ¼ cup cheese over the top, and scatter the chicken over the broccoli. In a bowl, beat the cream with an electric mixer till soft peaks form, fold into the cheese sauce, pour evenly over the chicken and broccoli, and bake till bubbly and golden brown, about 35 minutes.

5. Serve hot.

German Kidney, Onion, and Wild Mushroom Casserole

**Makes
6 servings**

Why German chefs have a special knack with kidneys, liver, sweetbreads, and other organ meats I don't know, but whenever I see a stew or casserole such as this one on restaurant menus while traveling in Germany, I never fail to order it. Buy only veal kidneys unless you have acquired a taste for the less tender and more pungent beef and pork ones, and before chopping the kidneys, be sure to first cut them in half and remove the membranes and knobs of interior fat. Any wild mushrooms can be used in this casserole, and the more assertive the flavor, the better.

6 tablespoons (¾ stick) butter

2 pounds (about 4) fresh veal kidneys, trimmed of fat and membranes and coarsely chopped

½ pound fresh morel or chanterelle mushrooms, chopped

1 cup dry white wine

1 tablespoon grainy brown mustard

1½ cups beef broth

½ cup half-and-half

¾ pound tiny white boiling onions, peeled

Salt and freshly ground black pepper to taste

2 tablespoons chopped fresh parsley leaves

1. Preheat the oven to 350°F. Butter a 1½- to 2-quart casserole and set aside.

2. In a large, heavy skillet, melt about half the butter over moderate heat, add the kidneys, brown quickly, about 2 minutes, and transfer to a plate. Add the mushrooms to the skillet, stir for about 3 minutes, and transfer to another plate. Melt the remaining butter in the skillet, add the wine and mustard, stir well, and cook till any liquid is almost evaporated, 6 to 7 minutes. Add the broth and half-and-half, continue to cook till the sauce thickens, 8 to 10 minutes, and remove from the heat.

3. Layer the kidneys over the bottom of the prepared casserole, layer the onions over the kidneys, layer the mushrooms over the onions, and season with salt and pepper. Pour the sauce over the casserole, cover, and bake for 30 minutes.

4. Sprinkle the parsley over the top and serve hot.

Buffet Shrimp, Pasta, and Cheese Casserole

Makes at least
8 servings

How, when, and why a friend in Charlotte, North Carolina, came up with this elaborate, unusual buffet casserole has not been fully explained, but suffice it to say that whenever Beverly serves the rich dish, there's never a morsel left. She believes that fresh jumbo shrimp have just the right firm texture for this casserole, and she emphasizes that the shrimp must not be overcooked. A large tossed salad and hot rolls are all that is needed to serve with the dish—along, of course, with plenty of iced tea.

2 large eggs
1 cup evaporated milk
1 cup plain yogurt
½ pound feta cheese, crumbled
½ cup shredded Swiss cheese
⅓ cup chopped fresh parsley leaves
⅓ cup chopped fresh basil leaves
1 teaspoon dried oregano, crumbled
4 garlic cloves, minced
½ pound dried angel hair pasta, cooked according to package directions and drained
1½ pounds large (preferably jumbo) fresh shrimp, boiled till just cooked through, drained, peeled, deveined, and coarsely chopped
One 16-ounce jar medium-hot salsa
⅓ pound mozzarella cheese, shredded

1. Preheat the oven to 350°F. Grease a shallow 3-quart casserole and set aside.

2. In a large bowl, whisk together the eggs, milk, and yogurt, add the feta and Swiss cheeses, parsley, basil, oregano, and garlic, and stir till well blended.

3. Spread half the pasta over the bottom of the prepared casserole, layer half the shrimp over the pasta, and spoon the salsa evenly over the top. Spread the remaining pasta over the salsa and pour the egg mixture over the top. Layer the remaining shrimp on top, sprinkle the mozzarella cheese evenly over the shrimp, and bake till golden, about 30 minutes.

4. Let stand for about 10 minutes before serving.

Belgian Salmon, Green Pea, and Juniper Casserole

Aromatic, slightly smoky juniper berries are used almost as much in Belgium as in the Scandinavian countries to add distinctive flavor to all sorts of stews, casseroles, stuffings, and sauces, and the way the berries, along with the licorice-tasting chervil, enhance the salmon in this casserole is amazing. Too astringent to be eaten raw, juniper berries are usually sold dried in finer markets and must be crushed before using.

Makes 4 to 6 servings

1½ pounds fresh salmon fillets, skinned and coarsely chopped
Salt and freshly ground black pepper to taste
2 juniper berries, finely crushed
¼ teaspoon dried chervil, crumbled
Juice and grated rind of 1 lemon
1¼ cups plain yogurt
One 10-ounce package frozen green peas, thawed
1 cup shredded Swiss cheese
1½ cups dry bread crumbs
3 tablespoons butter, melted

1. Preheat the oven to 375°F.

2. Butter a shallow 1½- to 2-quart casserole and arrange the fish over the bottom. Season with salt and pepper, sprinkle with the juniper berries, chervil, and lemon juice, cover with a sheet of foil, and bake for 15 minutes.

3. Add the lemon rind, yogurt, peas, and cheese and stir gently till well blended. Sprinkle the bread crumbs evenly over the top, drizzle the butter over the crumbs, and bake till golden brown, 25 to 30 minutes.

4. Serve hot.

English Kedgeree

Originally a spiced East Indian dish of rice, lentils, and onions, kedgeree was totally Anglicized in the eighteenth century, when the English added flaked smoked fish, hard-boiled eggs, and cream and transformed the dish into a popular breakfast specialty. Today in Britain, kedgeree can be lightly curried, enhanced with many spices, or flavored with no more than cayenne pepper, and when I feature my version at a formal brunch, I might just as easily pack the mixture into a loaf pan for quick, even baking (15 to 20 minutes at 350°F) as simply stir it in a pot. I've also learned that this is an ideal way to use up any leftover poached or baked fresh salmon.

**Makes
4 servings**

1 pound smoked haddock, whitefish, or salmon fillets, skinned and boned

1 cup milk

1 cup water

1 thick strip lemon rind

1 small bay leaf

Salt and freshly ground black pepper to taste

4 tablespoons (½ stick) butter

1 medium onion, finely chopped

¾ cup basmati or long-grain rice

1 teaspoon grated nutmeg

1 cup chicken broth

3 large hard-boiled eggs, finely chopped

⅓ cup finely chopped fresh parsley leaves

½ cup sour cream

Cayenne pepper to taste

1. Place the fish in a large saucepan or skillet and add the milk, water, lemon rind, bay leaf, and salt and pepper. Bring to a boil,

(continued)

reduce the heat to low, and simmer till the fish flakes easily, 12 to 15 minutes. Drain the fish and discard the lemon rind and bay leaf.

2. In a large saucepan, melt half the butter over moderate heat, add the onion, and stir till softened, about 2 minutes. Add the remaining butter, the rice, and nutmeg and stir for about 1 minute. Add the broth, bring to a boil, reduce the heat to low, cover, and cook till the rice has absorbed all the liquid, about 17 minutes.

3. Flake the fish well and add it to the rice. Add the eggs, parsley, sour cream, and cayenne and stir till well blended and hot. Serve immediately.

Retro Tuna and Rice Casserole

Popularized by the Campbell Soup Company during the 1940s and '50s to promote cream of celery soup, the original tuna casserole was made with noodles, green peas, possibly a few chopped pimentos, and a buttered bread crumb topping (not the infamous crushed potato chips). Over the years, the variations have been endless, some delicious, others pretty wretched. My version features flavorful brown rice, green peas, pimentos, canned mushroom soup, and a sensuous cheese topping, and I stand solidly behind its integrity. If the tuna mixture looks a little too thick for your taste, add a little more milk.

Makes 4 servings

1 cup brown rice, cooked according to package directions
One 10¾-ounce can Campbell's cream of mushroom soup
½ cup milk
Two 6-ounce cans chunk light tuna packed in oil, drained and flaked
1 cup frozen green peas, cooked according to package directions and drained
3 tablespoons chopped pimentos
Freshly ground black pepper to taste
2 tablespoons dry bread crumbs
½ cup shredded sharp cheddar cheese

1. Preheat the oven to 375°F. Generously butter a 1½-quart casserole or baking dish.

2. In a large bowl, combine the rice, soup, and milk and mix till well blended. Add the tuna, peas, pimentos, and pepper and stir till well blended. Sprinkle the bread crumbs evenly over the bottom of the prepared casserole and scrape the tuna and rice mixture into the casserole. Sprinkle the cheese evenly over the top, and bake till bubbly and golden, 25 to 30 minutes, and serve hot.

Caribbean Crabmeat Casserole

Makes
6 servings

The chiles, herbs, lime juice, and rum give this crabmeat casserole a distinctive Caribbean personality unlike that of any other version, but what really sets off the delectable flavor is the way the crabmeat is slightly browned during the final baking. Just be careful not to overcook the casserole, which will dry out the crab. More economical but equally delicious for this dish is crab claw meat, so long, that is, as you don't mind picking it over carefully for shells and cartilage.

1 cup milk
2 fresh jalapeño chile peppers, seeded and minced
1 teaspoon dried thyme
1 bay leaf, crumbled
Salt and freshly ground black pepper to taste
2 cups dry bread crumbs
1 pound fresh lump crabmeat, flaked
4 slices bacon
1 small onion, minced
3 tablespoons minced fresh parsley leaves
2 tablespoons fresh lime juice
2 tablespoons light rum
4 tablespoons (½ stick) butter

1. In a saucepan, combine the milk, half the chiles, thyme, bay leaf, and salt and pepper and bring almost to a boil. Reduce the heat to low, simmer for 15 minutes, let cool completely, and strain into a bowl. Add the bread crumbs and let soak for about 15 minutes. Squeeze the bread crumbs almost dry, place in a bowl, add the crabmeat, stir well, and set aside.

2. Preheat the oven to 350°F. Butter a 1½-quart casserole and set aside.

3. In a skillet, fry the bacon over moderate heat till crisp, drain on paper towels, and crumble. Add the bacon, onion, parsley, lime juice, and rum to the crabmeat mixture and stir till well blended.

4. In a large skillet, melt the butter over moderate heat, add the crabmeat mixture, and stir till golden, about 10 minutes. Scrape the mixture into the prepared casserole and bake till lightly browned on top, about 15 minutes.

5. Serve hot.

More economical but equally delicious for this dish is crab claw meat.

Roman Spaghetti Carbonara

One of the most sublime Roman dishes ever conceived, spaghetti carbonara depends as much on chopped pancetta for its integrity as on the right ratio of pasta to sauce. Lean regular bacon can be substituted for the cured, unsmoked, unique Italian-style, but the result will not be the same—even if a little chopped prosciutto is added. Likewise, if you're skittish about eating raw eggs, you're better off choosing another pasta dish. Although a classic carbonara is made with only egg yolks, most Italian chefs today lighten the dish by using whole eggs. Use only genuine Parmigiano-Reggiano cheese for this dish.

**Makes
6 servings**

1 pound dried spaghetti
½ pound pancetta, chopped
1 tablespoon olive oil
2 medium onions, finely chopped
¼ cup chopped fresh parsley leaves
½ pound Fontina cheese, diced
Salt and freshly ground black pepper to taste
4 large eggs, beaten
Grated Parmesan cheese to taste

1. Bring a large pot of salted water to a boil, add the spaghetti, and cook till al dente, about 8 minutes. Remove from the heat.

2. Meanwhile, fry the pancetta in a large skillet over moderate heat till almost crisp, add the oil and onions, and stir till softened, about 5 minutes. Add the parsley, Fontina cheese, and salt and pepper, reduce the heat to low, and simmer for about 10 minutes, stirring often.

3. Drain the spaghetti and transfer to a large serving bowl. Add the eggs and toss till well blended. Add the cheese sauce, toss well again, and serve immediately topped with the Parmesan cheese.

Hungarian Beef Noodle Paprikash

Whether it's made with ground beef, pork, or lamb, a spicy, creamy Hungarian noodle paprikash is not only quick and easy to prepare but also virtually guaranteed to inspire sighs of satisfaction from all concerned. An authentic paprikash always has plenty of zip, meaning that every effort should be made to use a "hot" Hungarian paprika (available in finer markets) instead of the milder, sweeter products that fill most grocery shelves. Some Hungarian cooks like to enhance their paprikash by adding a small chopped dill pickle to the sauce.

Makes
4 servings

3 tablespoons vegetable oil
1 pound ground beef round
2 medium onions, finely chopped
1 medium green bell pepper, seeded and finely chopped
1 garlic clove, minced
3 tablespoons hot paprika
½ teaspoon dried thyme, crumbled
Salt and freshly ground black pepper to taste
3 cups beef broth
½ pound dried egg noodles
1 cup sour cream

In a large skillet, heat the oil over moderate heat, add the beef, and stir till no longer pink, about 10 minutes. Add the onions, bell pepper, garlic, paprika, thyme, and salt and pepper and stir till the vegetables soften, about 7 minutes. Add the broth and noodles, bring to a boil, reduce the heat to low, and simmer till the noodles are tender, about 15 minutes. Add the sour cream, stir till the sauce is thickened, about 3 minutes, and serve immediately.

Midwestern Johnnie Marzetti

Makes
6 servings

Popular throughout much of the American Midwest, this strange ground meat and pasta concoction was most likely created in the 1920s at a restaurant in Columbus, Ohio, called Marzetti's, but the dish's true origins are as vague and varied as its ingredients—depending on which state or city or town you happen to be in. Ground veal, pork, or sausage is used in some versions; virtually any style of pasta is permissible; and the sky's the limit when it comes to the preferred types of cheeses. The bottom line is that when a Johnnie Marzetti (or "Johnnie Mars") is prepared with care, it's one of the best American casseroles around.

¼ cup olive oil
1½ pounds ground beef round
2 medium onions, finely chopped
½ green bell pepper, seeded and finely chopped
½ pound mushrooms, finely chopped
2 garlic cloves, minced
Salt and freshly ground black pepper to taste
One 28-ounce can crushed tomatoes with juice
1 teaspoon dried oregano, crumbled
One ¾-pound package medium-wide dried egg noodles
½ pound Romano cheese, shredded
3 ounces mozzarella cheese, shredded
¼ cup dry bread crumbs
2 tablespoons butter, melted

1. In a large, heavy skillet, heat the oil over moderate heat, add the beef, breaking it up with a fork, and stir for about 5 minutes. Add the onions, bell pepper, mushrooms, garlic, and salt and pepper, stir well, and continue cooking till the beef and vegetables are slightly browned, about 8 minutes. Add the tomatoes and oregano and stir till well blended. Bring to a simmer, cook for about 15 minutes, and remove from the heat.

2. Preheat the oven to 350°F. Grease a 2-quart casserole and set aside.

3. In a large pot of boiling salted water, cook the noodles according to package directions till just tender and drain.

4. Spoon about half the meat sauce over the bottom of the prepared casserole, spread the noodles evenly over the sauce, and sprinkle half the Romano cheese over the top. Spoon the remaining sauce over the noodles and sprinkle the remaining Romano plus the mozzarella over the top.

5. In a small bowl, combine the bread crumbs and butter, toss well, scatter the crumbs over the casserole, and bake till lightly browned, about 30 minutes.

6. Serve hot.

Orecchiette Pasta with Sausage and Wild Mushroom Sauce

Makes 4 to 6
servings

Orecchiette ("little ears" in Italian) is a perfect pasta for holding a rich, earthy sauce such as this one, and while ground beef or pork can be substituted for the sausage, the textural blend of the chunky diced sausage and sturdy pasta is so beguiling that it's a shame not to try the combination. Other pastas appropriate for this type of sauce are rigatoni, fusilli, and farfalle, and any variety of bosky wild mushroom is better than ordinary bland agarics. Also, here is another time when only freshly grated Parmigiano-Reggiano cheese should be used.

¼ cup olive oil
1 pound sweet Italian sausage, finely diced
2 medium onions, finely diced
1 small green bell pepper, seeded and finely diced
2 garlic cloves, minced
½ pound shiitake, cep, or chanterelle mushrooms, diced
½ teaspoon dried oregano, crumbled
Salt and freshly ground black pepper to taste
One 28-ounce can crushed tomatoes with juice
1 pound dried orecchiette
3 tablespoons butter
½ cup grated Parmesan cheese

1. In a large, heavy skillet, heat the oil over moderate heat, add the sausage, and stir till lightly browned, about 10 minutes. Add the onions, bell pepper, garlic, mushrooms, oregano, and salt and pepper and stir till the vegetables are golden and the mushrooms begin to brown, 8 to 10 minutes. Add the tomatoes and stir well. Bring to a boil, reduce the heat to low, and simmer for about 20 minutes, stirring several times.

2. Meanwhile, in a large pot of boiling salted water, cook the pasta according to package directions. Drain, place the pasta in a large bowl, add the butter, and toss till well coated. Add the sausage and mushroom sauce, toss till well blended, and serve piping hot in individual bowls with the Parmesan sprinkled over the tops.

Greek Pastitsio

This spicy, layered meat and pasta casserole is one of the glories of classic Greek cuisine, and, made in quantity, one of the best and most unusual ways I know to feed a crowd. Every region of Greece produces a different pastitsio, some made with ground pork, rabbit, or lamb; others with added chopped mushrooms or eggplant; and still others with more exotic pastas and cheeses. One secret to any great pastitsio is to bake the casserole just till the sauce is set and the filling is still soft and not at all dried out. No more is needed with this dish than a big tossed green salad or bowl of marinated dilled cucumbers.

**Makes
6 servings**

½ pound dried elbow macaroni

2 tablespoons olive oil

2 medium onions, finely chopped

1 pound ground beef chuck

One 14½-ounce can crushed tomatoes with juice

¼ teaspoon ground cinnamon

¼ teaspoon grated nutmeg

Salt and freshly ground black pepper to taste

4 large eggs

½ cup grated Parmesan cheese

2 tablespoons butter

1 teaspoon cornstarch

1½ cups milk, heated

1. Preheat the oven to 350°F. Grease a 12 by 9 by 2-inch baking dish and set aside.

2. In a pot of boiling salted water, cook the macaroni according to package directions and drain.

3. Meanwhile, heat the oil in a large skillet over moderate heat, add the onions, and stir till softened, about 5 minutes. Add the beef and stir till browned, about 5 minutes. Add the tomatoes and stir till most of the liquid has been absorbed, about 5 minutes. Add the cinnamon, nutmeg, and salt and pepper and stir well. In a bowl, whisk 2 of the eggs till frothy and, stirring constantly, add them to the meat mixture. Add half of the cheese and stir till well blended. Add the macaroni, mix well, and transfer to the prepared baking dish.

4. In a saucepan, melt the butter over moderately low heat, add the cornstarch, and stir till well blended. Gradually add the milk, whisking till slightly thickened. Whisking constantly, add the remaining 2 eggs and whisk till the sauce is smooth. Pour the sauce over the meat and macaroni mixture, sprinkle the remaining cheese over the top, and bake till the sauce is set and the top is golden, 40 to 45 minutes.

5. Let cool for about 10 minutes, then cut the pastitsio into squares.

One secret to any great pastitsio is to bake the casserole just till the sauce is set and the filling is still soft and not at all dried out.

Classic Chicken and Pasta Tetrazzini

Makes
6 servings

Created in either San Francisco or Charleston, South Carolina, for the coloratura soprano Luisa Tetrazzini when she toured America in the early twentieth century, chicken Tetrazzini was a rich, elaborate concoction involving the meat and giblets of a long-simmered hen, mushrooms, possibly nuts and olives, and a heavy sherry-Parmesan cheese sauce—all tossed with plenty of boiled spaghetti and topped with even more cheese. My version maintains the basic spirit of the original but is much easier to make and lighter as well as being one of the best ways I know to use up leftover roast chicken or turkey or even baked ham. If you do want to gild the lily by sprinkling extra Parmesan over the top, go right ahead. Do notice that this is not a layered but a mixed casserole.

6 tablespoons (¾ stick) butter
¼ pound mushrooms, chopped
¼ cup all-purpose flour
1 teaspoon salt
Freshly ground black pepper to taste
¼ teaspoon grated nutmeg
1 cup chicken broth
1 cup milk
1½ pounds cooked chicken, finely diced
½ cup black olives, drained, pitted, and chopped
½ cup slivered almonds
½ cup grated Parmesan cheese
1 large egg yolk, beaten
½ pound dried spaghetti or linguine

1. Preheat the oven to 350°F. Butter a 2-quart casserole and set aside.

2. In a small skillet, melt 2 tablespoons of the butter over moderate heat, add the mushrooms, stir for 5 minutes, and remove from the heat.

3. In a large, heavy pot, melt the remaining 4 tablespoons butter over moderate heat, add the flour, salt, pepper, and nutmeg, and stir for 1 minute. Gradually add the broth and milk and stir till the sauce begins to thicken, 5 to 7 minutes. Remove the pot from the heat, add the mushrooms, chicken, olives, almonds, cheese, and egg yolk, and stir till well blended.

4. In a large pot of boiling salted water, cook the pasta according to package directions for about 8 minutes, drain, and place in the prepared casserole. Pour the chicken mixture over the top, toss to mix well, and bake till crusty, 25 to 30 minutes.

5. Serve piping hot.

Creole Macaroni and Cheese with Crawfish

Makes 4 to 6 servings

This Creole variation of mac and cheese not only is intriguing but also couldn't be easier to make as a last-minute main course. Frozen crawfish tails can now be found in better markets and do have a distinctive flavor and texture, but if you have a problem finding them, use fresh shrimp.

> 1 pound dried elbow macaroni
> 3 tablespoons butter
> ½ pound extra-sharp cheddar cheese, grated
> 4 large eggs, beaten
> 1 cup milk
> 1 tablespoon Worcestershire sauce
> 1 pound frozen crawfish tails, thawed, peeled, and chopped
> Freshly ground black pepper to taste
> Tabasco sauce to taste

1. Preheat the oven to 350°F. Butter a 1½-quart casserole or baking dish.

2. In a large pot of boiling salted water, cook the macaroni according to package directions, drain, add the butter, and stir till the butter melts. Transfer the noodles to the prepared casserole, add the cheese, eggs, milk, Worcestershire, crawfish tails, pepper, and Tabasco, stir till well blended, and bake till bubbly and golden brown, 40 to 45 minutes.

3. Serve piping hot.

Chinese Pork Fried Rice

Fried rice with various diced cooked meats is a popular concept all over China, and when the dish is prepared with care, it's a far cry from the stodgy versions found in so many Chinese take-out locations in this country. Diced cooked beef, chicken, or shrimp can also be used in this recipe, as well as diced broccoli florets, bell peppers, mushrooms, or more exotic Chinese vegetables. Do note that this is one Chinese dish in which the grains of rice should not be viscous and sticky but relatively loose and dry. I like to serve this fried rice with no more than fresh pears and crisp Chinese wontons.

2 tablespoons soy sauce
1 tablespoon hoisin sauce
1 teaspoon rice vinegar
3 tablespoons peanut oil
2 large eggs, beaten
1 medium onion, minced
1 medium red bell pepper, seeded and minced
2 garlic cloves, minced
½ pound cooked pork, finely diced
4 cups cooked rice
One 10-ounce package green peas, thawed

1. In a small bowl, combine the soy sauce, hoisin sauce, and vinegar, stir till well blended, and set aside.

2. In a large skillet, heat 1 tablespoon of the oil over moderately high heat, add the eggs, and let them set for 1 minute. Stir till cooked (do not scramble), transfer to a plate, and cut into thin strips.

(continued)

I like to serve this fried rice with no more than fresh pears and crisp Chinese wontons.

3. Add the remaining 2 tablespoons oil to the skillet, reduce the heat slightly, add the onion, bell pepper, and garlic, and stir till softened, about 2 minutes. Add the pork and rice, stir well, and add the soy sauce mixture. Add the peas and stir till they are bright green and crisp-tender, about 3 minutes. Remove pan from the heat, stir in the egg strips, and serve immediately.

Hashes and Chilies

Chicken Hash with Almonds

Makes
4 servings

Chicken hash, like the roast beef or corned beef versions, can be crusted on one or both sides, but since it's so easy to dry out cooked chicken (and turkey) when transforming it into a hash, I much prefer to let it absorb the sauce in the skillet and maintain a soft, creamy texture. For this chicken hash, I like both the chicken and potatoes cut into fairly small dice, especially if you plan to serve it over toast—always an option.

2 medium boiling potatoes
3 tablespoons butter
1 medium onion, finely chopped
2 tablespoons all-purpose flour
2 cups chicken broth
¼ cup heavy cream
3 cups diced cooked chicken breasts
Salt and freshly ground black pepper to taste
¼ cup sliced toasted almonds

1. Peel and dice the potatoes and place in a saucepan with enough water to cover. Bring to a boil, reduce the heat to moderate, cook till tender, 6 to 8 minutes, and drain.

2. In a large, heavy skillet, melt the butter over moderate heat, add the onion, and stir till softened, about 2 minutes. Sprinkle the flour over the top and stir 2 to 3 minutes longer. Add the broth, bring to a boil, reduce the heat to moderate, and stir for about 3 minutes. Add the cream and stir about 1 minute longer. Add the potatoes, chicken, and salt and pepper and cook till the sauce is absorbed and the hash is quite firm but still moist, about 8 minutes.

3. To serve, transfer the hash to a serving platter, sprinkle the almonds over the top, and serve hot.

Parmesan Turkey Hash with Olives

I often think that the noble turkey exists mainly to make sumptuous sandwiches, salads, hashes, and casseroles with the leftovers, and nothing illustrates the principle better than this crusty hash enhanced with black olives, tarragon, and Parmesan cheese. The hash is great as is for a casual brunch or Sunday supper, but to make it a bit more elegant, you can either sprinkle a few extra tablespoons of Parmesan on the top and glaze the hash quickly under the broiler, or you can serve the portions topped with poached eggs sprinkled lightly with paprika. As with any good hash, the interior of this one should remain slightly soft and moist, while the exteriors should be nicely browned and crusted.

Makes 4 servings

2 tablespoons bacon grease
1 medium onion, minced
½ small green bell pepper, seeded and minced
1 garlic clove, minced
2 cups finely diced cooked turkey
2 cups mashed potatoes
½ cup finely diced pitted black olives
¼ cup grated Parmesan cheese
1 tablespoon minced fresh parsley leaves
¼ teaspoon minced fresh tarragon leaves
Salt and freshly ground black pepper to taste

1. In a large, heavy skillet, heat the bacon grease over moderate heat, add the onion, bell pepper, and garlic, and cook, stirring, till softened, about 8 minutes. Add the turkey, potatoes, and olives and cook, stirring, for 5 minutes longer. Add the cheese, parsley, tarragon, and salt and pepper and stir till well blended.

(continued)

Hashes and Chilies

2. Using a heavy spatula, press the mixture down and let cook till a brown crust forms on the bottom, about 10 minutes. Using two heavy spatulas, carefully flip the hash over in the skillet and cook till the other side is crusted, 8 to 10 minutes.

3. Slide the hash onto a plate, cut into 4 portions, and serve immediately.

Coffee Shop Corned Beef Hash

No old-fashioned coffee shop is worth its coarse meat loaf and chunky applesauce that doesn't also serve a compact, crusty corned beef hash—preferably topped with a poached or fried egg. All the major ingredients for this hash should be finely chopped, and to allow the flavors to blend and the texture to develop, it's always a good idea to chill this mixture for at least several hours before crusting the hash over fairly low heat. Of course, few short-order cooks today would take the extra time required to crust the hash slowly while keeping the interior relatively moist, but such an effort does make a difference.

> Makes
> 4 servings

1 pound lean cooked corned beef, finely chopped
2 medium boiled potatoes, finely chopped
1 medium onion, finely chopped
1 small green bell pepper, seeded and finely chopped
1 small dill pickle, minced
½ cup evaporated milk
⅛ teaspoon grated nutmeg
Salt and freshly ground black pepper to taste
3 tablespoons butter

1. In a large bowl, combine the corned beef, potatoes, onion, bell pepper, pickle, milk, nutmeg, and salt and pepper; mix till well blended, cover with plastic wrap, and chill for several hours or overnight.

2. In a heavy 12-inch skillet, melt the butter over low to moderately low heat, spread the corned beef mixture evenly in the skillet, press down firmly with a spatula, and brown till the underside is crusty, 20 to 25 minutes. Fold over in half like an omelette, slide onto a heated serving platter, and serve immediately.

> Hashes
> and Chilies

New England Red Flannel Roast Beef Hash

**Makes
4 servings**

Even James Beard was mystified by the origins of red flannel hash, wondering if the New England classic was correctly made with corned beef leftovers from a boiled dinner, the remains of a beef roast, or, indeed, even codfish. What is for sure is that any red flannel hash must have plenty of diced cooked beets, and that some recipes even insist that up to 85 percent of the volume should be beets. My particular recipe is inspired by the version at the Copley Plaza Hotel in Boston, where the hash was always served with hot cornbread, and I still have never tasted a better one. For the right compact texture, do make sure the major ingredients are finely diced.

3 slices bacon
1½ cups finely diced cooked beets
2½ cups finely diced boiled potatoes
1 medium onion, finely diced
2 cups finely diced roast beef
3 sprigs parsley, finely chopped
¼ teaspoon dried thyme, crumbled
Salt and freshly ground black pepper to taste
1 large egg
¼ cup heavy cream
1 tablespoon butter

1. In a large, heavy skillet, fry the bacon over moderate heat till crisp, drain on paper towels, crumble, and pour off all but about 2 tablespoons of fat from the skillet.

2. In a large bowl, combine the bacon, beets, potatoes, onion, roast beef, half the parsley, thyme, and salt and pepper, and mix till well blended. In a small bowl, beat the egg and cream together till frothy, add to the beet mixture, and stir till well blended. Divide the mixture into 4 rounds and press each down slightly with the palm of your hand.

3. Add the butter to the fat in the skillet over moderate heat, add the beef rounds, press each down further with a spatula to form cakes, and cook till crusty brown, about 10 minutes on each side. Transfer the hash to a heated platter, sprinkle the remaining parsley over the tops, and serve hot.

Swedish *Pitt i Panna* Meat Hash

Makes
4 servings

In Sweden, this popular hash can be made with finely diced cooked beef, lamb, ham, or a combination of all three, and some chefs insist that the hash is not authentic unless it is mixed with raw egg yolks. Instead, I bind the mixture with a little cream and serve the hash topped with poached eggs. Delectable!

2 tablespoons butter
2 tablespoons vegetable oil
5 medium potatoes, peeled and finely diced
1 large leek (white part only), rinsed well and finely diced
1 pound cooked beef or lamb, finely diced
½ pound cooked ham, finely diced
¼ cup heavy cream
1 tablespoon minced fresh parsley leaves
Salt and freshly ground black pepper to taste
4 poached eggs, kept warm

1. In a large, heavy skillet, heat the butter and oil over moderate heat, add the potatoes, fry till crisp and golden, stirring, about 15 minutes, and drain on paper towels. Add the leek to the skillet and stir till softened, about 3 minutes. Add the two meats and stir till lightly browned on all sides, about 10 minutes. Stir in the potatoes, cream, parsley, and salt and pepper and stir about 5 minutes longer.

2. To serve, mound equal amounts of hash on heated serving plates, make a depression in the center of each serving, and spoon an egg into each depression.

Lake Superior Mincemeat

Rich, spicy mincemeats have been made for centuries in European countries as a way of preserving meats and fruits intended for stuffings, pies, and puddings, and when the first settlers came to Minnesota and northern Michigan, they brought the tradition with them. Commercial mincemeat from the region is sold in jars at most grocery stores during the Thanksgiving and Christmas holidays, but none is as good as a homemade version that is allowed to mellow for a few weeks and used as a filling or cocktail spread. Because of its slightly sweet savor, I think ground buffalo (more and more available) particularly appropriate for mincemeat, but of course, virtually any form of beef or game can be used. Packed into tightly sealed decorative jars, mincemeat also makes an unusual and attractive gift.

Makes about 6 pints

1½ pounds ground beef round, venison, or buffalo

¼ pound beef suet, finely ground

2 tart apples, finely chopped

3 cups seedless golden raisins

1 cup chopped walnuts

2 cups packed light brown sugar

1 cup granulated sugar

3 cups apple cider

½ cup cider vinegar

¼ cup light rum

2 teaspoons salt

2 teaspoons ground cinnamon

2 teaspoons grated nutmeg

1 teaspoon ground cloves

1 teaspoon ground allspice

Freshly ground black pepper to taste

(continued)

In a large pot, combine all the ingredients and stir well. Bring to a boil, stirring, reduce the heat to low, cover, and simmer for about 2 hours, stirring from time to time. Let the mincemeat cool, then store in airtight containers in the refrigerator for up to 2 weeks or in the freezer for up to 1 year.

Pork, Bacon, and Sausage Hash with Apples

Ideal for breakfast or a casual brunch buffet, this spicy hash topped with chopped hard-boiled egg and served with buttery soft apple rings is made with three different types of pork for ultimate flavor. Be sure to use a cast-iron skillet for preparing this hash, and since the texture should be fairly loose and moist, don't try to crust both sides by turning it over in the skillet.

Makes 4 to 6 servings

3 slices bacon
1 medium onion, minced
1 garlic clove, minced
2 medium ripe tomatoes, peeled, seeded, and chopped
1 fresh red chile pepper, seeded and minced
1½ pounds lean pork, finely chopped
½ pound smoked pork sausage links, casings removed and finely chopped
3 tablespoons fresh lemon juice
Pinch of ground cloves
1 large hard-boiled egg, finely chopped
2 apples
2 tablespoons butter

1. In a large, cast-iron skillet, fry the bacon over moderate heat till almost crisp, drain on paper towels, and chop finely.

2. Pour off all but about 2 tablespoons of fat from the skillet, add the onion and garlic, and stir for 2 minutes. Add the tomatoes and chile pepper, stir well, and simmer till the mixture is thickened, about 8 minutes. Add the pork, sausage, bacon, lemon juice, and cloves and continue cooking for about 20 minutes, stirring often. During the final 10 minutes of simmering, preheat the oven broiler.

(continued)

Be sure
to use a
cast-iron
skillet for
preparing
this hash.

3. Brown the hash under the broiler till slightly crusty on top, about 5 minutes, transfer to a large serving platter, sprinkle with the chopped egg, and keep warm.

4. Core the apples and slice them into thin rings. In a large skillet, melt the butter over low heat, add the apples, and cook on both sides till golden, about 10 minutes total. Arrange the apples around the edges of the hash and serve immediately.

Seattle Geoduck Clam Hash

Indigenous to the coast of the Pacific Northwest, a vile-looking clam called geoduck (pronounced "gooey-duck") has a shell that measures about 6 inches and a neck that can extend up to 1½ feet long. Since the neck meat is as tough as abalone, it is either pounded for steaks or ground to make chowders and hashes, and more than once I've raved about the crusty hashes with this monster clam that are made in modest restaurants all over Seattle. Since the likelihood of finding even frozen geoduck outside the region is remote, you'll have to settle for minced littleneck, chowder, or steamer clams to make this hash. The results, however, are still impressive if you love fresh clams as much as I do.

**Makes
4 servings**

6 slices bacon
3 tablespoons butter
1 small onion, finely chopped
2 cups diced boiled potatoes
2½ cups minced fresh clams
Salt and freshly ground black pepper to taste
¾ cup heavy cream
4 large egg yolks

1. Preheat the oven broiler.

2. In a large, heavy skillet with a metal handle, fry the bacon over moderate heat till crisp, drain on paper towels, and crumble.

3. Pour off all but about 1 tablespoon of fat from the skillet and melt the butter in the fat. Add the onion and stir till softened, about 2 minutes. Add the potatoes and stir till golden, about 8 minutes. Add the clams and salt and pepper, stir for about 2 minutes, and
(continued)

press the mixture down with a spatula. In a small bowl, beat the cream and egg yolks together till frothy, pour over the clam mixture, cover, and cook till the custard is set, 2 to 3 minutes. Brown the hash under the broiler till slightly crispy on top, loosen the edges with the spatula, slide onto a heated serving platter, and sprinkle the crumbled bacon over the top.

4. Serve hot.

Texas Three-Alarm Chili

This is a classic Texas "bowl of red," the granddaddy of all American chilies, and since the chili freezes so beautifully, I can't imagine making it for less than eight people and preferably for up to a dozen. The alarm number of any chili (one to five) refers to its hot spiciness, so while I prefer a good jolt without the risk of incinerating my guests' palates, by all means adjust the chile peppers and Tabasco to suit tastes. Be sure to use only beef chuck for any Texas chili, and remember that long, slow simmering (at least 1 hour) is as important for success as the ingredients. As to whether genuine Texas chili should contain beans, I refuse to debate the heated issue. As to whether such toppings as grated cheddar cheese and chopped raw red onions are appropriate, why not?

**Makes at least
8 servings**

2 pounds ground beef chuck
2 large onions, finely chopped
2 garlic cloves, minced
2 medium green bell peppers, seeded and finely chopped
2 small fresh jalapeño chile peppers, seeded and finely chopped
8 tablespoons chili powder
2 teaspoons ground cumin
1 teaspoon dried oregano, crumbled
½ teaspoon ground coriander
½ teaspoon ground allspice
1 teaspoon salt
Freshly ground black pepper to taste
Tabasco sauce to taste
2 tablespoons cider vinegar
One 28-ounce can crushed tomatoes with juice
1 cup water
Two 16-ounce cans red kidney beans with liquid

(continued)

Hashes
and Chilies

1. In a large, heavy pot, break up the beef over moderate heat, stir till the meat has lost its pink color, and drain off all but about 2 tablespoons of fat. Add the onions, garlic, bell peppers, and jalapeños to the pot and stir till softened, about 10 minutes. Add all the remaining ingredients and stir well. Bring to a boil, reduce the heat to low, cover, and let the chili simmer for at least 1 hour, stirring frequently.

2. Serve piping hot in soup bowls.

Cincinnati Chili

People either love or hate Cincinnati chili, and while there can be no doubt that it is one of the strangest concoctions ever devised (exactly by whom remains debatable) in American gastronomy, it's also true that it can be one of our most subtle and delicious dishes when prepared carefully. In Cincinnati, the chili is made with either ground beef or lamb, and depending on who's making it, can be topped with not only grated cheddar cheese but also boiled kidney beans. All options are open with this chili, the one exception being the cocoa powder, without which the chili would lose its distinctive personality.

Makes 6 to 8 servings

3 tablespoons olive oil
2 medium onions, finely chopped
1 garlic clove, minced
2 pounds ground beef round or lamb shoulder
2 tablespoons chili powder
2 tablespoons unsweetened cocoa powder
1 tablespoon ground cumin
¼ teaspoon ground cinnamon
¼ teaspoon ground allspice
One 28-ounce can crushed tomatoes with juice
1 tablespoon tomato paste
2 tablespoons red wine vinegar
Salt and freshly ground black pepper to taste
1 pound dried spaghetti
6 ounces sharp cheddar cheese, grated (optional)

1. In a large, heavy pot or casserole, heat the oil over moderate heat, add the onions and garlic, and stir till softened, about 3 minutes. Add the meat and stir till browned, about 10 minutes. Add

(continued)

the chili powder, cocoa, cumin, cinnamon, and allspice and stir 1 minute longer. Add the tomatoes, tomato paste, vinegar, and salt and pepper, bring to a simmer, and cook the chili, uncovered, for 25 to 30 minutes. Remove the pot from the heat.

2. Shortly before serving, cook the spaghetti in a large pot of boiling salted water according to package directions and drain well. Divide the pasta among shallow serving bowls, top each with equal amounts of the chili, sprinkle the optional cheese over the top, and serve immediately.

Mexican Pork and Corn Chili

Mexicans were simmering pork and corn together hundreds of years before American pioneers combined the first ground or chopped beef and beans to make what we know as chili con carne, and today, chili made with ground pork and corn is still a staple south of the border (and in most southwestern American states). What gives this particular version a bit of distinction is the subtle flavor of beer, and the only things you need to serve with it are plenty of corn sticks and perhaps a few chopped jalapeños to sprinkle over the top.

**Makes
6 servings**

3 tablespoons corn oil
2 pounds ground lean pork
2 medium onions, finely chopped
1 small green bell pepper, seeded and finely chopped
2 garlic cloves, minced
2 tablespoons chili powder
2 teaspoons dried oregano
2 teaspoons ground cumin
Salt and freshly ground black pepper to taste
Tabasco sauce to taste
One 28-ounce can crushed tomatoes with juice
1 cup beer
½ cup beef broth
One 10-ounce package frozen corn kernels, thawed

1. In a large, heavy casserole or pot, heat the oil over moderate heat, add the pork, and brown, stirring. Add the onions, bell pepper, and garlic and stir till softened, about 5 minutes. Add the chili powder, oregano, cumin, salt and pepper, Tabasco,
(continued)

tomatoes, beer, and broth, bring to a boil, reduce the heat to low, cover, and simmer for about 1 hour.

2. Add the corn, stir, return the chili to a simmer, cover, and cook about 30 minutes longer or till the chili has the desired consistency.

3. Serve piping hot in soup bowls.

Italian-American Chili

In Italy, chickpeas (or garbanzos) are used to make not only minestrone but also all sorts of salads and stews, so it's little wonder that when Italian-Americans added chili to their many culinary adaptations, they substituted these buff-colored, nutty-flavored legumes for kidney beans. Just ten years ago, you would probably have had to grind your own Italian sausage for this chili, but today the ground product is available in virtually all markets. Although the chili can be made exclusively with sausage, the ground chicken does enhance the texture.

**Makes
6 servings**

3 tablespoons olive oil
1 pound ground hot Italian sausage (or links, casings removed and meat ground)
½ pound ground chicken
1 large onion, finely chopped
1 cup finely chopped fennel bulb
1 tablespoon balsamic vinegar
2 tablespoons finely chopped fresh basil leaves
2 tablespoons finely chopped fresh oregano leaves
1 teaspoon ground cumin
Salt and freshly ground black pepper to taste
2 cups canned chickpeas, drained
One 14½-ounce can crushed tomatoes with juice
1 cup chicken broth

1. In a large, heavy pot, heat the oil over moderate heat, add the sausage and chicken, and stir till lightly browned. Add the onion and fennel and stir till softened, about 5 minutes. Add the vinegar, basil, oregano, cumin, and salt and pepper, and stir till well blended. Add the chickpeas, tomatoes, and broth, bring to a boil, reduce the heat to low, cover, and simmer for about 45 minutes.

2. Serve hot in soup bowls.

Peruvian Chicken Chili with Peanuts

Makes
6 servings

Made with ground, chopped, or shredded chicken and lots of roasted peanuts, *ají de gallina* is a form of chili found all over Peru and one of the most delectable dishes anywhere. Typically, evaporated milk is used instead of crushed tomatoes to tame the garlic and jalapeños, and the suave chili is almost always served with wedges of hard-boiled eggs and black olives. Be warned that this chili has a real kick if you use all the jalapeños in the authentic recipe. Feel free to adjust.

¼ cup peanut oil

2 pounds ground chicken

2 medium onions, finely chopped

6 garlic cloves, minced

2 fresh jalapeño chile peppers, seeded and liquefied in a food processor

2 fresh jalapeño chile peppers, seeded and minced

1 teaspoon ground cumin

½ teaspoon ground allspice

Salt and freshly ground black pepper to taste

2 cups roasted chopped peanuts

½ cup grated Parmesan cheese

1 cup chicken broth

1 cup evaporated milk

1. In a large pot, heat the oil over moderate heat, add the chicken, and brown lightly, breaking it up with a fork. Add the onions, garlic, both the liquefied and minced jalapeños, cumin, allspice, and salt and pepper, and stir till the vegetables soften, about 5 minutes. Add the peanuts, cheese, broth, and milk, bring to a simmer, cover, and cook till the chili is smooth, 30 to 40 minutes.

2. Serve hot in soup plates.

Turkey Chili

I think I must have been inspired to come up with this meatless chili when I saw the first package of ground turkey in a grocery store case and wanted to use it to prepare something besides burgers. Since then, I've served the chili at more than one casual luncheon with a salad and warm tortillas, and I can only say there's never a spoonful left in the pot. By no means leave out the carrot, which along with the raisins gives the chili a subtle and appealing sweetness.

Makes 4 to 6 servings

3 tablespoons corn oil
1 pound ground turkey
1 medium onion, finely chopped
1 celery rib, finely chopped
1 small green bell pepper, seeded and finely chopped
1 carrot, scraped and finely chopped
1 garlic clove, minced
1 tablespoon chili powder
1 teaspoon ground cumin
Salt and freshly ground black pepper to taste
One 28-ounce can crushed tomatoes with juice
½ cup seedless golden raisins
One 15-ounce can red kidney beans, drained
Sour cream for garnish

1. In a large, heavy pot, heat the oil over moderate heat, add the turkey, breaking it up with a fork, and stir till lightly browned. Add the onion, celery, bell pepper, carrot, and garlic and stir till softened, about 5 minutes. Add the chili powder, cumin, salt and pepper, and tomatoes, stir well, reduce the heat to low, cover, and simmer for 30 minutes. Add the raisins and beans, return to a simmer, cover, and cook about 20 minutes longer.

2. Serve hot in soup bowls with dollops of sour cream on top.

Indian Lamb Chili

Makes
6 servings

Popular throughout India, *kheema* is like chili con carne made with ground lamb instead of beef and without the beans and chili powder. Instead, the dish might well include a few diced potatoes, chopped mushrooms, or green peas, and the seasoning is a virtual explosion of herbs and spices. Grated fresh ginger is essential to the right flavor of this chili, and if you love curry, it's not unheard-of for Indian chefs to add a teaspoon or so of curry powder to their *kheema*.

3 tablespoons vegetable oil
2 medium onions, finely chopped
3 garlic cloves, minced
1 small fresh hot chile pepper, seeded and finely chopped
2 pounds finely ground lamb
¼ teaspoon grated fresh ginger
¼ teaspoon ground cinnamon
¼ teaspoon ground cloves
1 bay leaf, crumbled
1 teaspoon ground coriander
½ teaspoon ground cumin
½ teaspoon ground turmeric
One 28-ounce can crushed tomatoes with juice
½ cup water
1 tablespoon fresh lemon juice
Salt and freshly ground black pepper to taste

1. In a large, heavy skillet, heat the oil over moderate heat, add the onions, garlic, and chile pepper, and stir till softened, about 5 minutes. Add the lamb, break up the lumps with a fork and blend well with the vegetables, and stir till the meat is browned, about 10 minutes. Add the ginger, cinnamon, cloves, and bay leaf and stir for about 5 minutes. Add the coriander, cumin, and turmeric and stir 5 minutes longer. Add the tomatoes, water, lemon juice, and salt and pepper and stir well. Bring to a boil, reduce the heat to low, cover, and simmer slowly for about 1 hour.

2. Serve hot in soup bowls.

Stuffed Dishes and Forcemeats

French Veal Birds

While living in France as a youngster when classic French cooking was the norm everywhere, nothing intrigued me more than these herby veal roll-ups, quaintly called *oiseaux sans têtes* ("headless birds"). They could be made with ground veal, pork, chicken, or even sweetbreads in finer restaurants, but I loved none more than those stuffed with spicy pork sausage meat that were served at my neighborhood bistro in Grenoble. If you grind your own sausage, be sure to add some crushed red pepper flakes or cayenne, and if you use a commercial product, choose the style labeled "hot." These birds can be partially baked in advance, then finished off when ready to be served.

Makes
6 servings

½ pound bulk pork sausage

2 medium onions, finely chopped

2 garlic cloves, minced

1 teaspoon dried thyme, crumbled

½ teaspoon dried rosemary, crumbled

½ teaspoon ground fennel seeds

1 cup bread crumbs

2 large eggs, beaten

2 tablespoons finely chopped fresh parsley leaves, plus more for garnish

Salt and freshly ground black pepper to taste

4 tablespoons (½ stick) butter

2 medium ripe tomatoes, peeled and seeded

1 cup finely chopped mushrooms

1½ cups beef broth

1 bay leaf

6 veal cutlets (about 1½ pounds)

¼ cup dry white wine

1. In a skillet, break up the sausage with a fork and stir over moderate heat till browned. Drain on paper towels, place in a bowl, and pour off the fat from the skillet. Add to the sausage half the onions, half the garlic, half the thyme, the rosemary, fennel, bread crumbs, eggs, parsley, and salt and pepper, mix till thoroughly blended, and set the stuffing aside.

2. Melt half the butter in the skillet over moderate heat, add the remaining onions and garlic, and stir for about 2 minutes. Add the remaining thyme, the tomatoes, mushrooms, broth, and bay leaf, and simmer the sauce for 12 to 15 minutes, stirring occasionally. Remove the bay leaf and set the sauce aside.

3. Preheat the oven to 350°F.

4. Place the cutlets between sheets of wax paper on a work surface and pound them lightly with a mallet till quite thin. Spread the cutlets out, add equal amounts of the stuffing to the center of each, roll the meat up over the stuffing, tucking in the edges, and tie the birds securely with string.

5. In a large, enameled baking dish, melt the remaining butter over moderate heat, add the birds, and brown on all sides. Add the sauce and wine, cover the dish, and bake for 1 hour.

6. To serve, remove the string from the birds and sprinkle parsley over the tops.

If you grind your own sausage, be sure to add some crushed red pepper flakes or cayenne.

Stuffed Dishes
and Forcemeats

Mexican Chicken Enchiladas

Makes
6 servings

These classic enchiladas are just as good made with ground beef or pork, and if you want to make them a bit fancier, add about ¼ cup of heavy cream to the tomato sauce and reserve a little of the stuffing to spoon over the tops. Do note that it takes only a minute or so to soften the tortillas in the oil; any longer and they will be soggy.

¼ cup corn oil
1 pound ground chicken
1 medium onion, minced
1 small green bell pepper, seeded and minced
1 garlic clove, minced
2 teaspoons chili powder
½ teaspoon ground cumin
½ teaspoon dried oregano, crumbled
Salt and freshly ground black pepper to taste
One 8-ounce can tomato sauce
6 corn tortillas

1. In a large skillet, heat 2 tablespoons of the oil over moderate heat, add the chicken, breaking it up with a fork, and stir till lightly browned. Add the onion, bell pepper, and garlic and stir till softened, about 3 minutes. Add the chili powder, cumin, oregano, salt and pepper, and tomato sauce, bring to a simmer, and cook for about 20 minutes, stirring from time to time.

2. Meanwhile, heat the remaining 2 tablespoons oil in another large skillet over moderately high heat, add the tortillas one at a time, cook just till softened, about 1 minute on each side, and drain on paper towels.

3. Stuff the tortillas with equal amounts of the chicken mixture, roll them up seam sides down, and serve hot.

Burmese Stuffed Zucchini

Due partly to religious restrictions, the Burmese eat very little meat, and when you do find beef or pork dishes in more cosmopolitan cities like Mandalay, they're usually in the form of small kabobs or sectioned vegetables stuffed with spicy ground meat mixtures such as this one used to enhance thick rounds of zucchini. If you want a more substantial and authentic stuffing, eliminate the flour and substitute about ½ cup of cooked rice.

Makes
6 servings

1 pound ground beef chuck
1 medium onion, minced
1 to 2 tablespoons all-purpose flour
1 tablespoon paprika
¼ teaspoon grated fresh ginger
¼ teaspoon ground cloves
Salt and freshly ground black pepper to taste
4 large zucchini, about 6 inches long and 3 inches in diameter, rinsed
¼ cup peanut oil
½ cup water

1. In a large skillet, break up the meat with a fork and stir over moderate heat till browned. Add the onion and stir till softened, about 2 minutes. Sprinkle the flour, paprika, ginger, cloves, and salt and pepper over the top and stir about 1 minute longer. Transfer the stuffing to a bowl and mix till thoroughly blended and smooth. Wipe out the skillet.

2. Cut the zucchini crosswise into 2-inch rounds and scrape out the seeds in the center, leaving a shell about ¼ inch thick all the way around. Stuff equal amounts of the stuffing into the center
(continued)

of each round, pressing with your fingers to compact it as firmly as possible.

3. Heat the oil in the skillet over moderate heat, add the water, and place the zucchini rounds in the liquid. Bring to a simmer and cook the rounds till the water evaporates and only the oil remains, turning them carefully to allow for cooking on both sides, 10 to 12 minutes. Continue cooking just till lightly browned and serve immediately.

Belgian Meat-Stuffed Tomatoes

While I relish nothing more in Brussels than perching on an outdoor terrace during summer and eating a ripe, juicy tomato stuffed with tiny, sweet North Sea shrimp lightly dressed with fresh mayonnaise, when my appetite is really on edge, I'm just as likely to opt for a more substantial perfect tomato stuffed with an herby meat mixture and served typically on a bed of buttered rice. If you like, you can use the remaining tomato pulp to mix with a little seasoned minced bell pepper and parsley to make a sauce in a blender or food processor to be spooned over the crusty tops.

Makes
4 servings

4 large ripe tomatoes
2 tablespoons butter
½ pound ground pork
½ pound ground veal
1 small onion, minced
1 garlic clove, minced
1 slice white bread, soaked in ¼ cup milk and squeezed dry
1 large egg, beaten
1 tablespoon minced fresh parsley leaves
1 teaspoon minced fresh basil leaves
1 teaspoon minced fresh thyme leaves
Salt and freshly ground black pepper to taste

1. Cut a ½-inch lid off the stem end of each tomato and scoop out most of the pulp, leaving walls about ¼ inch thick. Discard the lids and reserve about ½ cup of the pulp.

2. Preheat the oven to 350°F. Butter a medium baking dish and set aside.

(continued)

3. In a large skillet, melt the butter over moderate heat, add the meats, and stir till lightly browned, breaking up any clumps. Add the onion and garlic, stir till softened, about 2 minutes, and transfer the mixture to a bowl. Add the reserved tomato pulp plus all remaining ingredients and stir till well blended.

4. Stuff the tomatoes with equal amounts of the meat mixture, arrange in the prepared baking dish, and bake till slightly crusted on top, 35 to 40 minutes.

5. Serve hot.

Jamaican Chicken-Stuffed Plantains

Plantains, which are large, firm "cooking bananas" with a mild, mellow flavor, are popular throughout the Caribbean and Latin American countries and increasingly available in our better markets. I've eaten them every way imaginable, but perhaps the most memorable I ever tasted were stuffed with a spicy ground chicken forcemeat, battered, and deep-fried on the island of Jamaica. It is a little tricky at first stuffing the plantain strips tight enough so that no filling is lost during the frying, but once you learn to readjust the toothpicks correctly, the procedure is a cinch. I like to serve these plantains on beds of saffroned or lightly curried rice.

Makes 4 to 6 servings

6 slices bacon
3 large ripe plantains
1 pound ground chicken or turkey
2 medium onions, finely chopped
1 medium green bell pepper, seeded and finely chopped
2 garlic cloves, minced
2 ripe tomatoes, peeled, seeded, and finely chopped
½ teaspoon ground cinnamon
½ teaspoon ground allspice
Salt and freshly ground black pepper to taste
Vegetable oil for deep frying
2 large eggs, beaten

1. In a large, heavy skillet, fry the bacon over moderate heat till crisp, drain on paper towels, reserving the fat in the skillet, and crumble.

2. Peel the plantains, slice each one lengthwise into 4 strips, add the strips to the fat in the skillet, cook till golden, about

(continued)

I like to
serve these
plantains
on beds of
saffroned
or lightly
curried rice.

5 minutes, and drain on paper towels. Shape each strip into a circle, secure with toothpicks, and set aside.

3. Add the chicken or turkey to the remaining fat in the skillet, breaking it up, and stir till lightly browned, about 7 minutes. Add the onions, bell pepper, garlic, tomatoes, cinnamon, allspice, salt and pepper, and crumbled bacon and stir till the vegetables are tender, about 15 minutes. Let cool, then stuff each plantain circle with equal amounts of the chicken mixture, pressing with your finger and adjusting the toothpicks to compact the stuffing as tightly as possible.

4. In a deep, heavy skillet, heat about 3 inches of oil over moderate heat till a bread cube tossed in turns golden brown in about 30 seconds. Dip the stuffed plantains in the eggs and deep-fry in the skillet till golden brown, turning once. Drain briefly on paper towels and serve hot.

Spanish Eggplant Stuffed with Lamb

In Spain, baked eggplants are stuffed with all types of ground meats, game, poultry, and even fish, the difference being that the eggplants there are a considerably smaller, paler, and more tender variety than the large dark purple ones to which we're most accustomed. Baby (or Italian) eggplants are now available in our finer markets, and these are the ones you want for this delectable dish. If you must use the more common variety, look for the smallest, youngest, thinnest-skinned fruit you can find. Do remember that all eggplants are very perishable and should be used within a day or so of purchase.

Makes
6 servings

6 small eggplants, about 5 inches long
6 tablespoons olive oil, plus more as needed
¾ pound lamb shoulder, ground or finely chopped
1 medium onion, finely chopped
2 garlic cloves, minced
3 large ripe tomatoes, peeled, seeded, and finely chopped
½ cup finely chopped fresh parsley leaves
Salt and freshly ground black pepper to taste
½ cup grated Parmesan cheese
1½ cups sour cream
½ cup dry bread crumbs

1. Remove the eggplant stems and cut the eggplants in half lengthwise. With a spoon, carefully remove most of the pulp, discarding the seeds and leaving shells about ⅛ inch thick. Finely chop the pulp and set aside.

2. In a large, heavy skillet, heat 3 tablespoons of the oil over moderate heat, add the lamb, and stir till lightly browned. Add the onion and garlic and stir till softened, about 2 minutes. Add the eggplant pulp, the tomatoes plus their juices, parsley, and salt and

(continued)

pepper and stir well. Reduce the heat to low, cover the pan, and simmer till most of the liquid has been absorbed, about 10 minutes. Remove from the heat.

3. Preheat the oven to 350°F.

4. In another large skillet, heat the remaining 3 tablespoons oil over moderate heat, add the eggplant halves, and carefully cook on both sides just to soften, adding more oil if necessary. Drain the halves on paper towels.

5. Arrange the eggplant halves in a large, shallow casserole or baking dish, sprinkle each with a little cheese, then divide the lamb stuffing equally among the halves, pressing it down slightly. Spoon equal amounts of sour cream over the tops, sprinkle with the bread crumbs and remaining cheese, and bake till golden, 30 to 35 minutes.

6. Serve hot.

Dixie Stuffed Bell Peppers

In the American South, bell peppers are stuffed with ground beef, ham, pork, shrimp, or whatever other meat, poultry, or seafood might be on hand, but what makes most different from those prepared in other regions of the country is the addition of rice to the filling. Stuffed peppers make a delicious main course any time of year, but when I really prefer to serve them is in the summertime, when bell peppers are large and fleshy. All you need to accompany these peppers is a basket of hot buttered cornbread or corn sticks and maybe some pickled peaches.

Makes
6 servings

6 medium green bell peppers
1 pound ground beef chuck
1 medium onion, finely chopped
One 16-ounce can whole tomatoes, drained and finely chopped
½ cup water
½ cup long-grain rice
½ teaspoon salt
Freshly ground black pepper to taste
1 teaspoon Worcestershire sauce
5 ounces sharp cheddar cheese, shredded

1. Cut a wide circle around the stems of the peppers, scoop out and discard the seeds and membranes, and place the peppers in a large pot. Add enough water to cover, bring to a boil, cook for 5 minutes, and drain on paper towels.

2. In a large saucepan, break up the beef, add the onion, and cook over moderate heat till the meat is lightly browned, stirring. Drain off the fat. Stir in the tomatoes, water, rice, salt, pepper, and Worcestershire, bring to a simmer, cover, and cook till the

(continued)

rice is tender, about 20 minutes. Stir in 4 ounces of the cheese and mix till well blended.

3. Preheat the oven to 350°F.

4. Arrange the peppers cut side up in a large baking dish, stuff with equal amounts of the beef mixture, sprinkle the remaining cheese over the tops, and bake till the tops are golden and slightly crusty, 20 to 25 minutes.

5. Serve hot.

Chiles Rellenos

In Mexico, stuffed chile peppers can be a very elaborate dish involving various ground meat or poultry fillings and exotic sauces, whereas in South America and throughout the Caribbean, you're just as likely to find the peppers stuffed with no more than grated cheese, chopped chorizo sausage, or diced potatoes and served with no sauce. The most luscious chiles rellenos are usually stuffed with some form of picadillo, as in this recipe, and if you really want to gild the lily, feel free to add a little finely crumbled dry feta or grated Muenster cheese to the filling. The ideal chile for this dish is the snappy, tapered poblano, now available in many of our markets, but if necessary, you can use small green bell peppers.

Makes
6 servings

2 tablespoons corn oil
1 medium onion, minced
1 garlic clove, minced
1½ cups beef broth
One 8-ounce can tomato sauce
3 tablespoons tomato paste
Salt and freshly ground black pepper to taste
6 fresh poblano chile peppers
Vegetable shortening for deep frying
1 recipe for Latin American Picadillo (page 342)
½ cup all-purpose flour
4 large eggs, beaten

1. In a large saucepan, heat the oil over moderate heat, add the onion and garlic, and stir till golden, about 5 minutes. Add the broth, tomato sauce, tomato paste, and salt and pepper and stir till well blended. Bring the sauce to a simmer and let cook while preparing the peppers.

(continued)

2. Arrange the peppers in a large kettle with enough water to cover, bring to a boil, and cook till crisp-tender, 6 to 8 minutes. Drain on paper towels and, when cool enough to handle, cut a wide circle around the stems of the peppers and scoop out and discard the seeds and membranes.

3. In a deep fryer, begin heating enough shortening to cover the peppers to 375°F on a deep-fat thermometer.

4. Meanwhile, stuff the peppers with equal amounts of the picadillo, carefully roll in the flour, and dip in the eggs. Using tongs, lower the peppers into the hot fat, cook till golden, about 3 minutes, and drain on paper towels.

5. Serve the peppers topped with the hot tomato sauce.

Brazilian Bell Peppers Stuffed with Salt Cod Puree

If there's a way to utilize salt cod, Brazilian cooks know about it, and nothing is simpler and more delicious than these succulent baked bell peppers stuffed with a classic *bacalhau* made in seconds in a food processor. Do note that if you have a low tolerance for salt, the soaking water for the cod should be changed several times. The cod puree can also be used to stuff squash or tomatoes, and any left over is equally delectable spread on toast or crackers, glazed briefly under the broiler, and served as a canapé.

Makes
6 servings

1 pound boneless dried salt cod, soaked for at least 8 hours in water

2 pounds potatoes, peeled, cooked, and cut up

4 garlic cloves, minced

Freshly ground black pepper to taste

1 cup olive oil, plus more for drizzling

6 large red bell peppers

1. Cut the cod into pieces and place in a saucepan with enough water to cover. Bring to a low boil over moderate heat, reduce the heat to low, cover, and simmer till the cod flakes, 5 to 7 minutes.

2. In a food processor, combine the cod, potatoes, garlic, pepper, and oil, reduce to a coarse puree, and set aside.

3. Arrange the bell peppers in a large kettle with enough water to cover, bring to a boil, and cook till crisp-tender, 6 to 8 minutes. Drain on paper towels and, when cool enough to handle, cut a wide circle around the stems of the peppers and scoop out and discard the seeds and membranes.

(continued)

The cod puree can also be used to stuff squash or tomatoes.

4. Preheat the oven to 350°F.

5. Arrange the peppers in a large baking dish, stuff them with equal amounts of the cod puree, drizzle a little oil over the tops, and bake till slightly crusty on top, about 20 minutes.

6. Serve hot.

Tunisian Lamb-Stuffed Fennel Bulbs

Aware of my passion for aromatic, licorice-tasting fresh fennel in any shape or form, my good friend Paula Wolfert suggested I stuff the broad bases of a few bulbs with ground lamb enhanced by the Tunisian spice mixture known as *tabil* and bake them with a tomato sauce. Suffice it to say that the result is one of the most beguiling and sumptuous dishes I've ever tasted and still another example of what can be done creatively with ground meats. If you happen to object to the pungent nature of raw fennel (often called "sweet anise"), just remember that when cooked, its licorice flavor becomes sweeter, lighter, and more elusive.

Makes
4 servings

2½ teaspoons minced garlic
2½ teaspoons ground caraway seeds
2 teaspoons ground coriander seeds
2½ teaspoons crushed red pepper flakes
4 fennel bulbs
1 pound ground lamb shoulder
¼ cup minced fresh parsley leaves
2 teaspoons freshly ground black pepper
Salt to taste
3 tablespoons olive oil
2 large eggs, beaten
1 tablespoon grated Parmesan cheese
1 cup spicy tomato sauce (fresh or commercial)

1. In a small bowl, combine the garlic, caraway and coriander seeds, and red pepper flakes, mix till well blended, and set the spice mixture aside.

(continued)

2. Wash the fennel and trim the feathery foliage from the hard bases. Place the bulbs in a large pot with enough water to cover, bring to a low boil, and cook till tender, about 15 minutes. Drain and cut in half lengthwise.

3. In a bowl, combine the lamb, parsley, pepper, salt, and 1 teaspoon of the spice mixture and mix till well blended. In a large skillet, heat the oil over moderate heat, add the lamb mixture, breaking it up with a fork, and stir till nicely browned, about 10 minutes. Remove from the heat, let cool slightly, add the eggs and cheese, and mix till the stuffing is well blended.

4. Preheat the oven to 400°F.

5. Place 4 fennel halves cut side up in a greased baking dish, pile equal amounts of the stuffing over the tops, place the remaining fennel halves on top, spoon on the tomato sauce, and bake for 15 to 20 minutes.

6. Serve hot.

Greek Meat-Stuffed Grape Leaves

The Greek stuff grape leaves (dolmades) with everything from ground meats or poultry to minced seafood to a thick avgolemono sauce, and they serve them as appetizers, main courses, and even cold picnic snacks. My Greek grandfather loved nothing more than the warm lamb dolmades, elaborate feta and cucumber salad, and pita bread that my grandmother would serve at large family Sunday suppers, and while I do add beef to my stuffing for a more interesting flavor, this recipe is a good approximation of what I remember as a youngster. Brined grape leaves are available in jars at most fine markets, and if they're too salty for your taste, simply rinse them in warm water before stuffing.

20 grape leaves packed in brine
½ pound ground lamb shoulder
½ pound ground beef round
½ cup cooked rice
1 medium onion, minced
2 garlic cloves, minced
2 tablespoons minced fresh parsley leaves
¼ teaspoon ground allspice
Salt and freshly ground black pepper to taste
2 tablespoons fresh lemon juice
⅓ cup beef broth

1. Separate the grape leaves. Bring a large pot of water to a boil, drop in the grape leaves, cook for 5 minutes, and drain on paper towels.

2. In a large bowl, combine the remaining ingredients and mix till the stuffing is thoroughly blended.

(continued)

Makes 4 to 6 servings

3. Place a grape leaf vein side up on a work surface, place about 1 tablespoon of stuffing in the center, fold up the sides, and roll tightly to enclose the stuffing. Repeat with the remaining leaves and stuffing.

4. Arrange the stuffed leaves in layers, seam sides down, in a large, heavy kettle and cover with an inverted plate to weight them down slightly. Add enough warm water to reach the plate, bring to a boil, reduce the heat to low, cover, and simmer till the stuffed leaves are tender, 30 to 35 minutes.

5. Serve hot, warm, or cold.

Italian Meat-Stuffed Zucchini Blossoms

Orangish zucchini blossoms stuffed with various ground meats or poultry have been a staple in the kitchens of Parma and other northern Italian towns for ages, and now that the blossoms are more and more available in our summer farmers' markets, we too can experience how luscious this stuffed and fried delicacy can be. Zucchini blossoms are highly perishable and must be used the same day they're bought. Note also that there are both male and female blossoms, and only the male ones, on the vegetable's stem, are good to eat (the female, attached to the zucchini itself, are too mushy and have little flavor). This is still another time when only genuine Parmigiano-Reggiano cheese should be used.

Makes 4 to 6 servings

¼ cup olive oil
2 scallions (parts of green tops included), finely chopped
1 garlic clove, minced
½ pound ground pork
¼ pound ground veal
¼ pound finely chopped prosciutto
½ cup finely chopped fresh parsley leaves
Salt and freshly ground black pepper to taste
¼ cup grated Parmesan cheese
2 large eggs, beaten
12 large zucchini blossoms, gently wiped
2 tablespoons butter

1. In a large skillet, heat 2 tablespoons of the oil over moderate heat, add the scallions and garlic, and stir till softened, about 2 minutes. Add the pork, veal, and prosciutto and stir till the meats are lightly browned, about 10 minutes. Transfer the

(continued)

mixture to a bowl, add the parsley, salt and pepper, cheese, and eggs, and stir till well blended. Wipe out the skillet.

2. Carefully stuff equal amounts of the meat mixture into the zucchini blossoms and seal the edges by pressing them together as tightly as possible.

3. In the skillet, heat the remaining 2 tablespoons oil and the butter together over low heat, add the stuffed blossoms, and gently turn them to coat well. Cover, cook for about 10 minutes, turn gently, and cook about 10 minutes longer. Drain briefly on paper towels.

4. Serve hot or at room temperature.

Leeks Stuffed with Trout Mousse

Few people stop to realize how perfect the broad, flat, dark green leaves of leeks are for stuffing, especially when the younger, more tender version of the vegetable, used in soups, salads, and other dishes, is unavailable. Virtually any fish can be substituted for the trout in this recipe, but whichever you choose, be sure to chill the cut-up fillets for at least an hour so that the mousse stuffing will have a fine texture. These stuffed leeks make an elegant main course, but they are also ideal for a formal buffet.

Makes
6 servings

4 large leeks with no discolored leaves

1½ pounds fresh rainbow trout fillets, cut into pieces and chilled for at least 1 hour

2 tablespoons minced fresh chives

1 tablespoon minced fresh tarragon leaves

Salt and freshly ground black pepper to taste

2 large egg whites

1 cup heavy cream

1 teaspoon fresh lemon juice

¼ cup bottled clam juice

8 tablespoons (1 stick) butter, melted

1. Trim and discard the rootlets and leaf ends of the leeks, remove 12 large outer leaves, rinse well to remove any grit, and reserve the whole leeks for another use. Bring a large pot of water to a boil, add the leaves, blanch for 2 minutes, and drain. Refresh the leaves under cold running water, drain again, and pat dry.

2. In a food processor, combine the trout, chives, tarragon, and salt and pepper and process till well blended. With the motor

(continued)

running, add the egg whites, then gradually the cream and lemon juice, and blend to a fine mousse.

3. Preheat the oven to 375°F. Butter a large baking dish.

4. Spread the leek leaves out on a flat surface, spoon equal amounts of the fish mousse near the base of each leaf, and roll up the leaves snugly enough to enclose the mousse. Arrange the rolls seam side down in the prepared baking dish, pour the clam juice around the sides, brush the rolls generously with the butter, and bake till the mousse is cooked through, about 20 minutes, basting the rolls several times.

5. Serve hot.

Virtually any fish can be substituted for the trout in this recipe.

Polish Stuffed Cabbage Rolls

German, Austrian, and Hungarian home cooks all stuff cabbage leaves (or whole cabbages) with various ground meats, game, or poultry, but in Poland the concept is deemed such a culinary art that serious chefs wouldn't dream of stuffing any cabbage leaves that hadn't been first softened in hot salted water. Polish cooks also insist that the dish is always better made a day in advance to allow the flavors to mellow, then reheated in a low oven. These rolls are traditionally served with boiled parsleyed potatoes and a large bowl of sour cream.

Makes
6 servings

2 tablespoons lard
2 medium onions, finely chopped
2 tablespoons rice
1 tablespoon finely chopped fresh parsley leaves
1 tablespoon finely chopped fresh dill
1 teaspoon dried thyme, crumbled
Salt and freshly ground black pepper to taste
1½ pounds ground lean pork
1 slice white bread, soaked in ¼ cup milk and squeezed dry
24 green cabbage leaves, softened in hot salty water for about
    20 minutes
2 cups beef broth

1. In a large skillet, melt the lard over moderate heat, add the onions, and stir till softened, about 3 minutes. Add the rice and stir till transparent, about 5 minutes. Add the parsley, dill, thyme, and salt and pepper, stir till well blended, and transfer the mixture to a large bowl. Add the pork and bread and work with your hands till the stuffing is smooth, adding a little milk if necessary to give it a creamy consistency.

(continued)

**Stuffed Dishes
and Forcemeats**

2. Preheat the oven to 325°F.

3. Cut out the hard center ribs of the cabbage leaves. To make each cabbage roll, spread a leaf out flat, place a little of the pork stuffing in the center, fold the edges over the stuffing, and roll the leaf up tightly. Arrange the rolls in layers in a large casserole, pour the broth plus enough water over the top to almost cover, and bake, covered, till only about 1 cup of liquid is left, 2½ to 3 hours.

4. Serve 4 hot rolls per person.

German Red Cabbage Roulades and Sauerkraut

Although German cooks might stuff their cabbage rolls with ground pork, ham, or game, by far the most popular *rouladen* are made with ground beef that has enough fat to guarantee a moist texture. Germans also love to bake their rolls between layers of sauerkraut and use the sauerkraut juice as a cooking liquid for ultimate flavor. The result is a substantial, succulent dish that requires no accompaniment other than coarse, slightly sour pumpernickel bread and plenty of full-bodied beer.

Makes
6 servings

2 tablespoons lard
1 medium onion, finely chopped
1 carrot, scraped and finely chopped
1 garlic clove, minced
1 tablespoon minced fresh parsley leaves
1 tablespoon caraway seeds
½ teaspoon grated nutmeg
Salt and freshly ground black pepper to taste
1 pound ground beef chuck or brisket
1 tablespoon grainy mustard
1 slice white bread, soaked in ¼ cup milk and squeezed dry
24 large red cabbage leaves
1 pound sauerkraut, drained and liquid reserved
1 tablespoon tomato puree

1. In a skillet, melt the lard over moderate heat, add the onion, carrot, and garlic, and stir till softened, about 3 minutes. Add the parsley, caraway seeds, nutmeg, and salt and pepper, stir well, and transfer the mixture to a large bowl. Add the beef, mustard, and bread and mix with your hands till the stuffing is smooth.

(continued)

**Stuffed Dishes
and Forcemeats**

331

2. Cut out the rib of each cabbage leaf. To make each roll, spread a leaf out flat, spoon a little stuffing in the center, fold the edges over the stuffing, and roll the leaf up tightly.

3. Line the bottom of a heavy, ovenproof 2-quart casserole with a layer of sauerkraut and arrange a layer of cabbage rolls over the top. Repeat layering the sauerkraut and cabbage rolls, ending with a layer of sauerkraut. In a small bowl, blend the reserved sauerkraut liquid and tomato puree and pour over the top. Bring to a simmer over moderate heat, reduce the heat to low, cover, and cook slowly till the cabbage rolls and sauerkraut are very tender, about 2 hours.

4. Serve hot.

Ham- and Walnut- Stuffed Pears

Here's a clever idea for an easy, casual winter luncheon or brunch dish, and if you don't have any cooked ham on hand, ground cooked chicken or shrimp would be just as tasty. Likewise, if large, fresh, ripe peaches instead of pears are in season, by all means disregard the poaching and broiling procedures and simply stuff the peaches with the ham and walnut mixture for a chilled summer treat.

Makes
4 servings

½ cup fresh lemon juice
4 large firm ripe pears
½ pound cooked ham, minced
2 scallions (white parts only), minced
½ cup finely chopped walnuts
1 tablespoon minced fresh parsley leaves
1 tablespoon minced sweet pickle
4 ounces cream cheese, softened

1. In a large stainless steel or enameled skillet, bring about 1½ inches of water and half the lemon juice to a low simmer. Meanwhile, peel the pears, cut them in half lengthwise, core them, and drop them into the acidulated water. Return to a simmer and poach the pears till just tender, 2 to 3 minutes. With a slotted spoon, transfer the pears to paper towels to drain and brush them with a little of the remaining lemon juice.

2. Preheat the oven broiler.

3. In a bowl, combine the ham, scallions, walnuts, parsley, pickle, cream cheese, and the remaining lemon juice and stir till well blended. Stuff the pears with the ham mixture, mounding it, then arrange them on a broiler pan and broil about 4 inches from the heat till glazed, 3 to 4 minutes.

4. Serve 2 pear halves per person.

Pierre's Baked Flounder Stuffed with Clams

It used to amaze me the way my friend and neighbor, the famous French chef Pierre Franey, would excuse himself from cocktails at his home on Long Island and, in no time, prepare and place a splendid dish such as this one on the dinner table. Pierre loved to stuff flounder (or fluke) fillets with all sorts of chopped shellfish, but you could also use striped bass, red snapper, or sole and have the same succulent results. Do be warned that overbaking this dish toughens not only the clams but also the fish.

Makes 6 servings

6 tablespoons (¾ stick) butter
2 scallions (white parts only), finely diced
2 celery ribs, finely diced
1 small green bell pepper, seeded and finely diced
½ cup dry white wine
½ cup chopped fresh clams
1½ cups fresh bread crumbs
1 large egg, beaten
⅓ cup finely chopped fresh parsley leaves
¼ teaspoon dried thyme, crumbled
Salt and freshly ground black pepper to taste
12 small fresh flounder fillets (about 2½ pounds)
Juice of 1 lemon
½ teaspoon paprika

1. Preheat the oven to 400°F. Butter a large baking dish and set aside.

2. In a skillet, melt 2 tablespoons of the butter over moderate heat, add the scallions, celery, and bell pepper and stir till softened, about 3 minutes. Add the wine and cook for 2 minutes. Add the clams, bread crumbs, egg, parsley, thyme, and salt and pepper, stir well, and remove the stuffing from the heat.

3. On a work surface, place half the flounder fillets skin side down, spoon equal amounts of the stuffing over the tops, and smooth it with a knife. Cover with the remaining fillets and arrange the stuffed fillets in the prepared baking dish. In a small saucepan, melt the remaining 4 tablespoons butter over low heat, add the lemon juice, stir, and spoon the lemon butter over the fillets. Dust the fillets with the paprika and bake just till the flounder flakes, about 15 minutes.

4. Serve piping hot.

Do be warned that overbaking this dish toughens not only the clams but also the fish.

Norwegian Shrimp- and Dill-Stuffed Salmon

Makes
4 servings

Appropriately enough, this luscious dish was served to friends and me at a home on a fjord in Norway by the wife of a salmon farmer who was teaching us all about his vocation. What I remember most are, without question, the tiniest and sweetest North Sea shrimp I've ever tasted, so small, in fact, that they could have been used whole in the stuffing instead of being chopped. When cutting the salmon into slices, do be sure to use a very sharp knife and to draw the blade against the flesh in a single stroke to avoid ragged tears. Also, bake this dish only till the salmon flakes; otherwise, it will be dry and almost tasteless.

½ pound fresh shrimp
¼ cup sour cream
1 scallion (white part only), minced
1 tablespoon minced fresh parsley leaves
1 tablespoon minced fresh dill
1 tablespoon fresh lemon juice
Salt and freshly ground black pepper to taste
One 1½- to 2-pound fresh salmon fillet
1 large egg white
2 tablespoons butter, melted

1. In a saucepan, combine the shrimp with enough water to cover, bring to a boil, remove from the heat, and let stand for 2 minutes. Drain and, when cool enough to handle, shell, devein, and chop the shrimp finely. In a bowl, combine the shrimp, sour cream, scallion, parsley, dill, lemon juice, and salt and pepper, and mix till the stuffing is well blended.

2. Preheat the oven to 400°F. Grease a baking pan and set aside.

3. Remove any skin and bones from the salmon and carefully cut the fillet into 8 thin slices of equal size. Place 4 slices in the prepared pan and spoon equal amounts of the stuffing in the center of each slice. Brush the edges with egg white, place the 4 remaining slices of salmon on the tops, and press the edges to seal. Brush each with butter and bake just till the salmon flakes, 10 to 12 minutes.

4. Serve hot.

Pearl's Poached Sole Stuffed with Lobster

**Makes
6 servings**

Pearl Byrd Foster was one of my early mentors, and of all the remarkable dishes Pearl prepared and served at her tiny restaurant in New York City, Mr. & Mrs. Foster's Place, none impressed me more than the elegant lemon sole, flounder, or red snapper fillets that she would stuff with rich diced lobster meat. Of course, Pearl used only fresh lobsters that she'd steamed herself ("and those critters had better be kicking," I heard her tell the fishmonger more than once), but the frozen, uncooked lobster tails now available in most markets are perfectly acceptable for this stuffing. Please do not over-poach this dish.

4 tablespoons (½ stick) butter

1 pound fresh (or thawed frozen) shelled lobster tails, finely diced

1 scallion (part of green top included), finely diced

1 celery rib, finely diced

½ small green bell pepper, seeded and finely diced

Salt and freshly ground black pepper to taste

6 medium fresh sole fillets (about 2 pounds)

2 tablespoons minced fresh parsley leaves

1 cup chicken broth

2 tablespoons fresh lemon juice

2 tablespoons minced onion

1. In a large skillet, melt the butter over moderate heat, add the lobster, and stir for about 3 minutes. Add the scallion, celery, bell pepper, and salt and pepper, stir about 5 minutes longer, and transfer the stuffing to a bowl.

2. On a work surface, spread equal amounts of the lobster stuffing on the sole fillets, roll the fillets up carefully, and secure the edges with toothpicks.

3. In the same skillet, combine the broth, lemon juice, and onion, and bring to a low boil. Add the stuffed fillets to the liquid, return to a simmer, and poach till the sole flakes easily, 10 to 12 minutes.

4. Serve hot.

Sausage, Apricot, and Prune Forcemeat

Makes about
2¼ pounds

Use this forcemeat to stuff a crown roast of pork; turkey; roasted chicken; breast of veal; or baked bell peppers, zucchini, or squash. It is also delicious fried or broiled as patties.

2 pounds bulk pork sausage
1 medium onion, finely diced
1 celery rib, finely diced
2 garlic cloves, minced
½ cup finely diced pitted prunes
¼ cup finely diced dried apricots
1 cup soft fresh bread crumbs
2 tablespoons light brown sugar
½ cup minced fresh parsley leaves
1 teaspoon powdered sage
Salt and freshly ground black pepper to taste
1 large egg, beaten

1. In a large skillet, break up the sausage with a fork, fry over moderate heat till browned, about 10 minutes, and drain on paper towels. Pour off all but about 2 tablespoons of fat from the skillet, add the onion, celery, and garlic, and stir till softened, about 3 minutes.

2. In a large bowl, combine the sausage, vegetables, and all the remaining ingredients and mix with your hands till thoroughly blended. Cover with plastic wrap and chill for at least 1 hour to allow the flavors to blend.

French Pork Belly, Spinach, and Swiss Chard Forcemeat

The French use this forcemeat to fill the center of a crown roast of pork, and it also adds lots of flavor and moisture when stuffed into thick pork chops or a baked fresh ham. Fresh pork belly (from which bacon is cut) is now available in most fine markets.

Makes about 3 pounds

2 pounds fresh spinach, rinsed
2 pounds Swiss chard greens
2 pounds lean pork belly, finely chopped
2 medium onions, finely chopped
2 tablespoons finely chopped fresh parsley leaves
1 teaspoon dried thyme, crumbled
Salt and freshly ground black pepper to taste
2 large eggs, beaten
Dry bread crumbs as needed

1. Bring a large pot of water to a boil, plunge in the spinach and chard, and blanch for 2 minutes. Drain well, squeeze out all the liquid with your hands, and chop the greens finely.

2. In a large bowl, combine the greens, pork belly, onions, parsley, thyme, salt and pepper, and eggs, and mix till well blended. Add just enough bread crumbs, stirring, to give the forcemeat a firm consistency, and chill till ready to use.

Latin American Picadillo

**Makes
6 servings**

Most all Latin American countries have some version of spicy picadillo, which is used to stuff chiles rellenos and tacos, make savory pies, and enhance all sorts of baked vegetables. The forcemeat can be made with either ground pork or beef or a combination of the two meats, and in some countries, picadillo is so relished that it's simply served by itself over mounds of hot rice.

2 tablespoons corn oil
1 medium onion, minced
1 fresh jalapeño chile pepper, seeded and minced
1 garlic clove, minced
1 pound ground lean pork
2 large ripe tomatoes, peeled, seeded, and finely chopped
¼ cup minced seedless dark raisins
¼ cup minced green olives
¼ cup minced pimentos
¼ cup minced blanched almonds
¼ teaspoon ground cinnamon
⅛ teaspoon ground cloves
Salt and freshly ground black pepper to taste

1. In a large, heavy skillet, heat the oil over moderate heat, add the onion, jalapeño, and garlic, and stir till golden, about 5 minutes. Add the pork and stir till browned, about 8 minutes, breaking it up with a fork. Drain off the excess fat from the skillet, add the tomatoes and their juices plus all the remaining ingredients, stir well, reduce the heat to low, and simmer till the mixture is slightly thickened, about 10 minutes.

2. Serve the picadillo hot over mounds of rice, or use it to stuff baked chile or bell peppers or tacos.

Sausage

Fresh Bulk Pork Sausage

Makes about 3 pounds

Used to make fried breakfast patties, encase baked Scotch eggs, stuff all types of poultry and vegetables, and enhance various meat loaves and breads, this bulk pork sausage has been a staple in my kitchen for as long as I can remember. For the right slightly coarse texture, don't use a food processor for this sausage, and by no means reduce the amount of pork fat, which accounts not only for the sausage's soft, moist texture but also for much of its succulent flavor. Stored in a covered container or tightly wrapped foil, the uncooked sausage mixture keeps for 3 to 4 days in the refrigerator and freezes beautifully for up to about 3 months.

2 pounds boneless pork shoulder

1 pound fresh pork fat, chilled for about 30 minutes in the freezer

2 tablespoons salt

1 teaspoon freshly ground black pepper

2 teaspoons powdered sage

1 teaspoon crushed red pepper flakes

2 tablespoons cold water

1. Cut the pork and pork fat into large cubes and pass first through the coarse blade, then through the fine blade, of a meat grinder into a large bowl. Add all the remaining ingredients, moisten both hands with water, and knead the mixture till well blended and smooth. Wrap the sausage in foil or plastic wrap and store in the refrigerator for at least 2 hours before using.

2. To fry breakfast patties, form the mixture into patties with your hands, fry in a skillet over moderate heat till cooked through and nicely browned, about 10 minutes on each side, and drain on paper towels.

Old-Fashioned Country Pork Sausage Links

Great when fried for breakfast, added to casseroles, or braised with cabbage, leeks, or beans, these spicy links are even better smoked over various wood chips in a home smoker or even a kettle grill. To allow the flavors to mellow, I always chill the ground sausage overnight before stuffing it into a casing. So long as you're careful not to grind the meats to a paste, a food processor can also be used for this sausage. The uncooked links keep for 3 to 4 days in the refrigerator and for up to 3 months in the freezer.

Makes about 2½ pounds

> 2 pounds boneless pork shoulder butt, cut into pieces
> ½ pound pork fatback, cut into pieces and chilled for 30 minutes in the freezer
> 2 tablespoons light brown sugar
> 1 tablespoon sweet paprika
> 2 teaspoons crushed red pepper flakes
> 1 teaspoon powdered sage
> ½ teaspoon dried thyme, crumbled
> Pinch of ground allspice
> Salt and freshly ground black pepper to taste
> 5 to 6 feet sausage casing, rinsed and drained
> Butter or margarine for frying

1. Using a meat grinder with a sausage attachment, grind the pork and fatback together through the fine blade into a large bowl. Add all the seasonings, mix with your hands till well blended, cover with plastic wrap, and allow to mellow in the refrigerator overnight. Wash the grinder.

2. Return the sausage mixture to the grinder and stuff it into the casing according to machine instructions. Twist the casing to
(continued)

form 3- to 4-inch links, alternating the direction of twisting so that the links will hold together when cut apart.

3. To cook, fry the links in a little butter or margarine in a large skillet over moderate heat till browned on all sides, about 15 minutes, and drain on paper towels.

To allow the flavors to mellow, I always chill the ground sausage overnight before stuffing it into a casing.

English Farmhouse Bangers

British slang for link sausages originally made with ground pork, beef suet, and bread crumbs, bangers are traditionally served either with a hot English breakfast or with mashed potatoes at lunch or dinner. Bangers are, by nature, drier in texture and spicier than other British sausages, but the very best ones are never over-breaded or over-seasoned. If you prefer your bangers a bit moister, substitute a thick slice of white bread soaked in ¼ cup of milk and squeezed almost dry for the bread crumbs. Most English chefs prick their bangers repeatedly with a knife before cooking. The uncooked sausages keep for 3 to 4 days in the refrigerator or for up to 3 months in the freezer.

Makes about 2 pounds

1½ pounds boneless pork shoulder, cut into pieces
½ pound fresh pork fat, cut into pieces
½ cup dry bread crumbs
¼ cup minced fresh parsley leaves
½ teaspoon powdered sage
½ teaspoon dried marjoram
½ teaspoon paprika
¼ teaspoon grated nutmeg
Salt and freshly ground black pepper to taste
1 tablespoon brandy
4 to 5 feet sausage casing, rinsed and drained
Butter for frying (optional)

1. In a meat grinder with a sausage attachment, grind the pork and pork fat together twice into a large bowl. Add the bread crumbs, parsley, and all the seasonings (including the brandy), mix with your hands till well blended, cover with plastic wrap,

(continued)

and chill for at least 12 hours for the flavors to develop. Wash the grinder.

2. Return the pork mixture to the grinder and stuff it into the casing according to machine instructions. Twist the casing into 6-inch links, alternating the direction of twisting so that the links will hold together when cut apart.

3. To cook, prick the links all over repeatedly with a knife and either fry in a little butter in a heavy skillet over moderate heat, 12 to 15 minutes, or broil till nicely browned on all sides, 15 to 20 minutes.

Italian Fennel Sausages

Variously flavored with herbs or seeds, and with different ratios of meat to fat and different textures owing to the individual grinds, hot and sweet sausages are used in Italy to enhance soups and stews, stuff roasted meats and poultry, and make endless sauces for pasta. Perhaps the most popular Italian sausages are those redolent of fennel seeds, and while today commercial fennel sausages can be found in virtually all grocery stores in this country, few in my opinion can equal those you season and grind yourself. I don't recommend using a food processor for these fairly coarse sausages, since the risk of over-grinding is too great.

2½ pounds boneless lean pork, cut into pieces
½ pound fresh pork fat, cut into pieces
1 small onion, minced
1 garlic clove, minced
1 tablespoon crushed red pepper flakes
1 tablespoon salt
2 teaspoons freshly ground black pepper
2 teaspoons fennel seeds
1 teaspoon paprika
¼ teaspoon dried thyme, crumbled
¼ teaspoon finely crumbled bay leaf
¼ cup dry red wine
5 to 6 feet sausage casing, rinsed and drained
Olive oil for frying

1. Using the coarse blade on a meat grinder with a sausage attachment, grind the pork and pork fat together into a large bowl, add the onion, garlic, and all the seasonings (including the wine), and mix till blended thoroughly. Return the mixture

(continued)

to the grinder and stuff it into the casing according to machine instructions. Twist the casing for form 5- to 6-inch links, alternating the direction of twisting so that the links will hold together when cut apart.

2. To cook, fry the links in a little oil in a large skillet over moderate heat till browned on all sides, 12 to 15 minutes, and drain on paper towels.

Creole Chaurice

Used in Louisiana for over a century to enrich gumbos, jambalayas, and numerous bean dishes, this spicy, garlicky, distinctive sausage is also delicious when simply fried for breakfast or brunch. Creole chefs in New Orleans and elsewhere in the state produce both patties and links from the sausage mixture, but one of the most practical methods is to form it into large cylinders, chill them well to firm up the texture, then slice into rounds as needed. The sausage keeps for 3 to 4 days in the refrigerator and for up to 3 months in the freezer.

Makes about 3 pounds

2 pounds boneless lean pork, cut into pieces
1 pound pork fatback, cut into pieces
2 medium onions, finely chopped
3 garlic cloves, minced
½ cup finely chopped fresh parsley leaves
2 teaspoons crushed red pepper flakes
1 teaspoon dried thyme, crumbled
½ teaspoon ground allspice
½ teaspoon ground bay leaf
Salt and freshly ground black pepper to taste
Peanut oil for frying

1. Using the coarse blade of a meat grinder, grind the pork and fatback together into a large bowl. Add the onions, garlic, and all the seasonings and mix with your hands till well blended. Form the sausage into a large cylinder about 2 inches in diameter, wrap the cylinder tightly in foil, and chill overnight to firm up the texture.

2. When ready to cook, slice the cylinder into ½-inch-thick rounds, fry them in a little peanut oil till nicely browned on both sides, 12 to 15 minutes, and drain on paper towels.

Zarela's Chiapas

**Makes about
2 pounds**

For over two decades, Zarela Martinez has been recognized as possibly the finest Mexican chef in New York City, and none of her authentic regional specialties do I relish more at her lively restaurant, Zarela's, than this highly flavored sausage from the state of Chiapas. Zarela mostly serves the sausage in hot patties with a spicy chipotle sauce, but it's also delicious braised in links, sliced, smeared with mayonnaise and rolled in minced parsley, and served cold as an appetizer. Do be very careful when toasting the aniseed, for the seeds can burn quickly. These sausages can easily be made with packaged ground meats found in all grocery stores.

1 teaspoon aniseed
1 pound ground beef chuck
1 pound ground pork (preferably shoulder)
2 garlic cloves, minced
1 tablespoon freshly ground black pepper
2 teaspoons salt
½ teaspoon grated nutmeg
½ teaspoon dried thyme, crumbled
½ teaspoon dried oregano, crumbled
2 bay leaves, ground to a fine powder
½ cup brandy
Juice of 1 lemon
¼ cup lard

1. In a small, heavy skillet, toast the aniseed over moderate heat for about 1 minute, stirring constantly, and remove from the heat.

2. In a large bowl, combine all the remaining ingredients except the lard, add the toasted aniseed, and mix with your hands till the sausage is well blended. Cover with plastic wrap and chill the sausage overnight to develop the flavors.

3. To cook, form the sausage into patties. In a large skillet, melt the lard over moderate heat, add the sausages (in batches if necessary), brown for 5 to 6 minutes on each side, and drain on paper towels.

4. Serve hot.

These sausages can easily be made with packaged ground meats found in all grocery stores.

Greek Meatball Sausages

Makes about
2 pounds

Coming from Thessaly in mainland Greece, these full-flavored "meatball" sausages are actually shaped into ovals and served with mashed potatoes, yogurt, and possibly a tomato sauce. Traditionally, the sausages are made exclusively with ground lamb moistened slightly with wine-soaked bread, but since they still tend to be rather dry for my taste, I improve the texture by adding some fatty beef chuck—especially since I prefer the sausages without a sauce.

1 pound ground lamb shoulder
¾ pound ground beef chuck
1 medium onion, minced
2 garlic cloves, minced
¼ cup minced fresh parsley leaves
1 teaspoon ground cumin
Salt and freshly ground black pepper to taste
2 slices white bread (crusts removed), soaked in ½ cup
  dry red wine
1 tablespoon red wine vinegar
Olive oil for frying

1. In a large bowl, combine all the ingredients except the oil and mix with your hands till well blended and smooth. Using heaping tablespoons, form the sausage mixture into ovals about 2 inches long, place in a large, shallow dish or pan, cover with plastic wrap, and chill for about 1 hour.

2. To cook, heat a little oil in a large, heavy skillet, add the sausages, brown lightly on all sides, 12 to 15 minutes, and drain on paper towels.

3. Serve hot.

Polish Kielbasa

Once this popular smoked garlic sausage was sold only fresh in the Central European markets of our largest cities, but today most kielbasa is processed by American packers and sold everywhere fully cooked. There's nothing wrong with commercial kielbasa, but once you've taste the authentic, freshly cooked product in Warsaw (usually served with sauerkraut), the difference is immediately obvious. In Poland, fresh kielbasa is either simmered in beef broth for about an hour or used to enhance numerous stews and casseroles, but it (like fresh German bratwurst) is also delicious when grilled for 20 minutes or so and served with braised red cabbage and grainy mustard. Never is a food processor handier than for the making of kielbasa.

Makes about
3 pounds

2 garlic cloves, minced
3 tablespoons sweet paprika
1 tablespoon coarse salt
2 teaspoons freshly ground black pepper
1 teaspoon dried marjoram, crumbled
½ teaspoon dried summer savory, crumbled
¾ pound boned and trimmed beef shin, cut into pieces
¾ pound fresh pork fat
½ cup ice water
1½ pounds lean pork, cut into pieces
5 to 6 feet large sausage casing, rinsed and drained

1. In a small bowl, combine the garlic, paprika, salt, pepper, marjoram, and summer savory, and mix till well blended.

2. In a food processor, combine the beef, half of the pork fat, half of the ice water, and half of the garlic mixture, grind finely, and

(continued)

Sausage

scrape into a bowl. Add the pork, remaining pork fat, remaining garlic mixture, and remaining water to the food processor, grind coarsely, and scrape into the beef mixture. Blend thoroughly, cover with plastic wrap, and chill overnight.

3. Gather all but about 2 inches of the casing over the mouth of a sausage funnel, force the sausage mixture through the funnel into the casing, and tie a knot at the top end. Twist the casing tightly into desired links, alternating the direction of twisting so that the links will hold together when cut apart. Refrigerate, uncovered, for at least 12 hours and up to 3 days before cooking.

French Garlic Sausages

Whether eaten as part of a *choucroute garnie*, cassoulet, garbure, or elaborate composed salad, French *saucisson à l'ail* is one of the most sublime sausages ever conceived. Since the texture of these spicy sausages should be coarse, do not use a food processor, and by no means try to substitute salt pork for the fresh fatback. The sausages are also wonderful braised with cabbage or, even more simply, transformed into patties, browned for about 5 minutes on each side in a skillet, and eaten with warm French potato salad and plenty of Dijon mustard.

Makes about 2 pounds

1 pound pork shoulder, cut into pieces
½ pound fresh pork fatback (rind removed), cut into pieces
½ pound chicken livers, cut in half
3 garlic cloves, finely minced
2 slices white bread, soaked in ½ cup milk and squeezed dry
2 large eggs, beaten
1 teaspoon dried thyme, crumbled
½ teaspoon grated nutmeg
½ teaspoon ground allspice
½ teaspoon sugar
2 teaspoons salt
2 teaspoons freshly ground black pepper
5 to 6 feet sausage casing, rinsed and drained
2 tablespoons lard

1. In a meat grinder with a sausage attachment, grind together with the coarse blade the pork and fatback into a large bowl. Add the chicken livers, garlic, soaked bread, eggs, and seasonings and mix with your hands till the sausage is well blended. Cover with plastic wrap and chill overnight.

(continued)

2. Using the sausage attachment on the grinder, stuff the sausage into the casing according to machine instructions. Twist the casing to form 4- to 5-inch links, alternating the direction of twisting so that the links will hold together when cut apart.

3. To cook, melt the lard in a large, heavy skillet over moderate heat, brown the links well on all sides, about 15 minutes, and drain on paper towels.

Cajun Boudin Rouge

In Cajun Louisiana, *boudin* is a generic term for all rice sausages made with pork, veal, game, or poultry, but by far the most unusual is this "red pudding," which ideally should also contain some pig's blood for ultimate flavor. Traditionally in Cajun country, women make boudin rouge after a fall or winter hog-killing and serve it at festive parties called "boucheries," but elsewhere in the state, the distinctive sausage is now usually available year-round. The fresh sausage keeps for 3 to 4 days in the refrigerator, but because of the rice, it should not be frozen.

Makes about 3 pounds

2 pounds boneless pork shoulder butt
½ pound fresh pork fat (preferably jowl or fatback)
½ pound pork liver
1 medium onion, chopped
1 carrot, scraped and chopped
1 celery rib, chopped
3 cups cooked rice
½ cup chopped scallions (part of green tops included)
2 garlic cloves, minced
½ teaspoon dried thyme, crumbled
Salt and freshly ground black pepper to taste
Tabasco sauce to taste
5 to 6 feet sausage casing, rinsed and drained
Lard for frying

1. In a large pot, combine the pork butt, pork fat, liver, onion, carrot, and celery and add enough water to cover. Bring to a boil, reduce the heat to low, cover, and simmer till the meats are very tender, about 1½ hours. Transfer the meats to a platter, strain the broth into a bowl, discard the solids, and reserve the broth.

(continued)

2. Cut the meats into chunks, place in a meat grinder or food processor, grind coarsely, and place in a large bowl. Add the rice, scallions, garlic, thyme, salt and pepper, and Tabasco and mix with your hands till well blended, adding just enough of the reserved broth to keep the mixture moist.

3. Using the sausage attachment on the meat grinder, stuff the sausage into the casing according to machine instructions; or, if using a food processor, gather all but about 2 inches of the casing over the mouth of a sausage funnel and force the sausage through the funnel into the casing. Twist the casing to form 3- to 4-inch links, alternating the direction of twisting so that the links will hold together when cut apart.

4. To cook, melt a little lard in a heavy skillet over moderate heat, fry the links till browned on all sides, 12 to 15 minutes, and drain on paper towels.

German Bratwurst

It's no secret that German bratwurst is one of the world's great sausages, but what most people don't realize is how much more delectable homemade bratwurst can be than the precooked and often bland versions found in delis and markets. For the right smooth texture, for instance, a little veal must be ground with the pork, and in Germany, the sausage is always seasoned with not just caraway seeds and nutmeg but also a little ginger. Equally important is that bratwurst be either poached or steamed before being lightly grilled or fried in lard.

2 pounds pork butt, cut into pieces
½ pound veal shoulder, cut into pieces
½ pound fresh pork fat, cut into pieces
1 teaspoon grated nutmeg
1 teaspoon caraway seeds (or dried coriander)
½ teaspoon ground ginger
1 tablespoon salt
1 teaspoon freshly ground black pepper
1 teaspoon sugar
½ cup milk
6 feet sausage casing, rinsed and drained
½ cup lard

1. In a meat grinder with a sausage attachment, grind the pork, veal, and pork fat together into a large bowl. Add the seasonings, sugar, and milk and mix with your hands till well blended. Grind the mixture again and, using the sausage attachment, stuff the sausage into the casing according to machine instructions. Twist the casing to form 5- to 6-inch links, alternating (continued)

the direction of twisting so that the links will hold together when cut apart.

2. To poach, place the sausages in a large skillet with enough water to almost cover. Bring to a boil, reduce the heat to low, simmer for 20 minutes, and drain on paper towels. To brown the poached sausages, dry the skillet, melt the lard over moderate heat, add the sausages, and brown lightly on all sides, about 12 minutes in all. Drain on paper towels and serve hot.

In Germany, the sausage is always seasoned with not just caraway seeds and nutmeg but also a little ginger.

Spanish Chorizo

Mexico and most South American countries have their versions of this coarse, highly seasoned sausage (some Mexican cooks add even chili powder to their seasoning), but never have I tasted more delectable chorizo than that produced in Spain—especially when included in an elaborate paella. Dried and eaten as a cold cut or used fresh to enhance soups, stews, casseroles, and other dishes, the sausage is either refrigerated, uncovered, for at least 12 hours to dry and firm up or simply cooked like any other sausage. Tightly covered, fresh chorizo keeps for about 3 days in the refrigerator, while the dried form maintains its flavor and integrity for several weeks.

Makes about 2 pounds

1 tablespoon paprika
2 teaspoons crushed red pepper flakes
1 teaspoon coriander seeds, crushed
1 teaspoon cumin seeds, crushed
3 whole cloves, crushed
2 teaspoons salt
½ teaspoon sugar
¼ teaspoon black peppercorns, crushed
2 garlic cloves, minced
1½ pounds lean pork, diced
½ pound fresh pork fat, diced
⅓ cup dry red wine
4 to 5 feet sausage casing, rinsed and drained

1. In a small skillet, combine the paprika, red pepper flakes, coriander and cumin seeds, cloves, salt, sugar, and peppercorns and shake over moderate heat till the seeds start to crackle, about 1 minute. Transfer the toasted seasonings to a spice mill

(continued)

Sausage

363

or mortar and grind to a coarse texture. In a bowl, combine the seasonings with the garlic and mix till well blended.

2. In a food processor, combine the pork, pork fat, seasonings, and wine and grind coarsely. Transfer the sausage to a bowl, cover with plastic wrap, and chill for 1 hour.

3. Gather all but about 2 inches of casing over the mouth of a sausage funnel and force the sausage through the funnel into the casing. Twist the casing to form 3- to 4-inch links, alternating the direction of twisting so that the links will hold together when cut apart. Refrigerate the sausages, uncovered, for at least 12 hours and, covered, up to 3 days.

Swedish Meat and Potato Sausages

Brined, poached, then lightly browned, these spicy sausages are made primarily for Christmas in Sweden and have to be some of the most distinctive on earth. Do note that, unlike with most meat sausages, both the beef and pork used for these should be fairly lean, and the texture of the links should be almost loose. The sausages can be brined in the refrigerator for up to 2 days, but because of the potatoes, they do not freeze well. Traditionally, the sausages are served with stewed apples and possibly braised red cabbage flavored with caraway seeds.

Makes about 2 pounds

¾ pound ground beef round
¾ pound lean pork shoulder
6 cups grated potatoes
1 medium onion, minced
1 teaspoon grated nutmeg
1 teaspoon ground allspice
Freshly ground black pepper to taste
4 to 5 feet sausage casing, rinsed and drained
4 tablespoons (½ stick) butter

1. In a large bowl, combine the meats, potatoes, onion, nutmeg, allspice, and pepper and mix till thoroughly blended. Gather all but about 2 inches of the casing over the mouth of a sausage funnel and force the sausage loosely through the funnel into the casing. Twist the casing to form 5-inch links, alternating the direction of the twisting so that the links will hold together when cut apart. Place the links in a large pan with enough salted water to cover and chill till ready to use.

(continued)

2. To cook, place the brined sausages in a large pot with enough salted water to barely cover, bring to a simmer, poach the sausages for about 20 minutes, and drain on paper towels. In a large skillet, melt the butter over moderate heat, add the sausages, brown on all sides, 10 to 12 minutes, and drain on paper towels.

3. Serve hot.

Jasper's New England Veal Sausage

Jasper White is not only the godfather of Boston chefs but also one of the most creative chefs anywhere, exemplified by this coarse, garlicky, highly versatile sausage that he grills for an appetizer, braises with sauerkraut, buries in cassoulet, tosses with pasta, and stuffs into roasts and chops. Jasper is adamant about the sausage having sufficient fat for the right flavor and texture, and he also insists that all the ingredients be chilled before grinding. Shoulder is the preferred cut of veal for this sausage, but boneless veal breast and even "stew meat" found in grocery stores can be used. Do remember that salt pork is not fatback and should never be substituted.

Makes about 3 pounds

2 pound boneless veal shoulder, cut into pieces
1 pound fresh pork fatback (rind removed), cut into pieces
3 scallions (white parts only), chopped
5 garlic cloves, sliced
1 tablespoon chopped fresh parsley leaves
1 tablespoon chopped fresh thyme leaves
2 teaspoons chopped fresh tarragon leaves
½ teaspoon fennel seeds, crushed
1 tablespoon cracked black pepper
1 tablespoon coarse salt
½ teaspoon cayenne pepper
2 tablespoons ice water
6 feet sausage casing, rinsed and drained (optional)
4 tablespoons (½ stick) butter

1. In a large bowl, combine the veal, fatback, scallions, garlic, herbs, and seasonings. Mix well, cover with plastic wrap, and chill overnight.

(continued)

2. In a meat grinder with a sausage attachment, grind the meat mixture rather coarsely into a large bowl, add the ice water, and mix with your hands till the sausage is well blended. Form the sausage into patties, or, using the grinder and sausage attachment, stuff it into the casing according to machine instructions and twist the casing to form 4- to 5-inch links, alternating the direction of twisting so that the links will hold together when cut apart.

3. To cook, melt the butter in a large, heavy skillet over moderate heat, add the sausage patties or links, cook till nicely browned on all sides, 12 to 15 minutes, and drain on paper towels.

4. Serve hot.

Alsatian Sweetbread and Spinach Sausages

I first tasted these elegant sausages at the renowned L'Auberge de l'Ill restaurant in the small Alsatian village of Ill-haeusern and wasted no time discussing the details with Jean-Pierre Haeberlin. Since then, I've made the sausages with both ground sweetbreads and chicken and must say that both are equally detectable when combined with the other meats, spinach, and seasonings. Do note that sweetbreads must be well trimmed and soaked overnight and that all the meats should be chilled before grinding for the best texture. The sausages are delicious by themselves or with any butter sauce, such as beurre blanc.

Makes about 2½ pounds

1 pound calf sweetbreads, trimmed of all membrane and soaked in water overnight
1 pound fresh spinach, stems removed and leaves shredded
½ pound veal shoulder
½ pound fresh pork fat
2 scallions (white parts only), finely chopped
½ teaspoon ground coriander
½ teaspoon ground allspice
½ teaspoon grated nutmeg
Salt and freshly ground black pepper to taste
2 large eggs
1 cup heavy cream
5 feet sausage casing, rinsed and drained
4 tablespoons (½ stick) butter

1. Place the sweetbreads in a large saucepan with enough water to cover, bring to a boil, reduce the heat to low, and simmer for 5 minutes. Transfer the sweetbreads to a clean towel, wrap
(continued)

tightly but gently, squeeze to extract moisture, and chill for 1 hour.

2. Place the spinach leaves in another large saucepan, cover, and cook over low heat till wilted, about 10 minutes. Transfer to another clean towel and squeeze to extract moisture.

3. Cut the chilled sweetbreads, veal, and pork fat into pieces, combine with the scallions, seasonings, and eggs in a food processor, and grind coarsely. Add the cream and process till the mixture is smooth, about 15 seconds. Scrape the mixture into a large bowl, add the spinach, and mix till well blended.

4. Gather all but about 2 inches of casing over the mouth of a sausage funnel and force the meat mixture through the funnel into the casing. Twist the casing to form 4-inch links, alternating the direction of twisting so that the links will hold together when cut apart.

5. To poach, arrange the sausages in a large kettle with enough water to cover, bring to a boil, reduce the heat to low, simmer for 15 minutes, and drain on paper towels. To cook the poached sausages lightly, melt the butter in a large, heavy skillet, add the sausages, cook till golden on all sides, about 10 minutes in all, and serve hot.

Flemish Boudin Blanc

In France, these "white" sausages are generally made with finely ground pork, veal, and pork fat, with minimal seasoning, whereas in Belgium the tendency is to produce a lighter but full-flavored sausage by substituting chicken for the pork and adding lots of spices. Frankly, I love both styles, but I must say that when the Flemish version is served on a bed of buttery sautéed onions and apples, there's no better dish on earth. The texture of these sausages should be almost like that of quenelles, and so long as you don't grind the meats to mush, a food processor is preferable to a meat grinder. If you can spare the time, the sausages are much more delicious when allowed to cool in the poaching liquid overnight in the refrigerator.

Makes about
2 pounds

6 tablespoons (¾ stick) butter
2 medium onions, minced
½ cup dry white wine
¼ cup milk
¼ cup heavy cream
1 cup fresh bread crumbs
½ pound skinless, boneless chicken thighs, cut into pieces
½ pound lean veal, cut into pieces
½ pound fresh pork fat, cut into pieces
¼ teaspoon dried thyme, crumbled
¼ teaspoon ground allspice
¼ teaspoon grated nutmeg
⅛ teaspoon ground fennel seeds
1 tablespoon salt
Freshly ground black pepper to taste
2 large eggs
5 feet sausage casing, rinsed and drained
2 quarts chicken broth

(continued)

1 leek, half of green tops trimmed, split, rinsed well, and
   cut in half
1 celery rib, broken in half
1 carrot, scraped and cut into quarters

1. In a skillet, melt half the butter over moderate heat, add the onions, and stir till softened, about 3 minutes. Add the wine, bring to a boil, reduce the heat to moderate, cook till the liquid has evaporated, and set aside.

2. In a bowl, combine the milk, cream, and bread crumbs, stir well, and let sit while preparing the meats.

3. In a food processor, grind together the chicken, veal, and pork fat to a fine texture and scrape into a bowl. Add the cooked onions, bread crumb mixture, thyme, spices, salt, and pepper and mix till well blended. Add the eggs and beat the mixture with an electric mixer till well blended and smooth.

4. To make the sausages, gather all but about 2 inches of the casing over the mouth of a sausage funnel and force the meat mixture through the funnel into the casing. Twist the casing into 6-inch links, alternating the twisting so that the links will hold together when cut apart.

5. In a large kettle, combine the broth, leek, celery, carrot, and salt and pepper to taste, bring to a boil, and reduce the heat to moderate. Lower the linked sausages in a circle into the liquid, return to a steady simmer, poach for 25 to 30 minutes, and drain on paper towels. Cut the sausage into links.

6. To cook, melt the remaining butter in a large skillet over moderate heat, add the sausages, brown on all sides, 10 to 12 minutes, and drain on paper towels.

7. Serve hot.

Swiss Herbed Chicken Sausages

Throughout the Swiss Alps, nothing is more popular at quaint, rustic inns and chalets than platters of these long, herby sausages served with a thick onion sauce, plenty of crisp *rösti* potatoes, and perhaps some marinated cucumbers. For a moist texture, the chicken must be ground with a little pork fat, and while the 3 tablespoons of white wine might seem negligible, that's one ingredient that gives the sausages their special flavor and distinction. Be careful not to grind the meats too finely, and do feel free to experiment with different herbs.

**Makes about
2 pounds**

1½ pounds skinless, boneless chicken thighs, cut into pieces
½ pound fresh pork fat, cut into pieces
⅛ teaspoon dried marjoram, crumbled
⅛ teaspoon dried thyme, crumbled
⅛ teaspoon ground coriander
Salt and freshly ground black pepper to taste
3 tablespoons white wine
5 to 6 feet sausage casing, rinsed and drained
3 tablespoons butter

1. In a food processor, grind together the chicken and pork fat to a coarse texture, add the herbs, salt and pepper, and wine, and grind to a fine texture.

2. Gather all but about 2 inches of the casing over the mouth of a sausage funnel and force the sausage loosely through the funnel into the casing. Twist the casing into 7- to 8-inch links, alternating the direction of twisting so that the links will hold together when cut apart.

3. To cook, melt the butter in a large skillet over moderate heat, add the sausages, brown on all sides, 12 to 15 minutes, drain on paper towels, and serve hot.

Spicy Turkey Sausages

Ground turkey makes splendid sausages, if, that is, you use flavorful thigh meat (breasts and wings are much milder, and the tough sinews in legs often cannot be properly ground even in a food processor) and if the meat is well seasoned. Since even turkey thighs tend to be rather dry, however, a little pork fat is needed for moisture and succulence, and to round out the flavor, I've discovered that a little honey does wonders. You can take a chance with the packaged ground turkey usually found in markets during the Thanksgiving and Christmas holidays, but why not just wait till the thighs go on sale afterward at bargain prices?

2 pounds skinless turkey thigh meat
½ pound fresh pork fat
1 garlic clove, minced
1 teaspoon paprika
1 teaspoon ground fennel seeds
½ teaspoon powdered sage
¼ teaspoon ground allspice
2 teaspoons salt
Freshly ground black pepper to taste
2 teaspoons honey
¼ cup water
5 to 6 feet sausage casing, rinsed and drained
4 tablespoons (½ stick) butter

1. In a meat grinder with a sausage attachment, grind the turkey and pork fat together into a large bowl. Add the garlic, seasonings, honey, and water and mix with your hands till well blended. Grind the mixture again and, using the sausage attachment, stuff the sausage into the casing according to machine instructions. Twist the casing to form 6-inch links, alternating the direction of twisting so that the links will hold together when cut apart.

2. To cook, melt the butter in a large, heavy skillet over moderate heat, add the sausages, and brown on all sides, 12 to 15 minutes. Drain on paper towels and serve hot.

Since even turkey thighs tend to be rather dry, a little pork fat is needed for moisture and succulence.

Hungarian Fish Sausages

Makes about 1³/₄ pounds

Interesting ground seafood sausages are produced in a number of European countries, but when it comes to delectable fish sausages, what Hungarian chefs do with pike, carp, sturgeon, and other fish from local rivers elevates sausage making to a veritable art. Although you find stuffed links at markets and restaurants in towns all over Hungary, never was I more impressed than by the free-form, long, battered and fried ovals made from carp and served with a light mustard sauce and buttery potato croquettes at an offbeat restaurant in Budapest. Carp, with a firm texture that lends itself beautifully to grinding, is not easy to find in this country, but almost as good for these sausages is pike, perch, catfish, or even trout.

1½ pounds fresh fish fillets (pike, perch, catfish, or trout), cut into pieces

2 white rolls, soaked in ½ cup milk, squeezed dry, and shredded

4 large eggs

2 tablespoons minced fresh parsley leaves

1 teaspoon paprika

½ teaspoon salt

Freshly ground black pepper to taste

½ cup all-purpose flour

½ cup dry bread crumbs

½ cup lard

1. In a meat grinder, grind the fish coarsely into a large bowl. Add the soaked rolls, 2 of the eggs, parsley, paprika, salt, and pepper and mix with your hands till well blended.

2. Form the fish mixture into 5- to 6-inch-long ovals about 1 inch thick. In a shallow pan, combine the flour, bread crumbs, and remaining 2 eggs, mix till well blended, and roll the fish sausages in the mixture till lightly coated. Place the sausages on a plate, cover with plastic wrap, and chill for about 1 hour.

3. To cook, melt the lard in a large, heavy skillet over low heat, add the sausages, and cook slowly for 15 to 20 minutes, turning them to cook on all sides. Drain on paper towels, sprinkle with a little extra salt, and serve hot.

French Seafood Sausages

Cervelas aux fruits de mer (with or without a rich Nantua or cream sauce) is not only one of the glories of classic French cuisine but also one of the world's most distinctive ground seafood dishes. Basically a mousseline of fish studded with bits of lobster, scallops, and salmon, this elegant sausage is not that difficult to make so long as you pay careful attention to what you're doing—especially when beating the egg whites and cream into the ground fish over ice cubes. To prevent any possible loss of stuffing, I do recommend not cutting the links apart till after the whole sausage string has been poached. And personally, I prefer these beautifully flavored sausages with no sauce at all.

Makes about
2½ pounds

1½ pounds fresh white fish fillets (such as striped bass, red snapper, or grouper), cut into pieces
2 large egg whites
1½ cups heavy cream
1 cup finely diced cooked lobster meat
½ cup finely diced fresh scallops
¼ cup finely diced smoked salmon
½ cup minced fresh parsley leaves
¼ teaspoon paprika
⅛ teaspoon ground fennel seeds
1 teaspoon salt
¼ teaspoon freshly ground black pepper
5 to 6 feet sausage casing, rinsed and drained
4 tablespoons (½ stick) butter

1. In a meat grinder with a sausage attachment, grind the fish coarsely into a large bowl placed over another bowl of ice cubes. Add the egg whites and beat with a wooden spoon till the mixture is smooth. Gradually add the cream, beating till the mixture is thickened and firm. Add the lobster, scallops, smoked salmon, parsley, and seasonings and stir till well blended.

2. Grind the mixture again and, using the sausage attachment, stuff the sausage into the casing according to machine instructions. Twist the casing to form 5- to 6-inch links, alternating the direction of twisting so that the links will hold together when cut apart. Place the whole sausage on a large plate, cover with plastic wrap, and chill for about 1 hour.

3. To cook, arrange the sausage in a large kettle with enough water to cover, bring to a simmer, poach gently for about 45 minutes, and drain. In a large, heavy skillet, melt the butter over moderate heat, add the sausages, brown lightly on all sides, about 10 minutes in all, and drain on paper towels.

4. Serve hot.

Sauces

Bolognese Meat Sauce

Makes about
1 quart

Known in Italy as *ragù,* this rich meat sauce used to dress tagliatelle, tortellini, rigatoni, and other pastas, and to enrich lasagna, is most closely identified with the city of Bologna. The American version is commonly called "spaghetti sauce," but the difference between most American meat sauces and a genuine *ragù alla Bolognese* is like the difference between domestic Parmesan cheese and true Parmigiano-Reggiano. Only beef chuck should be used for this sauce, the milk is needed to balance the acidity of the wine, and the sauce must be slowly simmered for at least 2 hours to attain its sweet succulence and subtle texture. Italian chefs do not drain the fat off their sauce; I do. This sauce freezes beautifully in tightly covered containers for up to about 3 months.

¼ cup olive oil

1 medium onion, finely chopped

1 celery rib, finely chopped

1 carrot, scraped and finely chopped

2 tablespoons finely chopped fresh parsley leaves

1 pound ground beef chuck

⅛ teaspoon grated nutmeg

Salt and freshly ground black pepper to taste

½ cup dry white wine

½ cup milk

One 28-ounce can crushed tomatoes with juice

1. In a large saucepan, heat the oil over moderate heat, add the onion, celery, carrot, and parsley, and stir till the vegetables soften, about 5 minutes. Add the beef, breaking it up with a spoon, and stir till it loses all pink color, about 10 minutes.

2. Drain the fat from the pan, add the nutmeg and salt and pepper, and stir well. Add the wine, increase the heat slightly, and stir till the wine evaporates, about 10 minutes. Add the milk and stir till the milk evaporates, about 10 minutes. Add the tomatoes, stir well, reduce the heat to low, and simmer the sauce, uncovered, for about 2 hours, adding a little water if it becomes too thick.

Commander's Beef Debris Sauce

Makes about
2 cups

When legendary chef Paul Prudhomme was heading up the kitchen at Commander's Palace restaurant in New Orleans during the 1970s, I was there reporting on him when he got the idea of using the burnt debris left over from beef rib roasts to make a sauce for grilled filet mignon. From there evolved the notion of blackening beef bones and vegetables and adding crusted ground sirloin steak to the winey debris sauce, and suffice it to say that this has to be one of the most unusual and delicious sauces I've encountered anywhere. Spoon small amounts of the sauce over any steak, slices of roast beef, or even hamburgers. Be warned that the kitchen can become smoky and that it's best to make this sauce when all the windows can be opened.

½ pound beef bones (from sirloin steaks or rib roast), hacked into 1-inch pieces

4 medium onions, diced

4 scallions (parts of green tops included), diced

2 celery ribs, diced

1 large green bell pepper, seeded and diced

2 teaspoons salt

1 teaspoon freshly ground black pepper

½ teaspoon paprika

Cayenne pepper to taste

5 cups beef stock or broth

1 pound ground beef sirloin steak (fatty edges included)

¼ cup dry red wine

2 teaspoons brandy

1. Preheat the oven to 500°F.

2. In a roasting pan, combine the bones, onions, scallions, celery, and bell pepper, sprinkle with the salt, black pepper, paprika, and cayenne, stir well, and roast till all the ingredients are caramelized and burned black, about 2 hours.

3. Remove the debris from the oven, add the stock, mix well, reduce the oven to 350°F, and roast about 1 hour longer. In another pan, break up the ground sirloin and cook alongside the debris till dry and crusty.

4. Remove the debris from the oven, strain the sauce into a saucepan, and discard the solids. Add the sirloin, wine, and brandy to the sauce, bring to a boil, reduce the heat to moderate, and simmer till the sauce is reduced and slightly thickened, about 5 minutes.

Spoon small amounts of the sauce over any steak, slices of roast beef, or even hamburgers.

Ham and Curry Sauce

Makes about
1¹/₂ cups

This simple sauce adds real flair to baked or soft-boiled eggs and any number of steamed vegetables served at brunches. The sauce is already fairly rich, but if you want even more savor, use aged country ham and leave out the salt. No matter what dish might be involved, only about a spoonful of the thick sauce per serving is necessary.

1 cup chicken broth
1 cup heavy cream
2 teaspoons curry powder
½ teaspoon powdered sage
Salt and freshly ground black pepper to taste
5 to 6 ounces cooked ham, finely chopped

In a heavy saucepan, combine the broth, cream, curry powder, sage, and salt and pepper and stir well. Bring to a boil, reduce the heat to moderate, and simmer till the sauce is reduced almost by half, 10 to 15 minutes. Add the ham, stir till well blended, and keep the sauce hot till serving.

Bacon and Blue Cheese Dipping Sauce

This dipping sauce is so good that I could almost make a sandwich with it instead of serving it with some type of crusty bread or raw vegetable sticks or florets at cocktail parties or brunches. For a truly sensational sauce, use an artisanal apple-wood-smoked bacon and either genuine Stilton or Roquefort cheese. I like my dipping sauce fairly thick, but feel free to adjust the consistency to your taste during the final reduction.

Makes about
1½ cups

6 slices lean bacon
2 scallions (white parts only), finely chopped
2 tablespoons all-purpose flour
½ cup milk
½ cup lager beer
1 teaspoon Worcestershire sauce
Freshly ground black pepper to taste
½ pound blue cheese, finely crumbled or chopped

1. In a large, heavy skillet, fry the bacon over moderate heat till crisp, drain on paper towels, and crumble finely.

2. Pour off all but about 2 tablespoons of fat from the skillet, add the scallions, and stir till softened, about 2 minutes. Sprinkle the flour over the top and stir 3 minutes longer. Whisking, add the milk and beer, then add the Worcestershire and pepper, and bring to a boil. Return the heat to moderate and stir for about 5 minutes. Reduce the heat to low, add the bacon and blue cheese, and stir till the cheese is melted and the sauce is reduced slightly. Transfer the sauce to a crock and serve hot or at room temperature with croutons, bread sticks, crackers, or raw vegetable sticks.

Giblet Gravy

There are those who somehow manage to eat a turkey or roast chicken dinner without any gravy at all, but personally, I can't imagine not making pan gravy enriched with minced boiled giblets to be spooned not only over the meat but also on rice, stuffing, and even potatoes. You can simply deglaze the roasting pan with water boiled down to a desired consistency, but for a much richer gravy, I always use the strained broth in which the neck and giblets have been simmered. The amount of minced meat you add to the gravy depends, of course, on what type of bird you're roasting and how much liquid is involved, so adjust quantities accordingly. If you prefer a cream gravy (I don't), simply add a little milk or half-and-half to taste.

Neck and giblets from a small turkey or roaster chicken to be roasted
¼ cup all-purpose flour
Salt and freshly ground black pepper to taste

1. In a saucepan, combine the turkey or chicken neck and giblets and add enough water to cover. Bring to a boil, reduce the heat to low, cover, and simmer till tender, 30 to 45 minutes. Remove the neck and giblets from the broth, mince the neck meat and giblets, and set aside about ½ cup of the meats. Strain about 2¼ cups of the broth into a bowl.

2. While the roasted turkey or chicken is "resting," drain the liquid from the roasting pan, add the reserved broth to the pan, and stir over moderate heat, scraping up browned bits. Sprinkle the flour over the top and stir for about 3 minutes. Add the reserved neck meat and giblets and stir till the gravy is the desired consistency. Add salt and pepper to taste.

3. Transfer to a gravy boat and serve piping hot.

French Foie Gras Sauce

Leave it to the French to come up with this luscious sauce made with mashed foie gras and intended to enhance poached chicken breasts or grilled veal cutlets, steamed broccoli or asparagus, and a number of soft-boiled egg dishes. If you don't have any foie gras around the kitchen, about ½ pound of mashed or finely minced chicken livers sautéed for 5 minutes in butter can be substituted with acceptable results. In either case, since the sauce is so rich, very little is needed no matter how it's used.

Makes about 2 cups

4 tablespoons (½ stick) butter
¼ cup all-purpose flour
2 cups chicken broth
3 large egg yolks
½ cup half-and-half
½ cup canned duck or goose foie gras, mashed
Salt and freshly ground black pepper to taste

1. In a saucepan, melt the butter over moderate heat, add the flour, and whisk till the flour begins to brown, about 5 minutes. Add the broth and whisk till the liquid begins to thicken, about 10 minutes. Remove the pan from the heat.

2. In a bowl, whisk the egg yolks and half-and-half together till well blended, whisk about half of the hot sauce into the mixture, then add the mixture to the sauce.

3. Return the pan to the heat, add the foie gras and salt and pepper, and stir till the sauce thickens, about 5 minutes. Keep hot till serving.

Lobster Sauce

Use this luscious sauce to adorn broiled or grilled fish, seafood quenelles and croquettes, or fish cakes and loaves. If you don't have the fresh leftovers of steamed or boiled lobsters, you can make the sauce with the frozen or canned cooked lobster meat found in all markets. Do not fail to include the anchovy paste, which disappears subtly into the sauce and adds a distinctive flavor.

Makes about 2 cups

8 tablespoons (1 stick) butter
6 tablespoons all-purpose flour
2 cups bottled clam juice
1 cup dry white wine
¼ teaspoon salt
Freshly ground black pepper to taste
1 tablespoon anchovy paste
½ cup minced cooked lobster
Cayenne pepper to taste

In a heavy saucepan, melt 6 tablespoons of the butter over moderate heat, sprinkle the flour over the top, and whisk for about 1 minute. Gradually add the broth, whisking till the mixture is slightly thickened and smooth, about 10 minutes. Reduce the heat to low and simmer, uncovered, for about 30 minutes, stirring frequently. Add the wine, return to a simmer, cover, and cook till the sauce reduces to about 2 cups, about 10 minutes. Add the salt and pepper, anchovy paste, and remaining 2 tablespoons butter, stir till well blended, and simmer about 10 minutes longer. Add the lobster and cayenne and stir till the sauce is fully heated.

Italian Clam Sauce

This is the basic Italian clam sauce traditionally tossed with about ¾ pound of linguine or spaghetti boiled just till al dente. Some Italian chefs balk at the idea of including basil in a classic clam sauce, so let your own taste be your guide. The main point to remember is not to overcook the clams, which toughens them. Quick-frozen shucked clams can be used like fresh ones for the sauce so long as there's at least some liquor included, but once the clams have thawed, never refreeze them. I do not recommend any canned clams for this sauce, since they tend to be tough and can have a metallic flavor.

36 fresh littleneck clams, shucked and liquor reserved
½ cup or more dry white wine
½ cup olive oil
1 large garlic clove, minced
½ cup minced fresh parsley leaves
2 tablespoons minced fresh basil leaves (optional)
¼ teaspoon crushed red pepper flakes
Salt and freshly ground black pepper to taste
2 tablespoons butter

1. Pour the clam liquor into a bowl and combine it with enough of the wine to measure about 1½ cups. Chop the clams.

2. In a large, heavy saucepan, heat the oil over moderate heat, add the garlic, and stir till softened, about 1 minute. Add the clam liquor mixture, parsley, basil, red pepper flakes, and salt and pepper, cover, and simmer for about 5 minutes. Add the chopped clams and butter and stir till the clams are just firm, about 2 minutes. Keep the sauce hot till serving.

**Makes about
2 cups**

Sauces

English Creamed Shrimp Sauce

Makes about
2½ cups

The English love rich, creamy seafood sauces spooned over baked fish, various egg dishes, croquettes, and boiled artichoke bottoms, and in one London restaurant, I've even eaten a chopped shrimp sauce such as this one served by itself in a puff pastry shell for lunch. Chopped cooked lobster is equally delectable for this sauce.

8 tablespoons (1 stick) butter
¼ cup all-purpose flour
2 cups chicken broth
1 small onion, minced
2 tablespoons dry white wine
1 teaspoon Worcestershire sauce
Salt and freshly ground black pepper to taste
½ cup heavy cream
½ pound boiled fresh shrimp, shelled, deveined, and finely chopped

1. In a small skillet, melt half the butter over moderate heat, add the flour, and stir constantly till the mixture forms a smooth paste. Remove from the heat.

2. In a large saucepan, bring the broth to a boil, reduce the heat to moderate, and simmer till reduced to about 1 cup. Add the onion, wine, Worcestershire, and salt and pepper and stir till well blended. Add the reserved paste, stir well, and continue simmering till the sauce has the consistency of slightly whipped cream, about 20 minutes.

3. Remove the sauce from the heat, add the remaining butter, and stir till the butter melts. Gently stir in the cream, add the shrimp, return the pan to the heat, and stir till the sauce is hot.

Tuna Sauce

One of the most distinctive dishes in Italy's Piedmont is *vitello tonnato*, thin slices of cold poached veal tenderloin covered with a luscious ground tuna sauce spiked with both anchovies and capers. Given the high cost of veal, I often substitute poached chicken or turkey breast, and once I even used slices from a baked boneless pork loin with surprising success. The truth is that the tuna sauce is so sublime (and such a cinch to make) that it tastes good on virtually any bland meat, and frankly, I challenge anybody to come up with a more appealing summertime luncheon dish than a well-made *tonnato*.

Makes about 2½ cups

One 7-ounce can solid white tuna in oil, drained
5 canned anchovy fillets packed in olive oil, drained
1 tablespoon capers, drained
1 small onion, chopped
1 carrot, scraped and chopped
1 cup dry white wine
1 tablespoon water
1 teaspoon white vinegar
Freshly ground black pepper to taste
Extra-virgin olive oil as needed

In a blender or food processor, combine the tuna, anchovies, capers, onion, carrot, wine, water, vinegar, and pepper, and grind to a coarse puree. With the machine running, add enough oil to make a smooth sauce of the desired consistency. Transfer the sauce to a covered container and chill till ready to use.

Mediterranean Anchovy Sauce

Most Mediterranean countries have at least one boiled beef, lamb, or tongue dish that is enhanced by a garlicky anchovy sauce, and as unlikely as this may sound to most Americans, take my word that nothing is more delicious when the meats are cooked properly and careful attention is paid to the quality of ingredients in the sauce. This sauce is also superb spooned over steamed or boiled fresh artichoke bottoms or used as a dip for cooked artichoke leaves.

½ cup dry red wine
2 tablespoons extra-virgin olive oil
1 teaspoon fresh lemon juice
10 canned anchovy fillets packed in olive oil, drained and finely chopped
10 black olives cured in brine, pitted and finely chopped
2 garlic cloves, minced
Cayenne pepper to taste

In a saucepan, whisk together the wine, oil, and lemon juice till well blended and smooth. Add the anchovies, olives, garlic, and cayenne, bring to a simmer over moderate heat, and stir till the sauce is smooth, about 10 minutes. Serve warm or at room temperature.

Acknowledgments

A large book such as this one could not have been realized without my world-wide network of professional chefs, colleagues, and friends who've always been there to inspire, suggest new ideas, share recipes, and even test some dishes. The list of names is long, but particular thanks goes to Jeremiah Tower, Paul Prudhomme, Delia Smith, Jasper White, Paul Bocuse, Zarela Martinez, Thom Chu, Gören Lindquist, Fay Schwartz, Roberta Gosman, John Mariani, George Lang, Laura Donnelly, and Jean-Pierre Haeberlin.

Always available to answer numerous nagging questions and offer savvy advice were my fellow foodaholics and close pals Jean Anderson, Paula Wolfert, Fran McCullough, and Damon Lee Fowler, and never too busy to teach me more about varieties and cuts of meat, poultry, and seafood and show me special grinding techniques has been my veteran butcher in Amagansett, New York, Brian Brunges.

Finally, my most earnest thanks to my long-time, dedicated editor at Wiley, Justin Schwartz, and to my indefatigable agent, Jane Dystel, both of whom have shepherded this book lovingly from its inception to the final anchovy sauce.

Index